Keeping
College
Affordable

Keeping College Affordable

Government and Educational Opportunity

MICHAEL S. McPHERSON
MORTON OWEN SCHAPIRO

THE BROOKINGS INSTITUTION
Washington, D.C.

Library of Congress Cataloging-in-Publication data

McPherson, Michael S.
  Keeping college affordable: government and
educational opportunity/Michael S. McPherson and
Morton Owen Schapiro.
      p.   cm.
  Includes bibliographical references and index.
  ISBN 0-8157-5642-9—ISBN 0-8157-5641-0 (pbk.)
  1. Student aid—United States.   2. Student aid—
United States—Statistics.   3. College attendance—
United States.   4. College attendance—United States—
Statistics.   5. Federal aid to higher education—United
States.   I. Schapiro, Morton Owen.   II. Title.
LB2337.4.M3   1991
379.1'214'0973—dc20   91-19442
                                                        CIP

9 8 7 6 5 4 3 2 1

The paper used in this publication meets the minimum
requirements of the American National Standard for
Information Sciences—Permanence of Paper for Printed
Library Materials, ANSI Z39.48-1984

Set in Linotron Times Roman
Composition by Monotype Composition Co.
Baltimore, Maryland
Printed by R. R. Donnelley and Sons Co.
Harrisonburg, Virginia

THE BROOKINGS INSTITUTION

The Brookings Institution is an independent organization devoted to nonpartisan research, education, and publication in economics, government, foreign policy, and the social sciences generally. Its principal purposes are to aid in the development of sound public policies and to promote public understanding of issues of national importance.

The Institution was founded on December 8, 1927, to merge the activities of the Institute for Government Research, founded in 1916, the Institute of Economics, founded in 1922, and the Robert Brookings Graduate School of Economics and Government, founded in 1924.

The Board of Trustees is responsible for the general administration of the Institution, while the immediate direction of the policies, program, and staff is vested in the President, assisted by an advisory committee of the officers and staff. The by-laws of the Institution state: "It is the function of the Trustees to make possible the conduct of scientific research, and publication, under the most favorable conditions, and to safeguard the independence of the research staff in the pursuit of their studies and in the publication of the results of such studies. It is not a part of their function to determine, control, or influence the conduct of particular investigations or the conclusions reached."

The President bears final responsibility for the decision to publish a manuscript as a Brookings book. In reaching his judgment on the competence, accuracy, and objectivity of each study, the President is advised by the director of the appropriate research program and weighs the views of a panel of expert outside readers who report to him in confidence on the quality of the work. Publication of a work signifies that it is deemed a competent treatment worthy of public consideration but does not imply endorsement of conclusions or recommendations.

The Institution maintains its position of neutrality on issues of public policy in order to safeguard the intellectual freedom of the staff. Hence interpretations or conclusions in Brookings publications should be understood to be solely those of the authors and should not be attributed to the Institution, to its trustees, officers, or other staff members, or to the organizations that support its research.

For our children,
Steven and Sean, Matt and Alissa,
and our wives,
Marge and Mimi

Foreword

RAPIDLY RISING COLLEGE tuitions in the 1980s have focused public attention on the ability of families and the nation to afford higher education. Both state and federal governments play a large role in the finance of American colleges and universities, mainly through operating subsidies to institutions by the states and financial aid grants and loans to students by the federal government. But are these state and federal subsidies keeping college affordable for Americans of all economic and social backgrounds? More broadly, are the nation's scarce resources being used as effectively as possible in its higher education investments?

In this book Michael S. McPherson and Morton Owen Schapiro examine the effects of student aid policies of the last twenty years. They address several vital questions. Has federal student aid encouraged the enrollment and broadened the educational choices of disadvantaged students? Has it made higher education institutions more secure and educationally more effective, or has it raised costs and prices as schools try to capture additional aid? Has federal student aid made the distribution of higher education's benefits, and the sharing of its costs, fairer? And what are the likely future trends in patterns of college affordability?

Drawing on their analysis, the authors highlight some of the main aspects of policy choice on which debate has focused, as well as some that have been neglected. Building on their conclusion that student aid works, they propose reforms that would bolster the role of income-tested aid in student financing. They recommend a number of incremental reforms that could improve the effectiveness of existing federal aid programs and present a bold proposal to replace a large part of current state operating subsidies to college and universities with expanded federal student aid.

Some of the material in chapters 1, 2, and 9 appeared in a different form in Michael McPherson's essays *How Can We Tell If Student Aid Is Working?* and "Appearance and Reality in the Guaranteed Student Loan Program," in *Radical Reform or Incremental Change? Student*

ix

Loan Policy Alternatives for the Federal Government, both published by the College Board. Michael O'Malley and Larry Litten collaborated with the authors on the research underlying chapter 5; Gordon Winston collaborated on the research underlying chapter 4.

Michael McPherson, formerly a senior fellow in the Brookings Economic Studies program, is the Herbert Lehman Professor of Economics at Williams College; Morton Schapiro is chairman of the economics department at the University of Southern California. The authors thank Michael O'Malley, Mary Skinner, Scott Blasdell, John Staudenmayer, Ian Smith, Collin Roche, and Ivan Yen for research assistance. Richard Spies of Princeton University, Kay Hanson of the Consortium on Financing Higher Education, Laurent Ross of the American Council on Education, and Kenneth C. Green of the Higher Education Research Institute at the University of California, Los Angeles, assisted in the project by making data available and helping to prepare it. Carole H. Newman, Christine C. de Fontenay, and Robert Davis of the Brookings Computer Center assisted in data preparation. Valuable comments on an early version of the manuscript were provided by Henry J. Aaron, David W. Breneman, Arthur H. Hauptman, and Janet Hansen. Rozlyn Coleman edited the manuscript, and Roshna Kapadia verified the factual information. The index was prepared by Ward and Silvan.

Financial support for this project was provided by the Andrew W. Mellon Foundation, the Teagle Foundation, and the Spencer Foundation.

The views expressed in this book are those of the authors and should not be ascribed to any of the persons consulted during its preparation, or to the officers, trustees, or staff members of the Brookings Institution.

BRUCE K. MACLAURY
President

June 1991
Washington, D.C.

Contents

xi

Appendixes

Tables

Figures

I

Introduction

SINCE WORLD WAR II, education beyond high school has become an increasingly routine feature of American life. It has been an expansion that gained particular momentum during the 1960s and 1970s, when both state and federal governments took steps to ensure that a postsecondary education was available to all Americans regardless of economic background—in the states, largely through the development of a broad network of open-enrollment community colleges; at the federal level, through the development of a set of student aid programs that targeted needy students.

In the last decade, however, while belief in the importance of education remains strong, perhaps even stronger than ever, worries about the future affordability of college and the effectiveness of governmental efforts to broaden postsecondary opportunity have become more prominent. A decade of rapid real tuition increases in both public and private higher education has led parents of even considerable means to worry about how they will pay for their children's college educations. In addition, two decades of substantial federal investment in need-based financial aid have left postsecondary enrollments of lower-income and minority students substantially below those of other students, casting doubt on how well student aid promotes equal opportunity in education. Certainly some of the enrollment shortfall for lower-income and minority students can be blamed on their too often inadequate elementary and secondary educations, but it remains true that even for students who are highly qualified socioeconomic status remains a powerful determinant of their progression from high school to college. In fact, as table 1-1 shows, progression rates to college did not improve at all for talented lower-income students between the high school classes of 1961–63 and the high school class of 1980.

Our purpose in this volume is to analyze the role of governmental subsidies for higher education—especially though not exclusively the role of federal student aid subsidies—in keeping college affordable for

Table 1-1. *High School Graduates Entering Postsecondary Education in the Year Following Graduation, by Academic Skill and Socioeconomic Status, Selected Years, 1961–80*
Percent

Skill quartile[a]	Year of graduation	Socioeconomic status		
		Low	Middle	High
1	1961–63	13.5	23.8	41.5
	1972	17.8	20.8	34.6
	1980	20.8	25.8	39.7
2	1961–63	23.5	35.8	55.0
	1972	25.3	34.7	52.6
	1980	31.1	39.3	68.1
3	1961–63	37.5	51.0	76.5
	1972	37.7	50.5	71.5
	1980	46.7	59.4	77.4
4	1961–63	59.5	77.3	91.0
	1972	58.2	67.6	84.4
	1980	58.0	76.3	86.4

Sources: Data are from Project Talent, National Longitudinal Study, and High School and Beyond, as compiled in the Eureka Project (1988, p. 35).
a. One is the lowest skill quartile; four the highest.

Americans of all economic and social backgrounds. This notion of affordability means more than simply keeping tuition low; affordability must also concern the income available to pay tuition. And in addressing the questions of income and affordability, the budget constraints facing the nation as a whole as well as individual families come into play. Thus, it is our aim to provide evidence that will show whether the nation's scarce resources are being used as effectively as possible with regard to higher-education investments.

That government has a legitimate role to play in improving the accessibility of higher education is not a claim that needs extended defense. Even in the narrowest economic terms, an argument can be made that educational investments generally pay returns more than equal to their costs, and that without government intervention difficulties in paying for education would certainly lead to underinvestment by potential students. This argument for the economic efficiency of investing in education can be broadened still further through recognition of the widely acknowledged (but hard to quantify) positive externalities that a college education generates.[1]

1. For useful, critical surveys of these externality arguments, see Hartman (1973, pp. 271–92) and Bowen (1977). Some externalities accrue not only through the effects of education on individual behavior but also through the contributions that a healthy higher-education sector makes

Beyond these broad efficiency concerns lie important arguments about social equity. A college degree remains a very important credential regulating access to the professions and to influential positions in public life. The value of equal economic and social opportunity argues strongly for making access to these favored careers as wide as possible. Moreover, advanced education is an important good in its own right, opening an individual's personal and intellectual horizons. Although education, like any other good, must be traded off against other valued ends, there is a strong argument that access to education, like access to medical care and to employment, deserves a privileged position in the distributive system of American society.[2]

These arguments, of course, go only to show that *effective* programs of governmental support for higher education deserve the nation's backing. Whether the existing programs deserve that backing and whether reform could make them more effective are, however, contestable questions and among our principal concerns in this volume.

An Overview of College Financing

In the fall of 1986, about 11.2 million people were enrolled as undergraduates at postsecondary institutions in the United States.[3] Of this total, only half were enrolled as full-time, full-year students, of whom 80 percent were of "traditional college age" (23 years or less). Among those attending part time or part year, only 41 percent fell into that traditional age group. As for where undergraduate students attend school, about 38 percent of total enrollment were in public four-year colleges and universities, 17 percent in private four-year colleges and universities, 38 percent in public colleges with programs of two years or less, and just 1 percent in private colleges of two years or less. The final 5 percent or so were enrolled at profit-seeking vocational and

toward national investment in research. A very thoughtful treatment of the economics of public support for higher education is in Nerlove (1972).

2. For a well-reasoned and carefully qualified defense of this position, see Gutmann (1987, chaps. 6 and 7).

3. The data in this and the subsequent paragraph are from the National Postsecondary Student Aid Survey (NPSAS), as reported in National Center for Education Statistics (1989, table 260, pp. 284–85), and Korb and others (1988, table 2.3, p. 12).

technical institutions, with the bulk of these students in programs of two years or less.[4]

The distribution of full-time enrollment across institutional categories has been quite different from that of total enrollment, since in every category except public two-year colleges more than 70 percent of all students attended full time (only 36 percent of two-year college students did).[5] Thus, public two-year college students accounted for 38 percent of all enrollments, but only 22 percent of full-time enrollments.

The financing of higher education varies substantially across these institutional sectors. In public higher education, the most important source of revenue is appropriations from state and local governments, which provided over 60 percent of educational and general revenue at these institutions in the 1985–86 academic year.[6] Unlike the federal programs that target needy students, state and local appropriations have served principally to keep tuition low for all students in public higher education. As a result, student tuition and fees (including all payments from student aid) supplied only 18 percent of revenue at public institutions in the 1985–86 academic year.

At private, nonprofit institutions the most important sources of revenue are tuition and fees, providing around half of educational and general revenue. The next most important source for these institutions is federal support, which supplies 22 percent of revenue.[7] Although similar figures for proprietary vocational and technical institutions are not available in comparable detail, they presumably get almost all their revenue from student charges (including payments from federal student aid).

The federal government contributes to the financing of undergraduate education principally by providing subsidies to students through the following three aid programs.

Pell grants provide aid directly to students and are awarded through a need-based formula. In the 1989–90 academic year, the maximum

---

4. The NPSAS data, from which these figures are drawn, may underestimate the number of proprietary school students, because students were surveyed only once during the academic year and a large fraction of proprietary school students are in programs of less than one year. By our example, the actual enrollment percentage for proprietaries may be closer to 6 or 7 percent.

5. Of the small number of students in private two-year colleges, 67 percent attend full time.

6. See table 2-1 for the data in this paragraph.

7. Most federal appropriations go to support research. Such funding, therefore, is concentrated on a few select universities. In addition, while federal funding for the campus-based student aid programs appears in these figures, Pell grant and guaranteed loan funds do not.

award was $2,300. No student can receive an award exceeding 60 percent of the cost of attendance at his or her institution.[8]

Guaranteed loans insure banks against default risk and, for the bulk of the loans that are made, subsidize the interest payments of students.[9] Subsidized loans, provided under the Stafford loan program, are available only to students who attend at least half time and who have a "demonstrated need" for assistance, as determined by their family resources and the cost of attendance at the school where they are enrolled. The federal government pays all interest while the students are in school and during certain other grace periods (for example, during enrollment in the Peace Corps). In addition, interest rates are fixed at levels that have typically been below market rates for comparable loans—for borrowers receiving loans after July 1, 1988, the interest rate is generally 8 percent for the first four years of repayment and 10 percent after that. The maximum loan is $2,625 a year for first- or second-year undergraduates and $4,000 for undergraduate students who have completed two years of study and have achieved third-year status.[10]

Campus-based programs provide money directly to institutions; the funds are earmarked for distribution as student aid. There are three such programs: supplemental educational opportunity grants (SEOGs), which institutions award to students who qualify on the basis of financial need; Perkins loans, which are made by colleges and universities di-

---

8. Pell grants are available only to undergraduate students who attend at least half time. In the 1988–89 academic year, more than 3 million students received Pell grants, with an average award of $1,372, according to preliminary figures from College Board (1989b, p. 10).

9. At the undergraduate level, the federal government guarantees and subsidizes loans to undergraduates through the Stafford loan program. In addition, parent loans to undergraduate students (PLUS) and supplemental loans to students (SLS) are available to families who are not eligible for Stafford loans or have borrowed as much as they are eligible for under the Stafford program. These loans carry a federal guarantee and their interest rates are regulated. However, they have no subsidy for interest charged while still in school, and have variable interest rates, which are adjusted each year. For the 1989–90 award year the interest rate on these loans was 12 percent. Maxima for PLUS and SLS loans are $4,000 a year to a total of $20,000, in addition to any borrowing under the Stafford program. Preliminary figures for 1988–89 indicate that 203,000 people borrowed an average of $3,133 under PLUS and 807,000 people (including graduate as well as undergraduate students) borrowed an average of $2,567 under SLS. See College Board (1989b, p. 10).

10. The total amount of guaranteed-loan debt that an undergraduate can have outstanding is $17,250 over five years. In the 1988–89 academic year, 3.6 million students borrowed an average of $2,559 under the Stafford program. This figure includes graduate student borrowers. See College Board (1989b, p. 10).

rectly to students at a subsidized interest rate from a fund provided by federal resources; and work-study programs, which pay colleges 70 percent of the cost of their providing jobs to students who have financial need. The maximum SEOG award is $4,000 a year. Perkins loan recipients can borrow up to $4,500 a year, with undergraduates limited to a total of $9,000 at an interest rate of 5 percent.[11]

The largest of these programs in terms of expenditure is the Pell grant program, which totaled $4.5 billion in the 1989 fiscal year.[12] Close behind it in federal expenditure is the Stafford program of federally guaranteed loans, which in 1989 was supported by appropriations of $4.1 billion and generated $9.2 billion in new loans.[13] The three campus-based programs are much more modest in size, with appropriations over the three programs totaling only $1.2 billion in the 1989 fiscal year. For the most part, discussion of federal student aid in this volume will concentrate on the Pell, Stafford, and SEOG programs.[14]

The most recent academic year for which we can pull together a picture of government contributions to higher education is 1985–86. Of the total college and university revenue of $81 billion in that year, the federal government contributed about $8.1 billion of it through student aid.[15] This compares to payments from state and local governments of over $30 billion. The federal and state contributions are, of course, distributed quite differently among types of institutions. Some 98 percent of state expenditures on higher education are devoted to

11. The 561,000 students receiving SEOG awards in the 1988-89 academic year had an average award of only $701. There were 803,000 Perkins borrowers in the same year, with an average loan size of $1,070. College work-study recipients numbered 765,000, with students receiving an average $923 each. See College Board (1989b, p. 10); these are preliminary figures.

12. The data in this paragraph are from College Board (1989b). Figures for the 1989 fiscal year are preliminary.

13. The figures on guaranteed loans include graduate students. The guaranteed student loan programs are the only student aid programs that function as an entitlement in the federal budget. Congress must appropriate the requisite funds to pay the costs on outstanding loans and regulations permit loans to be made to all qualified borrowers. Notice that the federal appropriation reflects the current cost of outstanding loans and is not an estimate of the future cost of new loans. These financing issues are further discussed in chapter 8. In addition to the $9.2 billion in Stafford loans, guaranteed loans under the SLS and PLUS programs totaled $2.7 billion in 1988–89. The appropriation figures include costs associated with these programs.

14. We also refer to Stafford loans by their traditional label—the GSL, or guaranteed student loan program. Pell grants used to be called BEOGs—basic educational opportunity grants.

15. The 1988–89 figure for federal contributions through student aid is $9.9 billion. The $81 billion figure for 1985–86 excludes revenue from auxiliary enterprises (such as dormitories) of $10.7 billion and from hospitals of $8.2 billion. Figures are from National Center for Education Statistics (1989, table 269, p. 292).

Table 1-2. *Student Aid Distribution, by Sector of Postsecondary Education, Academic Year 1986–87*
Amounts in dollars

| Distribution category[a] | Sector | | |
	Public	Private nonprofit	Proprietary
Percent of students receiving aid			
Total	38.0	65.3	84.0
Federal	28.5	48.4	80.6
State	12.5	25.4	10.3
Institution based	8.8	39.0	4.1
Other	6.0	11.2	3.7
Average student charges[b]			
(inclusive of student aid)	3,805	9,676	5,198
Average aid amount for aided students	2,887	5,633	4,025

Source: Data for distribution and amounts of aid are from Korb and others (1988, tables 4.1 and 4.6, pp. 24, 37). Data for student charges in public and private nonprofit institutions are from National Center for Education Statistics (1989, table 258, pp. 281–82). Student charges at proprietary institutions weight the expenses that are reported in Korb and others (1988, tables 2.3 and 3.1, pp. 12, 17) by the fraction of students living in each of three kinds of housing situation.

a. Aid distributions for an institutional type do not total 100 percent because some students receive aid from more than one source.

b. Student charges include tuition, fees, room, and board.

public institutions. The federal expenditures are spread wider, with about one-half going to public institutions, one-quarter to private, nonprofit institutions, and the final quarter to profit-seeking trade and vocational schools.[16] The relatively large percentage of support going to proprietary institutions, relative to their enrollments (which are between 5 and 7 percent of the total), reflects the fact that their student bodies are disproportionately drawn from lower-income groups and the fact that their tuition charges are high enough to qualify their students for substantial amounts of federal aid.

Under this complex system of college finance, the net price that any particular student will pay at any particular institution, after allowing for all subsidies, will depend on a number of factors. Table 1-2 shows how aid distributions and average student charges vary over the three sectors, public, private nonprofit, and proprietary. The sticker price (total student charges before aid is taken into account) in private, nonprofit institutions averages about 2.5 times that in public institu-

16. The NPSAS reports proprietary students getting 15 percent of federal aid, public students getting 55 percent, and private nonprofit students getting 30 percent. However, as noted above, there is evidence that the NPSAS substantially underestimates the enrollment of, and hence the amount of funds going to, proprietary students. The figures in the text adjust the NPSAS figures to accord approximately with other sources describing the distribution of aid across sectors, including College Board (1989b), which bases its estimates on data from the federal programs.

tions. The relatively low costs to students in public higher education reflect the subsidy to tuition that is provided to all students through state appropriations covering institutional operating costs. Notice, however, that students in private and proprietary institutions are much more likely to receive student aid than are those in public institutions and that the average aided student in a nonpublic school receives substantially more aid. It is also noteworthy that in all three sectors federal aid reaches a substantial fraction of students, playing a particularly prominent role at proprietary institutions, with more than 80 percent of these students receiving such aid. Institution-based aid plays a major role only in private, nonprofit higher education, where 39 percent of all students receive such aid. Determining the overall effects of this complex mixture of governmental and institutional practices, then, is a demanding task—a task made all the more complicated by the fact that the financing system has changed substantially in recent decades.

The Effectiveness of the Student Finance System

State subsidies to institutions have for more than a century been the largest component of government support in the overall structure of higher-education finance. Since World War II, however, the biggest change in the financing system has come through the expanded role for need-based student aid. Although scholarships to especially able and needy students have always been part of the college financing picture, the systematic introduction of needs-tested aid in the 1950s, followed by two decades of large-scale federal support for student aid, has resulted in a complex set of programs. To some observers this combined system of need-based aid and state operating subsidies is seen as fundamental to the existing college and university financing system, providing crucial services to disadvantaged students and contributing to the financial health and stability of higher education as a whole. Others see it as a wasteful and ill-structured mess, spending money ineffectually and distorting the incentives of students and institutions.

How can the effectiveness of this financing system be best evaluated? Given the predominance of the federal government in the provision of financial aid to individual students—it supplies approximately three-quarters of student assistance dollars—it makes sense to concentrate a good deal of analytical effort on assessing the effectiveness of this federal effort.[17] Moreover, federal policy has considerable leverage on other components of the system. A focused effort to modify federal aid policy can induce both states and institutions to respond; decentralized efforts by individual states or schools, though also important, cannot in the nature of things have comparable systemwide effects. Thus, careful consideration of federal policy really forces the analyst to examine the financing system comprehensively.

Our discussion of federal policy can be usefully organized around three central questions. First, have government financing efforts expanded educational opportunity? Have they, that is, encouraged the enrollment and broadened the educational choices of disadvantaged students? Second, have government financing efforts made higher education institutions work better, by making them financially more secure and educationally more effective? Or have they instead had perverse effects—as, for example, in the allegation that federal student aid has caused private institutions to raise prices in an effort to capture additional aid? Third, have government financing efforts made the distribution of the benefits of higher education, and the sharing of its costs, fairer?

Our agenda is thus broader than most found in discussions of financing effectiveness. Many policy analysts have fallen into the habit of focusing on federal programs, taking the state and institutional contributions to financing as largely given, and then further equating the issue of federal aid effectiveness with how much and how well student aid affects the enrollments of lower-income students. This is natural, since helping deprived students is a central purpose of the aid effort and since it appears somewhat measurable. But limiting inquiry only to the effects of aid on access for lower-income students produces an unreasonably narrow framework for assessing the role and impact of student aid in the overall higher-education financing system.

To elaborate for a moment on that last point, take first the question of fairness. Why can't we say that our concern about the fairness of the system would be settled by finding out if aid allows poor students to go to college who otherwise couldn't? A simple test of this criterion would let us limit discussion to our first, and more comfortable, question about the accessibility of education. But it seems clear that a lot of the

17. College Board (1989b, table 1, p. 6).

energy in the student financing debate comes from questions about who *should*, and not simply who *can*, carry the burden. Once a system is put in place that helps some families, one needs systematic rules about where to draw lines in determining whom to help and in what amounts. Those concerns have, for example, been at the heart of the continuing wrangle over how far up the income scale subsidies should extend.

Even if one considered the relatively straightforward need of poor families, concerns about college financing are not resolved by the purely numerical success of getting more of their members into higher education. Some lower-income families have made extraordinary sacrifices to send their children to college without aid. And most people, we believe, would feel strongly that it is unfair to ask that kind of sacrifice of some parents while others have a much easier time of it. Surely this kind of judgment should figure in our assessment of the financing system. This is so even though for those families who actually make the extraordinary sacrifice, the student aid just improves the family living standard and does not boost enrollment.

The impact of government finance on institutions and on the financial stability of higher education similarly must be in the picture. Although we pin the label "student aid" on some of the dollars that federal and state governments disburse, the fact is that those dollars inevitably become part of the overall stream of financial resources on which colleges and universities rely. In the immortal words of David Stockman, federal aid dollars help colleges and universities "finance their budgets."[18] It is quite likely that federal aid policies affect college pricing and aid policies, admissions policies, curricular and staffing decisions, and so on, just as state financing policies surely do. Government finance thus affects the *supply* as well as the *demand* for education. This is certainly clear for the states, with their central role in operating public institutions. Moreover, the history of the federal student aid programs makes it fairly clear that Congress anticipated and implicitly endorsed the notion that federal aid would contribute to the financial health of colleges.[19] Such factors must be part of the story.

18. "Now you are going to get a lot of pressure from the colleges on it. They're not worried about the student, they're not worried about equity in America; they're worried about financing their budgets." David A. Stockman, in Jonathan Fuerbringer, "GOP Leadership Seeking a Freeze in Social Security," *New York Times*, February 8, 1985, p. 1.

19. See the illuminating treatment in Gladieux and Wolanin (1976).

Considerations in Assessing Federal Policy

As must be clear by now, we intend to focus much of our analytical effort on evaluating the role of the federal government in higher-education finance, keeping a close eye on the key fact that it is only one influential but not necessarily dominant player in the overall financing system. More particularly, the analyses that follow bear on assessing the impact of the federal aid system on the three main questions of opportunity, institutional health, and distributive fairness.

The Impact of Student Aid on Lower-Income Enrollment

Although there is more to the story, a central purpose of federal student aid has been to provide needy students with the resources needed to encourage them to attend college and broaden their choices among colleges. How well has that strategy worked?

Attempts to answer this question come up against one preeminent obstacle: need-based federal student aid is only one strand in a highly complex and varying web of factors determining students' educational decisions. It would be most convenient if one could "rewind the tape" of the last twenty years and see what higher education would look like if there had never been, say, Pell grants. Or, a subtler counterfactual, one could see what would have happened if Pell grant award maxima had kept pace with the growth in college costs and the formulas for determining aid eligibility had been left in place over the period, rather than being subjected to the substantial variations these awards experienced.

But that's impossible. Basically only two kinds of substitutes exist for replaying history. One, the "before and after" study, involves looking at the actual historical record to see how the world with federal student aid is different from the world without it. The trouble is that one can never be sure if the results that show up in the actual record were produced by factors other than or additional to student aid— precisely the sort of possibility that could be ruled out if one could replay history according to some desired script.

The alternative is to build a statistical model of the processes that generate the historical outcomes, estimate the parameters of that model, and then try to simulate two separate histories by running the model with and without a measure for federal aid. The danger here—besides the pitfalls of statistical estimation—is that the model may omit some of the key relationships that shape real-world change. Suppose, for example, that federal student aid has indirect effects on the behavior of institutions: more generous aid may make them raise their admissions standards. The actual historical record will be shaped by these indirect effects, but the simulated history will not.

Since neither approach is adequate in itself, the obvious solution is to use both approaches and see if the two sets of findings can be reconciled. This we attempt in chapters 2 and 3. Chapter 2, on the recent history of financing and enrollment in higher education, includes a discussion of the historical data on enrollments and an attempt to detect the effects of changes in federal aid programs on that data. Chapter 3 reviews the literature on enrollment determination, looking especially at empirical studies of the effect of student aid on enrollment. That chapter also provides a new econometric study of the historical evidence. These chapters, which together use both a historical and empirical approach, offer a reasonably consistent picture of the impact that aid has on the enrollment of lower-income students. Our basic conclusion is that reductions in the net price charged to students (total charges less aid received) significantly increase the propensity of lower-income students to attend college, but do not increase the enrollment of middle- and upper-income students.

A further aspect of expanded educational opportunity is the length of a student's stay after his or her initial enrollment. If student aid simply induces a student to enroll and then quickly drop out, it would be hard to credit the increased enrollment with much genuine increase in opportunity. Although we do not undertake any fresh quantitative work in this area, it is reassuring to note that other studies have found that aided students are as likely to persist as other students.[20] That is, other things being equal, an aided student is as likely or more likely to remain in school, or to receive a degree, as a nonaided student. Thus, it seems justified to assume that expanded enrollment of aided students typically implies a genuine improvement in their educational opportunity.

State operating subsidies also have the plain effect of keeping tuition for lower-income students below what they would otherwise be, thus

20. See, for example, Porter (1989) and St. John, Kirshstein, and Noell (1988). The latter paper provides further references to the literature.

encouraging lower-income enrollment. They do it, however, at substantial cost. State subsidies reduce the net price for all students at public institutions, and the evidence we discuss in chapter 3 suggests that price reductions for middle- and upper-income students have no measurable effect on whether they enroll in college. In addition, other evidence points to a considerable recent rise in the share of public-sector students who come from affluent families, suggesting that while the number of students who benefit from these operating subsidies is rising, it is not necessarily a sign of improved access or expanded opportunity.

Institutions and Student Aid: The Supply Side

It is not possible to assess the effectiveness of student aid without attention to its impact on how, and how well, institutions operate. This issue was pushed into the headlines in the mid-1980s by then Secretary of Education William Bennett's strong insistence that increasing student aid does not help needy students cope with college costs, because the main effect of aid is simply to cause schools to raise their prices.[21] Certainly, the nation's experience with medicare and other federal programs has increased everyone's awareness that government subsidies can sometimes contribute substantially to price increases. Yet it would be remarkable if literally *all* federal aid were simply absorbed in aid-induced tuition increases—and we will show that no credible evidence supports such a claim. But it would also be just as remarkable if schools' decisions about pricing and the allocation of their own aid funds were entirely independent of federal student aid policy.

In fact, it is not impossible that aid and tuition are linked in just the opposite way from the secretary's hypothesis. It is possible that *decreases* in federal student aid, or other forms of federal support, may *raise* the prices some schools charge. If schools feel obliged, either for competitive or humanitarian reasons, to replace lost federal aid for needy students, that revenue has to be made up from other sources. And the revenue source that most institutions (especially private institutions) have some control over is tuition. This would provide a link between tuition and aid exactly inverse to the one Secretary Bennett emphasized.

In chapter 4, we address this issue in two ways. First, we examine historical trends in pricing and other dimensions of institutions' finan-

21. William Bennett, "Our Greedy Colleges," *New York Times*, February 18, 1987, p. A31.

cial decisionmaking in relation to trends in federal student aid and other forms of government support for higher education. Second, we use data from individual institutions to estimate the impact of various forms of external support on institutional financial behavior. Both sets of information let us test the Bennett hypothesis statistically, and when we do so we find no significant effect of changes in federal student aid on changes in tuition at private institutions. Interestingly, we do find that *public* institutions that receive increases in federal student aid do raise their tuitions more rapidly.

It would, however, be a mistake to limit assessment of the institutional impact of aid to the narrow question of pricing. Federal financial aid may, for example, influence the amount of money schools devote to instruction; alternatively, federal aid may replace student aid funding from the schools' own resources or else, like a matching grant, induce them to spend more of their own resources on student aid. For that matter, federal spending to support research may well leak over into other areas, affecting the price and quality of undergraduate instruction. Chapter 4 also examines similar questions concerning the impact of state operating subsidies on tuition at public institutions and on institutional quality.

Thus, while analysts have, comparatively speaking, lavished attention on the demand-side implications of student aid, they have hardly touched the supply side. It has been like having studies of agricultural price supports ignore the behavior of farmers, or studies of housing subsidies ignore the builders. It is our hope that the empirical work in chapter 4 particularly will begin to fill this gap.[22] From that work we find significant relationships between various external financial variables and institutions' choices about sticker price, institution-based financial aid, and their expenditures on instruction.

Distributive Effects of Aid

Student aid plays a strategic role in determining how the burden of paying for college is shared—shared among families, governments, and institutions, and, within families, how it is shared between the

22. Such studies connect with the literature on public choice and on the behavior of the not-for-profit sector more generally. Hoenack and Pierro (1986), as well as our own chapter 4, provides further references to this aspect of the study of higher education.

generations. Student aid is, of course, far from the only factor influencing these processes of "burden sharing."[23] State operating subsidies have a major influence on public institution tuition. Increasingly, too, there is interest in new devices to rearrange the burden—tax-preferred college savings instruments, college prepayment plans, and the like. Although these programs do not yet amount to much quantitatively, the attention they have received underscores the importance of distributive fairness when evaluating the nation's system for financing undergraduate education.[24]

Closely related to the issue of who should pay the costs of higher education is the question of who goes where to college. How does the quality or range of educational opportunities available to a student depend on his or her social background? There is perhaps special concern about the college destinations of high-achieving high school students. Are the educational futures of such students decisively shaped by their economic circumstances, or does the combination of government student aid and other forms of support provide them with a wide range of alternatives? A different but familiar concern is the perception that the middle class is being squeezed out of elite private higher education by rising costs, so that only the wealthy or the grant-assisted poor can afford to attend. In chapter 5, we assemble a variety of data that illuminate these "choice"-related issues, aiming to see how the college destinations of students have changed over time and trying to determine how financial considerations may have dictated their decisions.

Not everything we report in chapter 5 is encouraging—we find that the representation of students from middle-income backgrounds has declined at both public universities and highly selective private institutions. For the elite private institutions, at least, there is evidence that this decline may be explained in part by a tendency for middle-income families to underestimate the amount of aid that would be available to them. Yet despite these recent declines, middle-income students are still well represented in public universities and elite private institutions. But what another twenty years of rapid price increases might do to patterns of college affordability is difficult to say. Future trends in

23. See Johnstone (1986) for a comparative treatment of this issue at the international level.
24. For a more extensive treatment, see Hauptman (1990b). While not a major focus of this study, we discuss these new financing schemes in chapters 7 and 8.

affordability will depend on how rapidly college costs increase, on how much governments and donors contribute to defray those costs, on how rapidly family incomes grow, and on how much student aid is available to help meet the college costs of needy students. Chapter 6 provides an analysis of future affordability trends based on a range of projections that allows all these parameters to vary. The results underline the crucial role of stable, economywide growth in output and productivity as well as the importance of nontuition revenue at colleges in keeping the costs of higher education manageable.

Dimensions of Policy Choice

The goal of keeping college affordable, as we understand it, involves much more than keeping the sticker price to families as low as possible. As we argued at the outset, our concern is as much with using the nation's resources wisely as it is with keeping the cost of college to individual families low. Drawing on our empirical work, chapters 7 and 8 highlight some of the most important and most widely debated policy issues, along with others that have been relatively neglected.

Chapter 7 focuses on issues surrounding the targeting of financial assistance—whom to support and through what mechanisms. The basic logic of the financial aid system as a whole, and of its federal component in particular, has been heavily shaped by the principles of "need-based" student aid. Originally worked out by a group of colleges in the 1950s to guide the allocation of their own student aid resources, these principles, and the practical means of implementing them, have now been thoroughly resolved. They amount to a rather sophisticated system for taxing the income and assets of the families of financial aid recipients to ensure that they contribute to college costs according to their ability to pay.[25]

The system is, however, built around a series of assumptions and compromises that deserve attention. For example, needs analysis takes into account both the cost of the institution attended as well as the

25. Implementation of this system raises a variety of fascinating technical issues, many of them at a level of detail beyond the reach of this study. Over the years, the College Scholarship Service and the American College Testing Program, two of the major providers of needs-analysis services to colleges, have produced a number of valuable studies of the technical aspects of the student aid system.

family's resources: the more expensive the school, the "needier" the family. While this seems a sensible way for colleges to allocate their own resources, it is less clear that the federal government should operate this way. The issue is tied up with the question of how federal student aid should figure into the finance of a mixed public-private system of colleges, where the price facing some students (and therefore their financial need) is held down by state operating subsidies to public institutions.

A second issue related to needs analysis concerns the treatment of adult and independent students, a growing population in higher education which now receives more than half of all Pell grants.[26] Needs analysis was conceived originally to assess the financial resources of parents of young high school graduates, and its ad hoc translation to fit the situation of independent adult students is in many ways unsatisfactory.

A final issue raised in chapter 7 is the remarkable growth of vocational and technical training as an activity supported by the student aid programs. The principal federal programs are impartial between academic and vocational programs and among for-profit, private nonprofit, and state-run providers of services. It is fairly clear that Congress never expected nor intended that a quarter of all federal student aid funds should go to students learning trades at profit-seeking vocational institutions. Is there now reason for concern that either the level or the form of support for these activities—or for the vocational training provided at community colleges—is inappropriate?

Chapter 8 focuses on another dimension of burden sharing—the distribution of the costs and benefits of higher education over time. There is considerable evidence that, even viewed narrowly as an investment in higher earnings, higher education provides a good return. Currently, the American higher education system relies substantially on intergenerational finance—on each generation's contributing to the costs of the next generation's higher education, through taxes and parental contributions. An alternative would be to have each generation borrow enough to pay all or most of the cost of its own education. Chapter 8 discusses the feasibility of this alternative and considers the question of how this distribution of the burden of paying for college may matter economically and educationally. We also address some

26. College Board (1989b, table 8, p. 12).

other investment-related topics in higher education, including the notion of tailoring student aid policies to meet special labor market needs, and that of investing more heavily in the education of more able students through the use of merit aid.

Our conclusions about desirable directions for public policy are presented in chapter 9. To put them briefly, we believe the evidence shows that federal student aid fulfills its purpose, in three related senses. First, using student aid to reduce the price facing lower-income students causes more of them to enroll in college. Second, the presence of federal student aid, and accompanying institution-based aid, makes the distribution of educational opportunity across colleges broader and the pattern of burden sharing fairer. Finally, we find no evidence that perverse effects of aid on college pricing or resource allocation are significant. Under present arrangements, federal aid functions as a complement to state operating subsidies in the overall financing system, since state subsidies are the largest source of government finance and state institutions enroll the bulk of the students. Our assessment is that, viewed in this way, the contributions of federal student aid are positive and important but could be strengthened through a number of incremental reforms.

A more ambitious program of reform would call for rethinking the balance between the federal and state roles in the undergraduate financing system. Our judgment is that in the long run the best way to strengthen the undergraduate financing system is to increase the role of "ability-to-pay" pricing in the higher education system. The alternative is to rely on low tuition across the board as the means of providing access to college for lower-income students. This is a very expensive strategy for state governments, and one that they may be increasingly unwilling to follow. To the extent that state budgets are squeezed and operating subsidies are reduced, maintaining a low-tuition strategy forces states to reduce educational quality at state-supported institutions. If, on the other hand, they make up for reduced operating subsidies through higher tuition, the effects on lower-income access are likely to be devastating unless either states or the federal government provide more income-tested aid to the affected students. In chapter 9, we examine a possible solution to this dilemma—a redefinition of federal and state responsibilities for undergraduate student finance. Our proposal for the long run would make the federal government responsible for financing the educational costs of lower-income students, thus expanding the role of income-tested federal student aid while permitting states to raise tuition and thus reduce the magnitude of state operating subsidies without adverse effects on access. Such a "swap" of federal for state funding of the educational costs of lower-income students could, we believe, broaden opportunity, increase fairness, and raise the quality of higher education without increasing the nation's public investment.

II

Changing Patterns of College Finance and Enrollment

THIS CHAPTER summarizes the principal trends in the finance of under-graduate higher education and the pattern of postsecondary enrollment over the last half century. By taking a long view, some dramatic developments emerge. These include substantial growth in the share of enrollment at public institutions, a considerable increase in the fraction of young people who attend some kind of college, and a major increase in the role of the federal government in financing higher education. Over the long haul, though, it has been the growth in federal research support, rather than in federal student aid, that has been most prominent. Only in more recent decades has federal student aid come to play a more significant role.[1]

The first part of this chapter takes the long view, reviewing college finance and enrollment patterns since 1939. Later sections focus more closely on developments since the introduction of the major federal student aid programs in 1965 and 1972.

A Long-Run Perspective on College Finance

Tables 2-1 through 2-3 provide a schematic overview of the principal changes in college finance and enrollment since 1939. Table 2-1 shows how colleges' principal sources of revenue have changed over the last fifty years.[2] For public institutions, state and local government spending has been the most important source of support, and has plainly helped keep tuitions relatively low—with gross tuition (inclusive of student

1. In addition, that role has been subject to substantial fluctuations, both in the level of support and in the distribution of support among families and institutions.
2. Data after the 1985–86 academic year have not yet been released by the federal government.

Table 2-1. *Shares of Educational and General Revenue,*
Public and Private Institutions, Selected
Academic Years, 1939–86[a]
Percent

| Year | Gross tuition | Government[b] | | Gifts and endowment earnings | Other |
		Federal	State and local		
		Public institutions			
1939–40	0.20	0.13	0.61	0.04	0.01
1949–50	0.25	0.13	0.56	0.03	0.03
1955–56	0.13	0.17	0.62	0.04	0.04
1959–60	0.13	0.21	0.59	0.04	0.03
1965–66	0.14	0.23	0.54	0.03	0.05
1969–70	0.15	0.19	0.57	0.03	0.05
1975–76	0.16	0.18	0.61	0.03	0.02
1979–80	0.15	0.16	0.62	0.04	0.03
1985–86	0.18	0.13	0.61	0.05	0.03
		Private institutions			
1939–40	0.55	0.01	0.03	0.38	0.03
1949–50	0.57	0.12	0.04	0.23	0.05
1955–56	0.45	0.18	0.02	0.28	0.06
1959–60	0.43	0.25	0.02	0.25	0.05
1965–66	0.43	0.30	0.02	0.18	0.06
1969–70	0.44	0.26	0.03	0.19	0.08
1975–76	0.48	0.25	0.04	0.19	0.04
1979–80	0.47	0.25	0.04	0.19	0.05
1985–86	0.50	0.22	0.03	0.19	0.06

Sources: Data for 1939–66 are from Susan A. Nelson, "Financial Trends and Issues," in Breneman and Finn (1978, table 2-1, pp. 70–71). Data for 1969–86 are from National Center for Education Statistics (1989, tables 270 and 271, pp. 293–94).
a. Figures in table do not include revenue from auxiliary enterprises or from sales and services.
b. Government figures do not include student aid. Such aid is counted under gross tuition.

aid) providing between 13 percent and 25 percent of revenue at public
colleges and universities. Both the state and local government share
and the tuition share have been fairly stable over the period, although
a gradual rise in the share of public tuition can be observed starting
about 1959.[3]

For private institutions, the most important source of revenue has
been tuition. As with public institutions, the share of tuition in total
revenue is fairly stable, with a gradual upward trend visible from 1965
on. A decline in the share of support that private institutions derive from
gifts and endowment earnings is evident in the table. The importance of
federal support has varied considerably for private institutions, account-

3. For the 1949–50 academic year, the unusually high share of public tuition, 25 percent of
public institution revenue, was the result of the GI Bill. Federal tuition payments for veterans are
counted under gross tuition.

Table 2-2. *Enrollment at Public and Private Nonprofit Institutions, Selected Academic Years, 1939–88*[a]

	Total	Share	
Year	enrollment	Public	Private
1939	1,494	0.53	0.47
1949	2,659	0.51	0.49
1959	3,640	0.60	0.40
1965	5,921	0.67	0.33
1969	8,005	0.74	0.26
1975	11,185	0.79	0.21
1979	11,570	0.78	0.22
1985	12,247	0.77	0.23
1988	12,849	0.78	0.22

Source: National Center for Education Statistics (1989, table 3, p. 10).

a. For 1939 and 1949, data include all resident degree-credit students enrolled at any time during the academic year. Beginning in 1959, data include all resident and extension students enrolled at the beginning of the fall term. Data for 1988 are based on "early estimates."

ing for just 1 percent of revenue in 1939, 30 percent of revenue in 1965, and 22 percent in 1985. The share of federal support in public institutional revenue has shown a similar but more muted pattern of change.[4] Notice that in the table, student aid is reported under gross tuition and not under the government revenue figures—these latter figures include appropriations, gifts, grants, and contracts for colleges and universities.

While these figures in table 2-1 point to considerable stability in the funding sources of public and private institutions, enrollment patterns have not been nearly so stable. As table 2-2 shows, the shares of enrollment in the two sectors have changed markedly over the last half-century. In 1949, enrollment was divided almost equally between the public and private sectors, but by 1975, the public share had grown to 79 percent of all enrollment. Much of the growth in public enrollment during the 1960s occurred at two-year institutions. These institutions accounted for only 24 percent of public enrollment in 1963, but for 43 percent in 1975.[5] Interestingly, over this period of rapid growth in public enrollment relative to total enrollment, the level of private college enrollments continued to grow—it was simply the case that public institutions absorbed more of the rising enrollment. By the mid-1970s, rapid enrollment growth had subsided. Since then, the shares of enrollment in public and private higher education have been stable.

4. For the 1939–40 academic year, the surprisingly high figure for the federal share of public revenue, 13 percent, reflects the fact that the military academies are counted as public institutions.

5. National Center for Education Statistics (1989, table 149, p. 168).

Table 2-3. *Shares of Higher-Education Revenue, by Source, Selected Academic Years, 1939–86*

Year	Gross tuition	Tuition paid by				Nontuition revenue		
		Families	Insti-tutions	Government		Federal	State and local	Gifts and endowment earnings
				Federal[a]	State			
1939–40	0.37	0.35	0.02[b]	0.00	0.00[b]	0.07	0.33	0.21
1949–50	0.40	0.37	0.03	0.00	0.00[b]	0.12	0.32	0.12
1959–60	0.26	0.22	0.03	0.00	0.01	0.23	0.34	0.13
1965–66	0.26	0.21	0.04	0.00	0.01	0.26	0.33	0.09
1969–70	0.25	0.20	0.04	0.00	0.01	0.22	0.38	0.08
1975–76	0.26	0.16	0.04	0.04	0.02	0.20	0.43	0.08
1979–80	0.26	0.14	0.04	0.06	0.02	0.19	0.43	0.09
1985–86	0.29	0.18	0.05	0.05	0.02	0.16	0.41	0.10

Sources: Gross tuition and nontuition revenue are calculated from tables 2-1 and 2-2. Distribution of revenue among tuition-payers is calculated from tables 2-1 and 2-2 as well as from data in O'Neill (1973, table A-1, pp. 28–29); O'Neill (1971, tables 9 and 10, pp. 18–19), Gillespie and Carlson (1983, table A-1, p. 30), and College Board (1989b, table 1, p. 6).

a. Both veteran's educational benefits and social security benefits paid to qualified college students are excluded from federal tuition payments.

b. Figure is authors' estimate.

Yet, the swing that did occur in enrollment shares has major implications for overall financing patterns. Table 2-3 uses the enrollment weights reported in table 2-2 to examine the sources of higher-education revenue since 1939. Table 2-3 reports revenue shares for the major categories given in table 2-1, averaged over public and private institutions, and also breaks down gross tuition by its sources—showing the share paid by families directly and the shares paid by various forms of student aid.

The most striking trend in table 2-3 is the steady decline through 1979 in the overall share of tuition that is paid by families.[6] This decline was brought on by several forces. First, as the enrollment share of public institutions grew until the mid-1970s, the share of state and local spending grew along with it. Consequently, there was little pressure on tuitions and tuition payments as a share of total institutional revenue fell over the period. Second, the growth of federal grant and contract revenue from the end of the 1930s through the mid-1960s helped lower the share of gross tuition in overall revenue. Most of these federal funds

6. Recall that payments made under the GI Bill caused the tuition share in the 1949–50 academic year to be unusually high. The figures in table 2-3 report GI Bill tuition payments as if they were made by families rather than by the federal government. When veterans' tuition payments are treated differently, the share of revenue provided by families is dramatically reduced in 1949–50 as well as in 1969–70 and 1975–76, when Vietnam veterans received federal support. Our treatment here is based partly on the premise that trends stand out more clearly if we do not include these episodic events. Moreover, there may be a case for treating educational payments to veterans as deferred compensation rather than as student aid.

were directed toward financing research, although there were significant federal subsidies for dormitory construction in the 1960s. These vastly expanded research expenditures might be seen as largely separate from undergraduate instruction and finance, but we later present evidence that changes in federal grant and contract spending influence several aspects of institutional behavior, including the pricing of tuition and the spending on instruction.

A third reason for the declining share of family payments is that institutions and state governments gradually increased their student aid spending as a share of revenue. Thus the net tuition paid by families formed a decreasing share of total revenue. In addition, an even greater change in student aid spending was brought about by new federal programs. While federal student aid grants began to contribute to tuition payments in 1965, with the introduction of the educational opportunity grant program, it was not until 1972, with the launching of what is now the Pell program, that federal student aid grants made enough of a difference to show up in table 2-3. Since the 1975–76 academic year, the Pell program's impact has been substantial, reducing the share of higher education revenue provided by families by between 4 and 6 percentage points in each year.[7]

The cumulative effect of all these changes has been substantial. Over the period 1939–80, the educational and general revenue of colleges and universities has grown at 1.9 percent annually in real terms—a pace that roughly matches the growth in family incomes. However, because government payments covered a growing share of institutional revenue, real tuition grew at just 1.0 percent annually until about 1980. Government and institutional subsidies of tuition payments have further reduced the rate of growth in the burden on families. This shifting of burdens—through the expansion of public higher education and through a larger federal role—has substantially increased the affordability of college over the last fifty years for a wide segment of the American population, changing the nation's conception of higher education from that of a luxury available only to the elite to a normal experience for all qualified young adults.

The steady decline in the share of higher education revenue provided by families came to an abrupt halt after 1979, with the family share increasing by 4 percentage points in the 1979–86 period. Most of this

7. Table 2-3 does not take into account the federally financed educational loans provided to families—such loans are treated as part of the family's payments.

increase is explained by the increased reliance on tuition in the finance of both public and private institutions in the 1980s—a trend whose counterpart is a modest decline in the share provided by state and local government and a more substantial decline in the share provided by federal grant and contract payments. Links between changes in external funding and internal adjustments by institutions are the major topic of chapter 4.

As we look ahead, it seems unlikely that the steadily expanding government subsidies to higher education, which came to a halt at the end of the 1970s, are likely to resume. First, the public share of total enrollment cannot expand much further: the expanded role for state subsidies that accompanied a growing share of public enrollment is nearing its end. Second, postsecondary enrollments have grown so large that expanding the total government subsidy per student has become a very expensive proposition. These facts raise broad questions about future college affordability, which we examine in chapter 6. More immediately, these same facts underline the importance of examining how existing higher-education subsidies have been targeted and how effective they have been in meeting governmental goals.

College Financing Trends since 1965

In 1965, when Congress passed and President Lyndon Johnson signed the Higher Education Act, the principle that the federal government should bear an important share of responsibility for ensuring college opportunity for disadvantaged students was enacted into law. Although state governments were and have remained the largest financial contributors to public institutions (indeed, their share of total revenue grew as the community college movement expanded public enrollments during the 1960s and early 1970s), policy discussion has come increasingly to focus on defining and financing the changing federal role.

Table 2-4 shows the overall magnitudes of federal and other forms of student aid, expressed in constant dollars, for selected years since 1963. The overall change from the 1970s to the 1980s is dominated by so-called specially directed aid, funds provided to veterans and to children of social security recipients. However, it is not entirely clear whether the veterans' programs should be regarded as "student aid,"

Table 2-4. Aid Awarded to Students, by Source of Aid, Selected Academic Years, 1963–89
Millions of 1989–90 dollars

Source	1963–64	1970–71	1975–76	1979–80	1981–82	1983–84	1985–86	1987–88[a]	1988–89[b]
Federal programs									
Generally available aid									
Pell grants	0	0	2,154	4,108	3,114	3,491	4,176	4,103	4,679
Supplemental educational opportunity grants	0	429	463	546	490	451	480	460	412
State student incentive grants[c]	0	0	46	125	104	75	89	82	77
Work-study	0	727	679	976	845	854	768	697	741
Perkins loans	469	768	1,059	1,059	786	853	823	883	901
GSL, PLUS, and SLS[d]	0	3,249	2,915	6,438	9,782	9,472	10,348	12,500	12,461
Subtotal	469	5,173	7,315	13,251	15,121	15,196	16,684	18,726	19,270
Specially directed aid									
Social security	0	1,597	2,515	2,602	2,703	275	0	0	0
Veterans	276	3,588	9,619	2,925	1,830	1,435	994	837	779
Other grants	37	51	147	189	462	454	484	476	474
Other loans	0	134	104	69	148	329	436	322	315
Subtotal	313	5,371	12,384	5,785	5,143	2,493	1,913	1,635	1,568
Total federal aid	782	10,544	19,700	19,037	20,264	17,690	18,597	20,361	20,839
State grant programs	230	755	1,128	1,292	1,247	1,383	1,535	1,649	1,723
Institutionally awarded aid	1,234	3,089	3,302	3,096	3,043	3,602	4,301	5,006	5,409
Total federal, state, and institutional aid	2,247	14,389	24,129	23,425	24,555	22,675	24,433	27,016	27,970

Sources: Gillespie and Carlson (1983, table A-1, p. 30), Lewis (1988, 1, p. 6), and College Board (1989b, table 1, p. 6).
a. Figures are estimated.
b. Figures are preliminary.
c. State student incentive grants, or SSIGs, are federal matching funds for state need-based aid programs.
d. The acronyms represent guaranteed student loans, parent loans for undergraduate students, and supplemental loans for students, respectively.

since they might instead be seen as a form of deferred compensation. Moreover, although awards in both the veterans' and social security programs are contingent on college attendance, neither was designed with the principal aim of promoting higher education, and neither fits the model of need-based student aid, which dominates other federal student aid programs. Both programs were large in the mid-1970s, and have dwindled to almost nothing in the 1980s.[8]

When these programs are ignored, the "generally available" student aid programs administered by the Office (later Department) of Education predominate. The campus-based programs described in chapter 1 have not grown much in real terms since their inception in the mid-1960s, with the result that the guaranteed student loan (GSL) programs and the basic educational opportunity (later Pell) grant program have gradually become the main sources of federal student aid.

With respect to how federal funding has developed, the period from 1965 to the present can be usefully divided into four subperiods. From 1965 to 1973, a fairly modest total of "generally available" aid was divided between the GSL and the campus-based programs.[9] From 1973 to 1980, the federal aid budget grew rapidly, with expenditures on the newly introduced Pell program roughly keeping pace in percentage terms with the growing number of dollars lent through the GSL program. From about 1980 through about 1984, GSL growth continued to be substantial, while real growth in the Pell grant and the campus-based programs declined. In 1979, new guaranteed loans represented about 49 percent of the total volume of generally available federal student aid; in 1985, they were about 62 percent.[10] Since 1985, the Pell program has grown by 12 percent and guaranteed loans by 20 percent in real terms.

The targeting of these federal programs, across both students and institutions, has varied considerably. The following section examines the targeting of federal aid by income groups in some detail, focusing

8. The social security benefit was being phased out by 1982. As for the GI Bill, the lower spending results both from changes in the program and from the reduced number of young veterans claiming benefits after the Vietnam War ended.

9. The original GSL program (now called the Stafford loan program) has been, and still is, considerably larger than the other two components of the federal guaranteed loan program, PLUS and SLS. In table 2-4, we sum the three types of loans.

10. The shift toward loans is more dramatic when social security benefits and the GI Bill are included. In 1979, new guaranteed loans comprised about 34 percent of total federal aid, compared with 57 percent in 1985.

Table 2-5. *Distribution of Pell Grant Funds to Independent Students and Proprietary Schools, Selected Academic Years, 1973–88*
Percent

Year	Pell recipients who are independent students	Pell revenue going to students at proprietary institutions
1973–74	13.3	7.0
1975–76	29.8	9.0
1977–78	38.5	8.9
1979–80	33.8	10.5
1981–82	41.9	13.5
1983–84	47.5	18.8
1985–86	50.4	22.1
1987–88	57.6	26.6[a]

Sources: Gillespie and Carlson (1983, table 9, p. 26, and table A-12, p. 41); and College Board (1989b, tables 7 and 8, p. 12).
a. Figure is an estimate.

on that group of full-time students in "traditional" colleges and universities who are dependent upon their parents for financial support. Although when the programs were launched, this group constituted the largest set of aid recipients, and they remain an important group, the participation of other groups of students and institutions in federal student aid programs has grown substantially.

Table 2-5 illustrates this point through an examination of how Pell funds have been distributed in the 1970s and 1980s. While, in the early years of the program, the bulk of grant recipients were traditional-aged college students supported by their parents, this has changed so much that in recent years the majority of recipients are independent students, many of whom are adults.[11] An equally striking change has occurred in the distribution of Pell funds among institution types. Currently, as table 2-5 shows, students at proprietary vocational and technical institutions, most of which offer nondegree programs of less than two years, receive more than a quarter of all Pell grant funds—a figure that is up from only 11 percent in 1979–80. Yet, proprietary institutions enroll fewer than 7 percent of undergraduate students. While comparable figures for the distribution of loan funds are not available, they would probably show a similar pattern. These remarkable changes in the targeting of federal subsidies obviously raise major policy questions

11. Although the share of college students who are adult or independent has grown, it has not grown as fast as the share of Pell recipients who are independent. Chapter 7 discusses in greater detail the participation of adult students in government loan programs.

Figure 2-1. *Costs of Attendance at Public and Private Institutions,
1966–88*

Thousands of 1989–90 dollars

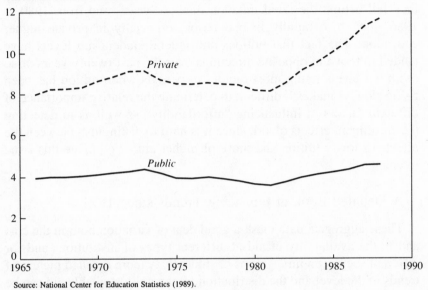

Source: National Center for Education Statistics (1989).

both about the suitability of traditional student aid programs as vehicles
for aiding adult and vocational students, as well as about the drain on
resources available for traditional students that results from the increased participation of other groups.

Student aid from state governments and institutions adds to the funds
provided to families to subsidize tuitions. (The states, it should be
remembered, contribute mostly through direct operating subsidies to
state-run colleges and universities.) The data in table 2-4 indicate that
these nonfederal sources of financial support have also fluctuated. Both
state and institutional grants grew substantially from the 1960s to the
1970s. From 1975 to 1989, state programs grew by 53 percent, while
institution-based aid, after holding steady in real terms in the 1970s,
grew by 78 percent in real terms from 1981 to 1989. The bulk of the
institution-based aid is awarded by private institutions, with much of it
taking the form of tuition discounts.

This changing picture of federal and other forms of student aid must
finally be seen against a background of changing tuition prices in higher
education. Figure 2-1 shows the course of public and private tuition

charges from 1966 to 1988. Here, three rough periods suggest themselves: from 1966 to the early 1970s tuitions rose relative to the price level, at a fairly modest rate; from the early 1970s until around 1980, they fell behind the rapid inflation of those years; and from 1980 to 1986, they rose rapidly in real terms, especially in private higher education. The fact that tuitions and federal student aid levels have tended to move in opposite directions over the past twenty years or so (with aid levels rising most rapidly in periods when tuition has been rising slowly) makes it difficult to determine the relative importance of different factors in influencing "affordability" as well as in detecting the enrollment effects of aid, since it is hard to distinguish between the effects of lower tuition and those of higher aid. We pursue this issue in chapter 3.

A Detailed Look at Financing Trends since 1974

These aggregate data mask a good deal of variation both in the cost and in the availability of aid at different types of institutions and for different socioeconomic groups of students. A more detailed picture of trends in the level and the distribution of generally available aid can be derived from the American Freshman Survey, an instrument administered yearly to freshmen enrolling at a large number of colleges and universities. Since 1974, the managers of the American Freshman Survey have included detailed questions on the sources and amounts of financial assistance received by surveyed freshmen. These responses provide a fairly complete picture of freshmen's *own perceptions* of how their education is being financed. These numbers should be interpreted cautiously, since students may be unclear not only about the amount but especially about the form (grant versus loan) and source (federal government versus state government versus institution) of the aid they receive.[12] Despite these limitations, however, the American Freshman

12. The survey is also forced to rely on self-reported family incomes. This survey is administered by institutions that elect to participate, and the setting in which it is administered may vary among institutions. As such, the sample of institutions is self-selected rather than random (institutions are only included in the sample if they survey a large fraction of their freshmen); as a result, the survey substantially underrepresents two-year colleges. Note also that we focus on data for full-time resident students, who are more likely to be enrolled at public and private four-year institutions than at public two-year institutions. Proprietary institutions, mostly vocational and technical institutions, are not included. The survey is conducted annually by Alexander W. Astin and (varying) other authors and published under the title *The American Freshman: National Norms for Fall*.

Survey data, which are used extensively below, provide a helpful baseline for years after 1974—a baseline that is not otherwise available on an annual basis.

The figures that follow focus on a limited subgroup of American undergraduates: young (ages 18–24), full-time freshmen in residence at traditional two-year and four-year colleges. This is the population that is most reliably sampled in the survey, and it provides a fairly well defined universe for comparisons over time.[13] Still, as noted above, a great many students—and an increasing portion of aided students—are outside this "traditional" category, because they are older or part-time, because they attend nontraditional institutions, or because they commute. Note that all data are reported in 1990 constant dollars, including the income classifications. The figures are adjusted using the consumer price index, or CPI, as the deflator.

Figure 2-2 summarizes trends in federal grant and loan awards received by full-time freshmen in public and private institutions. (Notice that the reported numbers are averages over *all* freshmen, including both recipients and nonrecipients of aid.) What stands out is the increase in per-student borrowing and the decrease in the real value of grants per student in the 1980s. It should be noted that the decrease in grants is more pronounced for this group of young full-time freshmen than it would be for a more broadly defined group, since an increasing percentage of federal grant money is going to older and part-time students as well as to students at "nontraditional," proprietary institutions.

Organizing the data by real family income allows us to trace changes in college affordability. The distribution of federal aid among income classes has by no means been constant over time. Figure 2-3 shows the variations in grants and loans according to income. One sees the substantial effects of the Middle Income Student Assistance Act (MISAA) of 1978 in increasing the grant and loan money available to middle- and (in the case of loans) upper-income students. During the years 1980 and 1981, when subsidized loans were available to all full-time students, regardless of income and need, the average student from

---

13. The specially directed aid programs (principally the GI Bill and the social security program) do not appear important in these data, apparently for two reasons. First, much of this money probably went to students outside the subsample reported here, which is limited to first-time, full-time freshmen who reside on campus, who are dependent on their parents for support, and who are 24 years old or younger. Second, many students who were recipients either of social security survivor benefits or of GI Bill assistance may not have reported it as student aid.

Figure 2-2. *Federal Aid per Student at Public and Private Institutions, 1974–84*

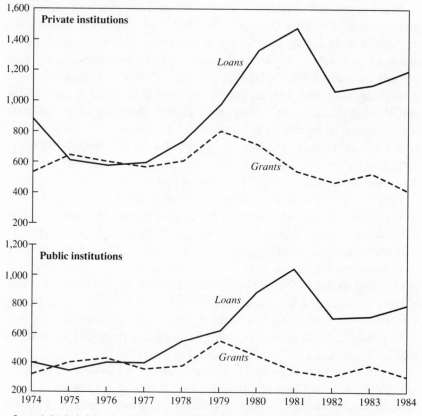

1990 dollars per student

Source: Authors' calculations from American Freshman Survey. The data include both aided and nonaided students.

a family with income over $100,000 (in 1990 dollars) borrowed more than $800 (in 1990 dollars).

Since 1981, the availability of subsidized loans to upper-income students has been sharply reduced. Moreover, the first half of the 1980s saw a substantial real decrease in the federal grants available to lower-income students. This partly reflects a squeeze on those federal dollars awarded in the Pell grant program, which (as shown in table 2-4) fell in real terms in the early 1980s before returning to roughly its 1979–80 level by 1985–86, and partly the awarding of more Pell grant funds to independent students and students at proprietary institutions. As

Figure 2-3. *Federal Grant and Loan Aid, by Family Income, 1974–84*

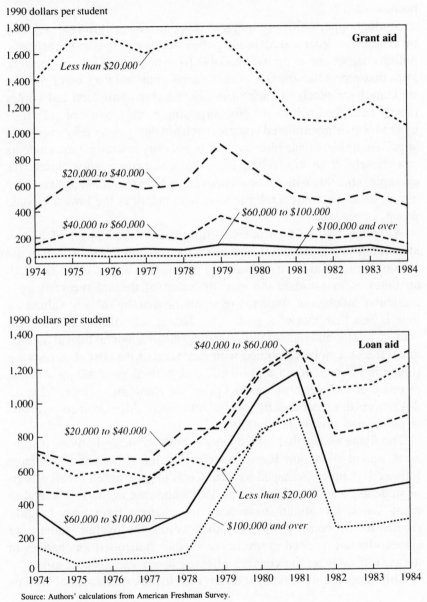

1990 dollars per student

Grant aid

Less than $20,000

$20,000 to $40,000

$40,000 to $60,000

$60,000 to $100,000

$100,000 and over

1990 dollars per student

Loan aid

$40,000 to $60,000

$20,000 to $40,000

Less than $20,000

$60,000 to $100,000

$100,000 and over

Source: Authors' calculations from American Freshman Survey.

figure 2-3 shows, the decrease in real grant money for lower-income students was accompanied by a rapid increase in the amount they borrowed.

Student opportunities throughout this period were affected not only by changes in federal student aid policy but by changes in the schools' tuition charges and in the aid available from nonfederal sources as well. Data that report the amount of nonfederal grant aid that lower-income students have received each year suggest that nonfederal aid comes mostly from the institutions. Not surprisingly, the amount of aid varies by the form of institutional control, such aid being especially important at private universities. Moreover, it is not only lower-income students who benefit from nonfederal grant aid. At private universities, for example, students with incomes between $20,000 and $40,000 receive almost as much nonfederal grant aid per student as the lowest income group.

Although no one measure can fully reflect the impact of aid on affordability, it is helpful to boil down the changes in tuition and in the various forms of aid to a manageable index. One way to construct such an index is to estimate the subsidy value of the aid received by a particular subclass of students, recognizing that the subsidy value of a loan is less than that of a grant. Per-student subsidies, combining all sources of aid, and putting the subsidy value of a federal loan at half the amount lent, can be combined with estimates of the cost of attendance (including books, room and board, and tuition) to come up with an estimate of the "net cost" or "net price" of attending college.[14] Figure 2-4 reports these net cost figures for students of different income levels at public and private institutions.

The figure shows that for students at both public and private institutions, and at all income levels, net costs for the 1970s and 1980s have followed a similar U-shaped pattern. Costs in general fell for all groups of students in the latter part of the 1970s and rose in the 1980s, and in many cases, the dollar amounts of the changes have been roughly similar for different groups. In other words, the overall student aid system did not succeed in insulating needier students from changes in the cost of college; the changes affected needy and affluent alike.

Still, there are some notable differences in the experiences of various

---

14. The estimate that the subsidy value of a loan is half of its face value is consistent with findings reported by Bosworth, Carron, and Rhyne (1987) and Hauptman (1985).

Figure 2-4. *Net Cost per Student at Public and Private Institutions, by Family Income, 1974–84*

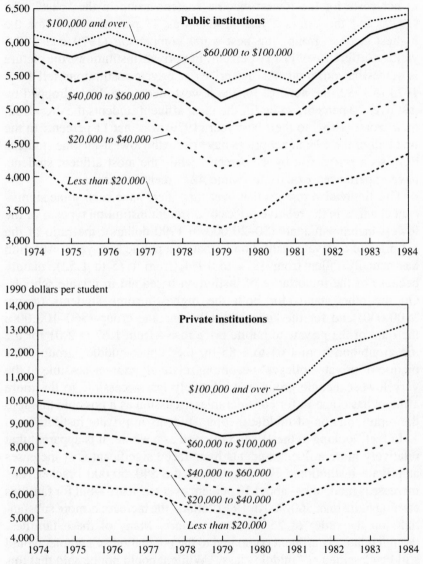

1990 dollars per student

Public institutions

$100,000 and over
$60,000 to $100,000
$40,000 to $60,000
$20,000 to $40,000
Less than $20,000

1990 dollars per student

Private institutions

$100,000 and over
$60,000 to $100,000
$40,000 to $60,000
$20,000 to $40,000
Less than $20,000

Source: Authors' calculations from American Freshman Survey.

groups. First, even when the dollar amounts of the changes in cost are similar for students at different income levels, percent changes in cost sometimes differ. Thus, for public institutions as a whole the difference in net costs for the lowest-income student group in the "best" year (1979) and the "worst" year (1984) was 33 percent, while for the highest-income group, the best-worst comparison (1979 and 1984) yields a difference of just 19 percent. For private institutions, the picture is somewhat different. As net prices at private institutions fell from 1974 to 1980, the net cost for the lowest-income students dropped by just over 30 percent, while for the most affluent students the drop from their worst (1974) to their best year (1979) was just 11 percent. In the first half of the 1980s, net prices have risen: the lowest-income students have seen prices rise by 42 percent, while the most affluent students have experienced exactly the same 42 percent increase.

This figure also implies that over time there have been some significant changes in the relative prices of different institution types. For the lowest-income students ($0–20,000 in 1990 dollars), the ratio of the net price of a private institution to that of a public four-year institution has actually fallen from 1974 to 1984 (from 1.75 to 1.52), mainly because of the importance of institution-based aid in private schools. On the other hand, for both the highest-income students (above $100,000) and for the "upper-middle" income group ($60–100,000) the ratio of the private to public price rose—from 1.67 to 2.01 for the top group and from 1.61 to 1.85 for the "upper-middle" group. This picture of private colleges' becoming relatively more accessible to the very lowest income group and relatively less accessible to the more affluent has come in for considerable discussion as a possible threat to the representation of middle-income students in private institutions.

In fact, looking at the 1974–84 period as a whole, it is apparent that relatively more affluent students have faced significant cost increases at private institutions. For families in the $40–60,000 bracket, this increase is moderate—about 10 percent over ten years—but for families earning more than $60,000 in 1990 dollars, the increase is more substantial—on the order of 25 percent or more. Many of these families, though relatively affluent compared to the population as a whole, would still be classified as "middle class." While it could not be said that this increase has damaged this group's access to college—since costs facing these families remain moderate at public institutions—there may well be an impact on "choice." This increase may well be related to the worries about "middle-class enrollment melt" at private institutions; this concern is discussed in greater detail in chapters 5 and 6.

Enrollment Patterns over Time

Trends in enrollment may also shed light on trends in affordability. Certainly over the very long run, from the 1930s to the present, the remarkable increase in participation rates and the broadening of the range of social groups represented in higher education are testimony to gains in affordability, gains that have been urged on by the expansion of public higher education and increased federal aid.

In examining the more recent era, it is useful to divide the historical data on the enrollment effects of government financing into three periods: that before 1974, preceding the introduction of the basic grants program; that from 1974 to 1980, when federal funding for student aid grew sharply in real terms; and that following 1980, when federal student aid funding first failed to keep pace with inflation and then later grew only slowly.

The pre-1974 evidence is scattered. Data on the distribution of student aid by income class are very hard to come by. Evidence on enrollment distributions is also shaky, partly owing to data availability problems, but also owing to the fact that large swings in military personnel levels and changes in recruitment policies during the Vietnam era complicate the interpretation of available data.

Nonetheless, fragmentary evidence suggests that the late 1960s and early 1970s were a period of rapid change in the socioeconomic composition of the United States college population. Davis and Johns have examined data on the distribution of college freshmen by income class, using the American Freshman Survey.[15] They found a marked increase in the fraction of students from families below the median and from within the bottom quartile of U.S. incomes in those years. Similar findings, relying partly on other data, are reported by the Carnegie Council and by Larry Leslie and Paul Brinkman.[16]

It seems implausible to attribute very much of this important change to the direct effects of federal student aid policy. The federal commit-

15. Davis and Johns (1982).
16. Carnegie Council (1980); Leslie and Brinkman (1988).

ment of dollars to the main Office of Education programs (the campus-based programs and the guaranteed student loans) remained modest through the late 1960s and early 1970s. Moreover, a large fraction of this federal support was in the form of guaranteed loans, which were not at that time targeted at the neediest students.

More likely, the proximate causes of the change in enrollment patterns can be found in changed policies at the state and institutional levels and in changed social attitudes. The most prominent state-level effort was the dramatic expansion in community colleges and urban state-run four-year colleges in the 1960s. These institutions were geographically closer to disadvantaged populations than traditional state universities and often adopted open admissions policies that encouraged the enrollment of educationally disadvantaged students, who are disproportionately from poor economic backgrounds. For many such students, the opportunity to conserve on spending by living at home has provided a dramatic increase in college affordability. Meanwhile, private colleges and universities expanded their own student aid efforts substantially in the late 1960s—by a factor of more than two from 1963 through 1971 after adjusting for inflation—and it may be that they targeted their funds more heavily at lower-income students. Finally, the strong societywide concern in the late 1960s for combating poverty and promoting racial equality should not be neglected. These forces led to stronger recruiting efforts directed toward disadvantaged youth and probably had effects as well on the college-going aspirations of minority and lower-income students.

While these effects probably outweighed any direct impact that federal student aid had on increasing lower-income enrollments in the 1965–74 period, the indirect effects of federal aid policy should not be overlooked. States and private institutions may well have been encouraged to strengthen their commitment to the higher education of disadvantaged students by the knowledge that the federal government was supporting those efforts, and seemed likely to increase that support. Student expectations may have been similarly affected. The anticipation of an expanded federal role in student finance in the 1970s may have produced some effect on enrollments even before the actual programs came into being; this effect, however, is unmeasurable.

The period 1974–85 saw an expanded federal aid commitment followed by a decline, as well as a shift in emphasis from grants to loans. As noted earlier, the period of expanding student aid was also a period

Figure 2-5. *Enrollment Rates, by Income Group, 1974–85*

Percent

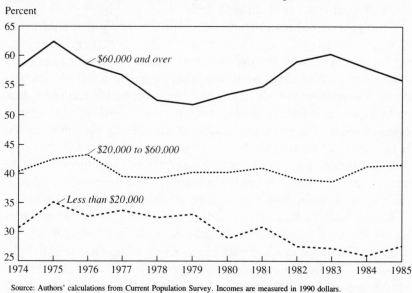

Source: Authors' calculations from Current Population Survey. Incomes are measured in 1990 dollars.

of declining tuition (in real terms), while in the 1980s tuitions rose as aid fell. As a result, all groups of students faced lower costs in the second half of the 1970s and higher ones in the 1980s.

Can we detect the effect of these swings in net costs on enrollment patterns and levels? Figure 2-5 shows enrollment rates, expressed as a percentage of the eligible population, for students of different income levels over the 1974–85 period.[17] In these enrollment graphs, there is no evident effect of net costs on enrollment for families with incomes above $60,000 (1990 dollars)—from 1974 through 1980, their enrollment rate averaged 56 percent, while from 1981 through 1985, it averaged 58 percent. For families with incomes between $20,000 and $60,000, there again appears to be virtually no effect from the increase in net price—the enrollment rate fell from 41 percent to 40 percent over the two periods.

A more distinct swing, however, is evident for the lowest income group, those with incomes below $20,000 in 1990 terms. This group's

17. These data are derived from the Current Population Survey. The figures include only students who are enrolled full time; the figures do not include most proprietary or vocational enrollment. Our sample is further limited to persons who are 18 to 24 years old, are financially dependent on their parents, and have completed less than four years of college.

enrollment rate averaged 33 percent from 1974 through 1980 but fell
to 28 percent from 1981 through 1985.

This general pattern is consistent with the theory that student aid
changes have played a significant role in either encouraging or discouraging the enrollment of lower-income students. As noted, net cost
changes in percent terms were somewhat larger for lower-income students, and econometric studies, which are described in chapter 3, lead
us to expect that that group will respond more sensitively to relative
price changes of a given magnitude. It thus seems plausible, on the
basis simply of examining these enrollment trends, that the change in
federal student aid policy, which contributed significantly to the
changes in the net cost facing lower-income students, played a substantial role in reducing lower-income enrollment rates in the 1980s.

It may well be that factors additional to changes in the net price
facing lower-income students contributed to the enrollment trends described. The 1980s saw a greater emphasis on admissions selectivity at
postsecondary institutions and a less aggressive federal stance toward
supporting affirmative action in admissions. Both trends may work
against students from educationally and socially disadvantaged backgrounds.

A slightly different way of looking at these data may also prove
illuminating. W. Lee Hansen has suggested that a look at relative
enrollment rates of more- and less-affluent students may help gauge the
impact of federal student aid—on the grounds that federal student aid
is the most obvious factor that should affect the enrollment behavior of
these two groups differentially.[18] He used Current Population Survey
(CPS) data to examine the enrollment rates for students from families
with dependents aged 18 through 24 for two, separate academic years,
1971–72 and 1978–79. He then calculated the ratio of the enrollment
rates of below-median-income to above-median-income families for
the two years and found that between 1971 and 1979 the ratios declined
for whites, blacks, men, and women. When a weighted average was
taken for whites and blacks and for men and women, the ratios again
fell between the two years.

The conclusion from this study is well known among researchers
and policymakers: these data force one to conclude that the greater
availability of student financial aid, targeted largely toward students

18. Hansen (1983).

from below-median-income families, did little, if anything, to increase access. The results certainly do not accord with expectations that access would increase for lower-income dependents relative to higher-income dependents."[19]

There are some obvious limitations in interpreting this kind of snapshot comparison at two points in time. First, year-to-year fluctuations may obscure underlying trends, so that increasing the number of years in the comparison is helpful. Second, controlling for variation in other factors that affect the demand for enrollment is not possible using this methodology. Such factors as overall economic conditions, changes in the rate of return to higher education, and changes in the opportunity costs of college enrollment (as produced, for example, by changes in the draft law) may influence the comparison if they affect income groups differently. Finally, this kind of comparison is not responsive to changes in the targeting of student aid. As noted, over the 1970s, the total amount of federal student aid not only increased substantially but also changed significantly in its distribution. A larger fraction of available aid was targeted at middle- and upper-income students in the late 1970s, tending to obscure any effect on differential enrollment rates that might have occurred.

Some of these limitations can be dealt with by extending the analysis to more years and by relating the enrollment fluctuations to what we know about year-to-year fluctuations in the amounts and direction of aid. Figure 2-6 presents data for the extended period 1975–84 and displays a three-year moving average of the ratio of the enrollment rates for the lowest (below $20,000) and highest (above $60,000) income groups (in 1990 dollars). The figure looks separately at white and black students. Although the trends are similar for both racial groups, the changes are much sharper for blacks than whites. The late 1970s saw a relative increase in the ratio of lower-income to higher-income enrollment, and the 1980s saw a decrease, with some recovery quite recently. For blacks the swing is marked—lower-income blacks enrolled at almost 70 percent of the higher-income black rate in 1979; by 1982 the ratio was only around 40 percent. For whites the change in the ratio was from about 60 percent to under 50 percent.

This narrowing of differences between upper-income and lower-income participation rates in the late 1970s was importantly influenced

19. Hansen (1983, p. 93).

Figure 2-6. *Ratio of Low- to High-Income Enrollment Rates,*
by Race, 1975–84

Ratio (low income / high income)

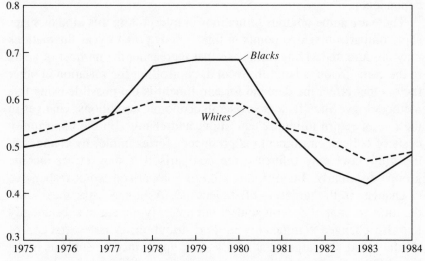

Source: Authors' calculations from Current Population Survey. Incomes below $20,000 in 1990 dollars are considered low.
Incomes above $60,000 are considered high. Figures are calculated using three-year moving averages.

by a decline in upper-income enrollment rates in the late 1970s, a
decline for which there is no obvious explanation. (It certainly was not
caused by the federal student aid policy, which was becoming more
generous to affluent students in those years.) Lower-income students
did not share in that decline, possibly because substantial federal student
aid was available to them. The underlying reasoning behind that suppo-
sition is that the forces (whatever they were) pressing down on higher-
income enrollments should have applied across the board; therefore,
the failure of lower-income enrollments to decline in the late 1970s is
backhanded evidence of the effectiveness of aid in bolstering enrollments in that group. This is a plausible, but not a very strong, argument.
The fact that in the 1980s a real decline in federal aid was accompanied
by a distinct drop in the lower-income enrollment rate, while the upper-
income rate stayed more or less constant, seems considerably more
convincing.

These data suggest that extending the Hansen time-series analysis to
more years, and taking closer account of changes in federal aid targeting, raises questions about the strong conclusion that federal aid has

been without effect. These extensions do not, however, deal adequately with one of the most important empirical concerns about such data: the need for an estimation method in which the strength of the relationship between cost variation and enrollment variation is systematically measured. We attempt to respond to that concern with the regression analysis in the next chapter.

III

Financial Aid, College Costs, and Enrollment

EVERYONE agrees that a central purpose of student aid is to encourage young people from lower-income families to attend college. There is much less agreement on how well existing student aid programs have accomplished this end. Does lowering the net cost of a college education increase the tendency of lower-income students to enroll? As noted in chapter 1, there is a broad disagreement on this issue between those who have searched the historical data for evidence of aid effects on enrollment and those who have used econometric methods to detect such effects. Typically, econometric studies have found significant effects, while such effects have proved harder to detect in the historical evidence.

Chapter 2 reviewed some of the relevant evidence about historical trends, and concluded that a carefully controlled statistical analysis of the historical time series is needed in order to isolate the separate effect of net cost on enrollment. The first section of this chapter reviews some of the principal findings from the econometric literature on aid. Following this is a report on an econometric analysis that uses some newly developed time-series data on enrollment and net costs. This analysis goes some distance toward resolving the controversy between historical trend analysis and cross-section econometric studies.

A Summary of the Literature

Over the years, a great many studies have attempted to estimate the impact of the price or the net cost of education on students' postsecondary education decisions.[1] A minority of those studies have tried to

1. A number of able surveys of this literature exist. One that provides references to many earlier studies is Leslie and Brinkman (1987).

44

measure the effect of student aid on enrollment decisions, while the rest have focused on the impact of tuition.[2] Although the studies differ widely in data sources and estimation techniques, they tend to agree on two main points. First, student decisions to enroll in college respond positively, and nontrivially, to both price cuts and aid increases. Second, decisions about where to attend school also respond nontrivially to changes in the relative prices of schooling alternatives.

Rather than simply review this large and complex literature, we believe it would be more enlightening to consider one exemplary study in some depth, elaborating the discussion with evidence from other studies. The focal study is that by Charles Manski and David Wise.[3] Their study, similar in its basic approach to several other studies of individual student behavior, relies on evidence concerning student characteristics and choices. The evidence has been taken from large-scale surveys of young high school graduates.

The Manski-Wise analysis proceeds in several steps. Starting from data for a sample of 1972 high school graduates, the authors first construct for each student a "choice set" of institutions to which the student could be admitted, with each set depending on that student's academic performance and geographic location. The authors then perform an analysis estimating the amount of aid that any given student would have been offered at each institution in his or her choice set.[4] The final step is to estimate a statistical model that best explains the choices they actually made among schooling and nonschooling alternatives.

More specifically, the authors develop in this last step an equation that calculates the probability that a person with certain characteristics (income, race, academic background, and so on) will select a school with certain characteristics (price, aid offer, quality, and so on). The parameters of this modeling equation are chosen to yield a "predicted"

2. In a later paper, Leslie and Brinkman provide a helpful review of those studies that focus more specifically on the effect of student aid on enrollment decisions. See Leslie and Brinkman (1988). See also McPherson (1988).

3. Manski and Wise (1983).

4. The National Longitudinal Survey of the High School Class of 1972 does not contain good information on the aid offers that students received from institutions that were in their choice set but that they did not attend. Manski and Wise deal with this problem by developing estimates from an equation relating the aid that a student actually received from the institution he or she attended to such variables as that student's academic achievement and family income as well as the institution's tuition and program (four-year or two-year).

enrollment pattern that matches the actual outcomes as closely as possible.[5] The equation can then be used to estimate how actual enrollment patterns would differ if some of these student or institutional characteristics were to change—if, for example, incomes or SAT scores rose, or if institutional costs rose.

In their work, Manski and Wise were able to show how changes in student aid policy can affect enrollment patterns. Specifically, they used their model to estimate how 1979 enrollment patterns would have differed had the Pell grant program not been available to students. Their sample of students was weighted to match the national population of 1979 high school seniors, and predictions were made for Pell awards during the 1979–80 academic year. Enrollment impacts of the grant program were then computed and compared with the hypothetical situation in which 1979 conditions are preserved but there is no Pell program. Their main finding was that the Pell grant program had a substantial effect on access. By their estimate, the Pell grant program left enrollments 21 percent higher than they would have been without it, with the increases heavily concentrated at two-year colleges and among students from lower-income families. The predicted response by income group varied greatly: there was a 59 percent enrollment increase for lower-income students, a 12 percent increase for middle-income students, and only a 3 percent increase for higher-income students.

As with most econometric studies, a detailed look at the Manski-Wise results exposes some puzzles. The large enrollment effect they find at two-year colleges stems from the fact that two-year enrollments are found to respond much more strongly to aid increases than to price cuts. They find no comparable result for other types of schools, nor is the result replicated in other studies. Moreover, theory suggests that grant increases should have a smaller effect than price cuts, because they are harder to learn about. If the unusually large aid effect that Manski and Wise find at two-year colleges is set equal to the smaller effect they find for price changes, the effect of the Pell program on total enrollment drops to 6 percent.

On the other hand, the effect of the Pell program on four-year college enrollments in the Manski-Wise study is puzzlingly small (virtually zero). Other studies, notably those by J. B. Schwartz, find

5. A maximum-likelihood technique was used in the estimation of their multinomial logit model.

substantial effects of public grants on four-year college enrollment.[6] It may be that a technical feature of the Manski-Wise estimation procedure produces an underestimate of the enrollment effect at four-year colleges.[7]

Several key features of the Manski-Wise findings on the access effects of Pell grants are corroborated by other studies. Leslie and Brinkman identified six studies, in addition to Manski and Wise's, that contained useful estimates of the effects of grant aid on enrollment levels.[8] While differing widely in data and technique, the studies all find substantial effects of grant aid on enrollment levels, and find those effects to be stronger among lower-income students. Eric Jensen, in a survey of the noneconomic literature, similarly concludes that there is strong evidence that financial aid positively affects access to college, especially among students from relatively disadvantaged backgrounds.[9] Arthur Hauptman and Maureen McLaughlin, in summarizing the econometric literature, agree that enrollments rise in response to additional aid availability and that lower-income students are more influenced by aid than are students from more affluent families.[10]

Estimates developed by Leslie and Brinkman suggest that the Pell program as it existed at the end of the 1970s should have raised lower-income enrollment by between 20 and 40 percent, implying an increase in total enrollment of roughly 10 to 20 percent.[11] They point out that these results indicate that roughly 500,000 to 1 million lower-income students and approximately 400,000 middle-income students are enrolled in college because of grant aid. The midpoint of the total of these figures is slightly over 1 million students, approximately 16 percent of all full-time students.

Further econometric support for this finding is provided by the many

6. Schwartz (1985, 1986).

7. In their simulation technique, Manski and Wise assume that the availability of Pell grants will not cause any increase in the applications to four-year colleges; the only effect that they allow for is increased enrollment among students who are admitted to a four-year school but who would not have actually enrolled without a Pell grant. Because, in their sample, about 65 percent of the eligible population are never admitted to a four-year college, this assumption sharply limits the potential effect they could find.

8. Leslie and Brinkman (1988). The six studies are Berne (1980), Blakemore and Low (1985), Carlson (1975), Carroll and others (1977), Crawford (1966), and Jackson (1978).

9. Jensen (1983).

10. Hauptman and McLaughlin (1988).

11. Leslie and Brinkman (1988).

studies that estimate the effect of tuition on enrollment behavior. Although changes in grant awards may not have identical effects on enrollment to changes in tuition, the size of those effects and their variation across income classes should be similar. It is therefore reassuring to note that most studies find that reductions in tuition have significant positive effects on enrollment levels and that the effects (in percentage terms) are larger for lower-income students.[12] Leslie and Brinkman find that the studies they survey generally agree that a $100 price cut (in 1982–83 academic year dollars) raises the national enrollment of 18–24 year-olds by about 1.8 percent. On the assumption that a price cut and a grant increase of equal size will have equal effect, the Pell program as it existed in 1979 should have boosted total enrollment by roughly 10 to 15 percent, compared to what enrollments would have been in that year without the program.[13] This is roughly comparable to estimates like those of Manski and Wise that try to measure the effect of grant aid directly.

Perhaps the most important limitation of the Manski-Wise effort and most of these other studies lies in their reliance on data that predate the major expansion in federal student aid beginning in the early 1970s.[14] For instance, Manski and Wise, in trying to simulate the effects of the Pell program, rely on estimates of student responsiveness to student aid grants available in 1972—grant programs which at that time differed significantly in structure and sources from the later Pell program. Within the last several years, a data set called High School and Beyond, which is based on a survey of 1980 high school graduates, has become available from the federal government. Though relatively few econometric studies of enrollment behavior based on these data are yet complete, the findings thus far suggest that these data will yield results broadly similar to those of earlier studies. J. B. Schwartz, for example, examined the effects of grants and loans on enrollment at four-year colleges and found that about 21 percent of lower-income

12. See Leslie and Brinkman (1987) for a comprehensive survey. For an analytically oriented survey that examines the relation between income levels and the price responsiveness of enrollment, see McPherson (1978).

13. This calculation assumes that an average Pell award was about $1,000 in 1979 dollars and that about half of all freshmen would have been eligible for Pell grants under 1979 rules. Manski and Wise (1983, p. 21) estimate an eligibility rate of around two-thirds and an average award of slightly below $1,000.

14. All but one of the econometric studies discussed by Leslie and Brinkman (1988) rely on pre-1973 data. Students first received awards from the Pell program in 1974.

enrollment at four-year colleges was accounted for by the Pell program and that higher-income enrollment was less strongly affected.[15] Edward St. John and Jay Noell, using High School and Beyond along with the National Longitudinal Survey of the High School Class of 1972, also found that financial aid had a positive impact on enrollment decisions, with scholarships and grants having the largest effect on minority applicants.[16] Empirically, then, grant aid appears to have a significant, positive effect on lower-income enrollment.

What is less clear, however, is how grants affect students' decisions about where to go to college. One reason for this is the lack of agreement about precisely what questions should be studied. Several studies have adopted the perspective of the individual institution, asking to what degree students with particular characteristics may be influenced to choose that institution by varying the amount or kind of aid they are offered. These studies, in effect, try to help institutions measure the effectiveness of their student aid packages as marketing or recruiting tools.

Other studies have considered the responsiveness of national enrollment to changes in the relative prices of different schooling alternatives, with student aid viewed as one source of relative price variation. Still other studies have tried to measure the impact that the nationwide pattern of student aid has had on the enrollment destinations of students.

It is important to recognize that each type of study is unique. It is conceivable, for example, that differences in aid offers may strongly influence which school was chosen from within a particular class of schools, but may not influence what class was chosen. To take a Chicago example, perhaps an offer of aid makes a big difference whether a student chooses Loyola or De Paul, or chooses the University of Chicago or Northwestern, but the aid has almost no influence on the choice between a Catholic comprehensive university and a secular research university. It is apparent that the outcome of any study of choice may be extremely sensitive to just how the alternatives facing students are specified and that attempts to generalize from disparate studies are hazardous.

There is also a major difference between asking how responsive students are to relative price changes and asking how large an impact

15. Schwartz (1986).
16. St. John and Noell (1988).

the national aid distribution has on choice. The latter question combines the issue of student responsiveness with the issue of how much the aid pattern might further contribute to relative prices, which is essentially a supply- rather than a demand-side question.

Despite these complications, some generalizations do emerge. Institutionally oriented studies tend to show that competitive aid packages can be effective in attracting students. Such studies rely on data that report the amount of aid offered by a particular institution compared with those offered by other institutions to which a sample of students were admitted. The usual finding is that the attractiveness of the aid package significantly affects student destinations.[17]

Michael Tierney examined the choices made by Pennsylvania students who had been admitted to schools with substantial cost differences. Tierney had exceptionally good information on the costs facing students at these institutions and on the students' personal and academic characteristics.[18] His studies, too, show that students respond to relative prices: as tuitions at private institutions rose relative to those at public institutions, the probability of matriculating at a public institution rose. However, when private institutions offered more grants and scholarships relative to public institutions, the probability of matriculating at a private institution rose.

In summarizing the literature, Jensen states that financial aid has a substantial influence on students who are accepted by two or more colleges. Leslie and Brinkman conclude that student aid is an effective way for institutions to compete—all else equal, an institution can increase its enrollment share by offering more aid. Manski and Wise also find that offers of financial aid can play an important role in affecting choice among schools.[19] However, in terms of the specific effect of the Pell program on choice, Leslie and Brinkman report that there is less agreement.

Is There Really an Inconsistency between Empirical Results and History?

On balance, researchers have found significant econometric evidence that enrollment responds strongly to changes in student aid. However,

17. See, for example, Ehrenberg and Sherman (1984) for a study of Cornell University.
18. Tierney (1980).
19. Jensen (1983); Leslie and Brinkman (1988); and Manski and Wise (1983).

despite substantial variation in aid over time, it is often suggested that the response of enrollment cannot be readily detected in national time-series data. Such conclusions, however, have not been based on econometric analysis. In this section, we hope to rectify that.

In chapter 2, we reviewed trends in enrollments and net costs over the 1974–84 period. Here, those data are employed in disaggregated form in an econometric examination of the effect of net college cost on enrollment. We examine the enrollment effect for three samples of schools: one that includes both public and private institutions, a second that includes only private institutions, and a third that includes only public institutions. Specifically, the analysis lets us test how the relationship between net cost and enrollment may be different for different income groups, and how these differences may affect the average propensity to enroll. In addition, we test to see whether men and women differ in their average propensities to enroll and test for the existence of long-run trends in enrollment that are related to income but not to net cost or gender. Unfortunately, sample sizes in the underlying CPS data base, from which the enrollment series is constructed, are not large enough to permit meaningful analyses of annual variations in the enrollment experience of blacks and other nonwhites. Therefore, the results we report here are limited to whites. A detailed technical presentation of this analysis is found in appendix A.

The statistical analyses we have performed let us examine the relations between enrollment rates and net prices for various gender and income groups over the 1974–84 period. This form of analysis has several significant advantages over studies that simply compare the net enrollment behavior of various groups of students at two points of time. First, our analytical technique uses information on enrollments and net prices for every year in the sample period, rather than using data from selected years only. Second, by including data for different income and gender groupings in the same analysis, we can test systematically for whether the behavioral relationships we observe differ between the groups. These two considerations interact in an important way. As noted in chapter 2, the distribution of federal financial aid between more- and less-affluent students fluctuated over the time period in question. By tracking these fluctuations and relating them to the enrollment behavior of particular income groups, we are able to take advantage of more information than we could in an analysis that simply averaged over income groups. Finally, these techniques permit us not

Table 3-1. *Estimated Effects of $100 (1978–79 Dollars) Increase in Net Price, Sticker Price, or Student Aid on the Enrollment of Lower-Income Students*[a]

Enrollment	Independent variable		
	Net price	Sticker price[b]	Student aid[b]
Public and private			
Change in enrollment			
Percentage points	−0.68*	−0.68*	0.69
Percent	−2.2*	−2.2*	2.2
Public			
Change in enrollment			
Percentage points	−0.38	−0.49	0.20
Percent	−1.6	−2.0	0.8
Private			
Change in enrollment			
Percentage points	−0.36*	−0.34*	0.38*
Percent	−6.0*	−5.7*	6.3*

Source: Authors' own calculations using data for the period 1974–84. Details of regression are reported in appendix A. Asterisk signifies that coefficient is significant at the 99 percent confidence level; if not so marked, coefficient is not statistically significant.
 a. Lower-income means having an annual family income less than $20,000 in 1990 dollars.
 b. Estimates for the effect of student aid control for sticker price and estimates for the effect of sticker price control for student aid.

only to search for the existence of effects of net prices on enrollment but also to estimate their approximate magnitudes.

Table 3-1 summarizes some of the principal findings of our study. Our most important and reliable finding is that increases in the net cost of attendance have a negative and statistically significant effect on enrollment for white students from lower-income families. Moreover, the size of this effect is similar to that found in cross-section studies of enrollment demand. Specifically, we find that for lower-income students (less than $20,000 family income in 1990 dollars) a $100 increase in net cost results in an enrollment decline of about 0.68 percentage points, which is about a 2.2 percent decline in enrollment for that income group. We noted earlier that Leslie and Brinkman find a consensus in the literature that a $100 increase in net cost reduces enrollment rates by 1.8 percent. Converting our estimates in 1978–79 dollars to the 1982–83 equivalent used by Leslie and Brinkman, we find that a $100 cost increase results in a 1.6 percent enrollment decline for lower-income students. However, it should be understood that the Leslie-Brinkman figure is in effect averaged over all income groups. Most other studies find higher price responsiveness among lower-income students. Manski and Wise's results, for example, suggest that a $100 increase in 1979 dollars leads to a 4.9 percent decline in lower-income enrollment.[20] Thus, our result, while lower than the Manski-Wise estimate, seems broadly consistent with typical cross-section findings. The important point is that our econometrically controlled time-series analysis supports the view that changes in costs lead to changes in enrollment for lower-income students.

The next step in our analysis is to break down our enrollment and cost measures into separate variables for public institutions and private institutions. Once again we find evidence of a negative net-cost effect for lower-income students attending private institutions (we estimate that a $100 increase in net cost lowers enrollment by about 6 percent among these students); for public institutions the net cost variable has a negative coefficient but is statistically insignificant. These findings are reported in table 3-1.

In a further refinement of the analysis, we break down net cost into its two components—the published tuition, or the sticker price, and the subsidy value of student aid. This step serves the purposes, first, of shedding light on the relative magnitudes of the aid and sticker price effects and, second, of pushing the data to see if anomalies or inconsistencies surface. For the combined public-private sample, we find an expected negative and significant impact of sticker price among lower-income white students; the aid effect is positive, as expected, but insignificant. It is interesting to note that the sizes of the estimated effects are virtually identical (and the same as the net cost coefficient reported above), suggesting that students respond equally to price cuts or aid increases. When public and private enrollment are considered separately, all the effects for lower-income students are as expected, with aid and price having statistically significant effects on private enrollment. Once again, the aid and price effects on private enrollment are similar in size.

Stepping back, we see that the results tell a consistent story about the behavior of lower-income white students. In our simpler sets of results, the variables measuring costs of attendance have significant effects in the expected direction. As we refine the analysis, we continue to find significant effects of reasonable magnitude without finding a single significant estimate that contradicts our theoretical expectations.

20. This coefficient is computed from information in Manski and Wise (1983, tables 7.2 and 7.4).

We find a very different picture when we look at the behavior of more-affluent students. We find no evidence in these data that increases in net cost inhibit the enrollment of these income groups. In fact, for the upper-income group ($60,000 and above in 1990 dollars), there is a fairly consistent positive effect of net cost on enrollment, which may mean that the high enrollment demand among affluent students leads to higher net costs for these students. For middle-income students ($20,000–$60,000), we find that net cost does not have a consistent effect on enrollment.

From our efforts to estimate the effects of net cost on enrollment, we also learn about the impacts of time and gender on enrollment behavior. To the extent that there has been a trend in enrollment over the 1974–84 period (after controlling for gender and net cost), it is negative. It is, however, a small decline. Finally, we find that, all things equal, women have a greater propensity than men to enroll in institutions of higher education. The effect is larger for the nonpoor.

Our finding that the time-series and cross-section results for lower-income white students are consistent with one another is a significant first step in resolving a long-standing controversy. It is important to appreciate that these findings for lower-income students would be obscured in an analysis that aggregated over income groups, since our evidence suggests (in line with the findings of cross-section studies) that the behaviors of these income groups are different.

This analysis indicates that changes in the net price facing lower-income students have significant effects on their enrollment behavior. An important policy issue, however, is whether changes in federal aid wind up changing net cost. If, for example, increases in federal aid lead to decreases in the amount of aid awarded by institutions or to increases in tuition, the effect of aid on net cost would be muted. While this is a difficult issue to address empirically, our conclusion is that these potentially offsetting effects may not be empirically important, at least at private institutions.[21] The time-series evidence on net cost further suggests that periods of generous federal aid coincide with periods of lower net costs for lower-income students, suggesting that increased aid does not necessarily lead to higher prices.

21. We deal with this issue in chapter 4.

Pushing the Analysis Forward: Where Do We Go from Here?

A more careful analysis of the time-series data has raised serious doubts about the hypothesis that federal student aid has failed to affect enrollment patterns in U.S. higher education significantly over the past two decades. Our assessment indicates that time-series evidence on the enrollment behavior of lower-income white students is consistent with the many econometric estimates of aid effects in the literature: increased student aid does raise the enrollments of lower-income students. As such, policymakers must carefully consider potential enrollment effects when determining student aid policy.

Further analysis of aid and enrollment patterns would certainly help clarify the needed direction for policy.

Thus, while this chapter's discussion has helped reconcile important points of disagreement in the literature, it also points to further areas of investigation. For one, time-series data on enrollment and net cost by student ability levels would help in measuring the nation's success in achieving a critical goal of aid policy—to enable high-ability students to pursue advanced education regardless of their income background.[22] Although it would be very expensive to maintain such data on an annual basis, useful work could be done by pooling data across those years in which large surveys such as High School and Beyond (the high school class of 1980) and the National Educational Longitudinal Study for the Class of 1988 (NELS88) are undertaken.

A second point is that future attempts to monitor the effectiveness of aid by inspecting enrollment trends should attempt to control for actual variations in net cost and other relevant variables. It would be desirable, for example, to include proxies for opportunity costs and rates of return to higher-education investments in regressions like ours. Reasonable proxies might be age-, sex-, and income-specific unemployment rates and education-related earnings differentials. Whenever the data allow, disaggregating aid by type (grant, loan, and work-study) and source (federal, state, local, and institutional) may reveal interesting differences among aid packages. Of course, developing data sets that would permit analysis of enrollment effects by race would be highly

22. Some evidence on this point appears in chapter 5.

desirable.[23] In addition, study of the supply-side effects of aid, such as we undertake in the next chapter, is needed to evaluate properly the various links among federal aid, institutional behavior, and enrollment patterns.

Finally, it would be useful to extend the time series to deal with the question of choice as well as access. Although we were able to estimate separate equations for enrollment at public and at private institutions, a high correlation between the public and private price variables impeded our efforts to include "cross-price" effects in these equations. Such cross-effects, for example, of public tuitions on private enrollment, have considerable importance for institutional and governmental policies. Conceivably, extending the data set over more years, or experimenting further with alternative estimation techniques, might permit meaningful estimates to be developed.

23. For an important attempt at identifying the role of race, see Kane (forthcoming).

IV

The Supply-Side Effects of Student Aid

OBSERVERS quite rightly think of federal student aid as a program for *students*—aimed at reducing the costs they face and at encouraging the enrollment of those from lower-income backgrounds. Yet federal student aid, like such other forms of government support as research grants and state operating subsidies, has also become an important source of financial support for many universities and colleges. Increases in federal student aid and in research funds, for instance, bolster demand for the services of higher education institutions, ultimately bringing in more revenue. Such increases may also free up institutional resources for other purposes. Increases in state operating subsidies contribute more immediately and more directly to the financial position of public colleges and universities, and may permit them to expand their instructional programs, reduce tuitions, or change their mix of services in other ways. Conversely, cutbacks in these or other areas of government support put pressure on budgets, causing universities and colleges to draw more resources from their endowments, cut back spending, or raise tuition to compensate for the lost revenue. To the degree that changes in government support influence instructional spending per student, they are likely to influence the quality as well as the quantity of education provided. The responses that institutions make to such changes may well be critical to understanding the effects of federal and state support and to evaluating its effectiveness. Empirically, however, we know little about these responses.

In this chapter, we investigate the effects of external financing on institutional behavior. To do so, we develop an empirical model that estimates the effect of various changes in government spending on a set of variables designed to measure the response of institutions to that spending. These variables include tuition and fees, institution-specific scholarship aid, and instructional spending. However, because external funding is only one factor in the complex process by which institutions

57

allocate resources, we broaden the exercise by developing a more complicated model that incorporates the effects of government funding into a framework capable of explaining general institutional behavior.[1]

Findings of Previous Research

Before proceeding to that model, however, we briefly show how the research that will be reported in this chapter fits into the growing but still quite limited empirical literature on the general behavior of governmental and not-for-profit institutions. This important subject has begun to receive considerable systematic attention from economists, legal theorists, and other social scientists.[2] But with respect to higher education institutions specifically, empirical work on behavior has been surprisingly rare. Among those few who have attempted it, Estelle James and also Stephen Hoenack and Daniel Pierro have developed models of how educational institutions alter resource allocation in response to changes in external constraints.[3] In particular, the piece by Hoenack and Pierro estimates the influence of state legislative appropriations on the behavior of a public university. To our knowledge, though, no systematic empirical work has been done on the role of other forms of government spending. Several studies of student aid, however, do note the potential importance of these issues.[4]

Empirical studies parallel to ours in approach have been performed for primary and secondary education, and they have instructive findings. An interesting example is the effort to measure the effect of state and federal grants on the spending patterns of local school districts. Not surprisingly, the results indicate that schools' responses depend on the type of subsidy and the manner in which it is distributed.[5]

1. If our analysis were limited to the effects of government funding, the relationships between variables could be incorrectly formulated, thus biasing the estimates. Moreover, because some of the additional variables are themselves influenced by institutional choices, we are led to a "simultaneous" model in which a range of feedback effects are incorporated.

2. See the useful collection of articles assembled in Rose-Ackerman (1986). Significant modeling work on institutional behavior in higher education includes Breneman (1976), Garvin (1980), and Hopkins and Massy (1981).

3. James (1978); Hoenack and Pierro (1986).

4. Hearn and Wilford (1985); Finn (1978).

5. See, for example, Tsang and Levin (1983) and Craig and Inman (1982).

In one study, Martin Feldstein examined the effects of federal educational funding on local school district spending.[6] The major question was whether local governments spent all this grant money on additional educational expenditures (as required under the terms of the program) or whether some of the federal money was instead used to replace state and local money or even to provide tax relief to local taxpayers. Feldstein found that an extra dollar of federal educational funding augmented total educational spending by 72 cents.[7]

In a somewhat broader study, Stephen Craig and Robert Inman examined the effects of different types of federal aid on the educational spending of state and local governments.[8] Their results indicate that different types of aid are in fact allocated differently. Each dollar of federal aid that is appropriated for local governments but is administered through the state ultimately increases local spending on education by 87 cents, while each dollar of federal aid that goes directly to the local government has a zero, or even negative, effect on total spending. The later finding indicates substantial substitutability between federal and local educational expenditures—local governments use federal aid to replace their own spending.[9]

In sum, studies such as these by Feldstein, Craig and Inman, and others are analogous to our present efforts—they raise the general question of how schools respond to changes in government support. So while relatively little work has directly addressed our specific concerns, a variety of studies do provide a methodological basis for our work and lead us to believe that meaningful empirical estimates can be obtained. With the context of our research thus established, we now turn to a discussion of our data, variables, and model.

The Data

The data set on which our subsequent trend and econometric analyses are based contains financial information on individual colleges and

6. Feldstein (1978).

7. See Craig and Inman (1982), Tsang and Levin (1983), and Gurwitz (1980) for discussions of this work.

8. Craig and Inman (1982).

9. The relevant literature is not limited to studies of education. Some of the work on the effect of government subsidies on the housing and health markets is germane. For the housing market, see Barnett and Lowry (1979). For the health market, see Sloan, Cromwell, and Mitchell (1978). For each of these markets, studies have tried to measure the extent to which the supply and

universities and has been constructed by merging three federally maintained data sets. The first one, the Financial Statistics Report from the Higher Education General Information Survey (HEGIS), describes the basic financial accounts of all public and private nonprofit, postbaccalaureate institutions in the United States, as well as a handful of "proprietary" trade schools that are run for profit. The second, the Fiscal-Operations Report and Application to Participate (FISAP) data base, provides more detailed information on institutional revenue, student aid spending, and students who apply for federal assistance under any of the so-called campus-based programs (direct loans, SEOGs, and college work-study).[10] The third, the HEGIS Enrollment Survey, reports full- and part-time enrollment for all institutions, and therefore lets us estimate full-time-equivalent enrollment, which we use to adjust the financial data to a full-time-equivalent basis. We have data for the academic years 1978–79 and 1985–86; the data set has been constructed as a panel, so that only schools with data for both years are included.[11]

Unfortunately, the data set we construct does lack two significant pieces of data that are hard to supplement from other sources: the amount of student borrowing through the federally guaranteed student loan program, and the amount of state grant aid provided to students. Except for these two items, coverage of the data is thorough. Painstaking efforts have been made to clean the data set of reporting and recording errors. In addition, we have dropped all proprietary schools, all private, nonprofit, two-year colleges, and all schools with fewer than two hundred undergraduates. The resulting sample contains a total of 1,934 institutions: 896 private four-year colleges and universities, 371 public four-year colleges and universities, and 667 public two-year colleges.

Analysis of Trends in College and University Finance

Table 4-1 reports various financial data for private four-year colleges and universities, public four-year colleges and universities, and public

demand for housing and health services respond to different forms of government expenditure in these sectors.

10. We are grateful to the American Council on Education (ACE) for preparing a single data set that combines the Financial Statistics Report and the FISAP data. We would particularly like to thank Laurent Ross of the ACE, who helped program and document the merge.

11. The academic year 1985–86 is the latest for which national data are available.

Table 4-1. *Revenue and Expenditure per Student,*
by Type of Institution

	Level in 1985–86 academic year (1990 dollars)			Percent change, 1978–79 to 1985–86 academic year		
Category	Public four-year	Public two-year	Private four-year	Public four-year	Public two-year	Private four-year
Revenue						
Tuition related						
Gross tuition and fees	2,110	905	7,716	29.7	24.6	28.7
Institutional financial aid	302	87	1,425	18.4	19.3	50.4
Federal financial aid	391	339	429	18.4	22.4	−2.1
Net tuition and fees	1,416	478	5,862	36.1	27.3	27.2
Gift and endowment earnings	1,542	350	6,871	−14.1	−49.0	109.8
Government grants and contracts						
Federal	1,064	219	1,939	−7.4	−17.5	−2.3
State and local	222	182	305	5.9	54.3	33.3
State and local appropriations	5,903	3,576	149	7.1	3.7	−4.8
Expenditures						
Instruction	4,270	2,487	5,109	7.3	5.6	18.8
Other educational and general						
Academic support	963	426	1,134	11.4	12.0	21.7
Student services	531	455	922	10.3	13.2	35.1
Institutional support	1,048	756	1,969	29.1	9.0	28.0
Operation and maintenance	985	589	1,337	1.9	9.5	14.0
Additions to physical plant	1,571	497	1,716	40.3	−21.1	58.9

Source: Authors' calculations from U.S. Department of Education, Higher Education General Information Survey, the 1978–79 and 1985–86 academic years (data tapes). See appendix B for a complete definition of each revenue and expenditure variable. Sample sizes among the types of institutions follow: 371 public four-year institutions; 667 public two-year institutions; and 896 private four-year institutions.

two-year colleges.[12] The table reports the levels of the financial variables in the 1985–86 academic year and also the percentage change in each variable between 1978–79 and 1985–86. The figures in the table are expressed in 1990 dollars and were calculated on a full-time-equivalent basis. Because differences in institutional wealth can make for substantial differences among these variables, table 4-2 reports data for private four-year colleges and universities, disaggregated by the level of endowment per student.[13]

12. Appendix B contains a glossary defining each of these variables. This appendix also describes the accounting framework within which these financial variables are defined. Another study analyzing trends in college costs is Hauptman (1990a).

13. We categorize private institutions according to endowment per student because this measure can serve as a proxy both for institutional wealth and for institutional "quality" (in that the size of an endowment helps determine the quantity and quality of educational inputs that an institution can supply). Institutional groupings were formed on the basis of 1978–79 endowment values, and the groupings were held constant over the period. Thus, the data reported here are

Table 4-2. *Revenue and Expenditure per Student at Private Four-Year Institutions, by Endowment per Student*

Category	Level in 1985–86 academic year (1990 dollars)				Percent change, 1978–79 to 1985–86 academic year			
	(1)	(2)	(3)	(4)	(1)	(2)	(3)	(4)
Revenue								
Tuition related								
Gross tuition and fees	5,935	6,735	7,505	9,468	23.0	26.5	27.9	32.5
Institutional financial aid	664	973	1,232	2,274	37.8	58.3	59.7	46.5
Federal financial aid	555	475	437	325	−1.2	−9.1	0.8	1.6
Net tuition and fees	4,716	5,287	5,836	6,869	24.8	26.2	25.2	30.2
Gift and endowment earnings	1,345	1,660	3,402	15,942	−30.1	−8.9	20.9	198.5
Government grants and contracts								
Federal	220	362	917	4,686	−36.4	−33.1	−21.5	4.9
State and local	109	189	426	393	13.6	39.9	71.4	13.8
State and local appropriations	101	127	131	204	14.0	21.7	−16.5	−10.6
Expenditures								
Instruction	2,796	3,351	4,496	7,973	12.6	15.5	15.8	22.1
Other educational and general								
Academic support	620	648	940	1,880	23.4	18.4	26.5	20.0
Student services	714	815	877	1,135	33.0	35.3	37.6	34.2
Institutional support	1,486	1,628	1,874	2,523	25.8	33.4	22.6	29.7
Operation and maintenance	775	953	1,157	2,027	15.7	14.1	12.0	14.4
Additions to physical plant	841	1,002	1,460	2,851	−6.8	46.4	46.5	88.3

Source: Authors' calculations from U.S. Department of Education, Higher Education General Information Survey, the 1978–79 and 1985–86 academic years. See appendix B for a complete definition of each revenue and expenditure variable. Levels of endowment per student are measured in 1978–79 dollars and are defined as follows: (1) signifies less than $400 per student; (2) $400–1,300; (3) $1,300–4,500; and (4) more than $4,500. The sample of private four-year institutions broke down fairly evenly among the different endowment levels: 205 institutions for level (1); 216 institutions for level (2); 225 institutions for level (3); and 250 institutions for level (4).

Tables 4-1 and 4-2 confirm some familiar impressions about higher-education finance in the United States, but they also contain a few surprises. Tuition per student (both including and excluding financial aid) is much lower in public than in private colleges and universities, a difference that is largely explained by the important role that state and local appropriations play in financing public institutions. Thus, while instructional spending per student per year differs by less than a thousand dollars in public and private four-year institutions ($4,270 and $5,109 respectively), gross tuition and fees differ by more than $5,500 per student.[14]

Interestingly, though, the gap in net tuition (tuition adjusted for

impervious to whether an institution might have sharply increased or reduced its endowment over the period.

14. Note that in addition to the difference in instructional spending per student, private institutions on average also spend more on other items (see table 4-1).

student aid) is considerably smaller than the gross difference: private four-year institutions "discount" their tuitions by an average $1,425, compared with only $302 at public four-year institutions. Combined with the fact that students at private institutions usually qualify for more federal aid than those at public institutions, the "net tuition gap" facing the average family is less than $4,500 per student. Moreover, this figure is an average over both recipients and nonrecipients of aid, so that the gap facing the average aid recipient is even smaller.

The data in table 4-1 mask considerable variation within the private sector. As table 4-2 shows, the wealthiest private institutions have gross tuition charges about $3,500 higher than those at the least affluent institutions—although the large role of "discounts" at the most affluent institutions implies that the gap in net tuition is much smaller, averaging a little more than $2,000 per student. Not surprisingly, gift and endowment earnings play a much larger role at the most affluent institutions.[15] Because the most prominent private research universities are also in the highest endowment category, federal grants and contracts are another important source of revenue for this endowment group, contributing $4,686 per student.

The differences in tuition across private institutions are mirrored in differences in spending. Instructional spending per student (which includes "self-supported research") increases substantially with institutional wealth, as does all other spending. It is significant that the differences in instructional and other kinds of spending exceed the differences in both gross and net tuition, implying that students at more affluent private institutions receive a larger educational subsidy, principally from gifts and endowment earnings, than do those at less affluent institutions where tuition must cover most costs.

Examining the rates of change in these revenue and expenditure categories sheds light on how different sectors in higher education fared from the late 1970s to the mid-1980s and also, to some extent, on how colleges and universities responded to changes in external funding. Perhaps most revealing is the relation between rates of change across different sectors' revenue categories and the rates of change across their spending categories. Thus, in table 4-1 we see that tuition

15. Our measure of gift and endowment earnings includes all capital gains to the endowment, both realized and unrealized. Typically, institutions "recognize" only a portion of these gains in their operating budgets, either saving the rest as an increment to the endowment or spending it as capital expenditures.

grew rather rapidly at private institutions (where it is an important source of revenue), increasing by more than 25 percent in real terms over the seven-year period. At the same time, instructional spending at private institutions, the largest spending category at both private and public institutions, also grew rather fast, increasing by 19 percent. In contrast, the principal source of revenue for public colleges and universities, state and local appropriations, grew much less rapidly (by 7 percent at four-year colleges and universities and by 4 percent at two-year colleges). Instructional spending also grew slowly at public institutions (by 7 percent and 6 percent at four-year and two-year colleges respectively).

A similar set of relationships exists within the private sector when it is disaggregated by institutional wealth, as in table 4-2. Interestingly, among variously endowed institutions, differences in the rates of tuition growth are relatively small, but differences in the growth rates of gifts and federal grants—which are important sources of revenue for the more affluent institutions—are much greater, with the more affluent institutions experiencing more rapid revenue growth. These different rates of revenue growth appear consistent with the rates of growth in instructional spending, which were noticeably more rapid at the more affluent institutions.

Other relationships are also suggested by the data. In table 4-1, for example, the actual decline in federal student aid going to private four-year institutions is accompanied by a rapid increase in institution-based aid, while in public institutions federal aid increased moderately and so did institution-based aid. We can also advance a tentative story about the relation between the growth of tuition and the growth in other revenue and expenditure categories in the public and private sectors. Rates of tuition growth are fairly similar across the sectors, with the most rapid growth in net tuition occurring, perhaps surprisingly, at public four-year colleges and universities. (Of course, the dollar increases are much larger in private higher education.) Yet expenditure increases were generally much more rapid in private higher education. One way of reconciling these facts is to suggest that tuition grew for different reasons in the two sectors. In private higher education, increases in instructional spending were financed by the relatively rapid growth in tuition and fees (and, at the more affluent private institutions, in other forms of revenue as well). In public higher education, the rapid growth in tuition and fees was used to compensate for the slow growth in state appropriations, which was having a dampening effect on instructional spending. Thus, similar patterns of tuition growth may derive from sharply different underlying behavioral relationships.

While we find these conjectures plausible, they are made at considerable peril. In the data a great many factors are changing simultaneously, and deciding which sets of relationships to focus on is by no means easy. For example, to return to the issue of institution-based aid, one might reasonably conjecture that the rapid growth in institutionally funded aid at private institutions resulted from the rapid growth in gift and endowment earnings in that sector, rather than from the decline in federal aid. Had wealth not grown over time, perhaps the decline in federal financial aid would have led to a decline in total scholarships, forcing students from lower-income families to flee private higher education for the less expensive public sector.[16] It seems most plausible that a combination of forces—the growth in institutional wealth at the more affluent private institutions and the cessation of growth in federal student aid at all categories of private institutions—explains the growth in institution-based aid. Such an interplay of forces may also be at work on other significant aspects of the data.

To test these various conjectures, and to estimate the magnitude of the behavioral relationships that exist, requires a statistically controlled model. Such a model lets us examine the relationship between any two variables while holding the effect of any other variables constant. It may also let us sort out the channels of influence between variables that may mutually affect one another (as, for example, if more rapid growth in tuition raises the growth rate of institutional student aid and, simultaneously, more rapid growth in institutional student aid raises the growth rate of tuition). Thus, we view this model as a first step toward understanding these important behavioral relationships.

An Econometric Model of College and University Finance

The "university" in our conception is a purposeful institution, in that it pursues the objectives—high quality in education, research, and

16. A possible weakness in this explanation is that institutionally funded aid grew rapidly even for the least affluent private institutions, where gift and endowment earnings are not an important source of income.

administration—that are valued by its various constituencies.[17] We are not convinced, however, that the university "maximizes" or "optimizes" anything. Instead, it seems more plausible to assume that university decisions are, in effect, the outcome of political struggles among constituencies. These constituencies may largely agree on what the broadly defined objectives of the institution are, but they will often disagree sharply about what weights should be attached to those objectives. University behavior will therefore be guided by all these goals, with the degree of response reflecting the influence of different constituencies.

For our purposes, we identify four major objectives shared by most institutions of higher learning. These are objectives that can readily be linked to institutions' resource allocation decisions.

—To maintain or improve the quality of education offered in the future. This objective implies that, all else being equal, institutions will prefer a larger endowment or a higher rate of saving to a smaller endowment or a lower rate of saving.

—To expand the applicant pool—either with the objective of attaining adequate enrollment (for nonselective institutions) or of increasing the institution's capacity to select preferred students. This will normally lead institutions to prefer a lower tuition to a higher one and to prefer a higher to a lower quality of undergraduate instruction.[18]

—To recruit a socioeconomically diverse student body. For most institutions, this will imply a desire to increase the number of disadvantaged and minority students, and will normally lead the institution to prefer a larger to a smaller rate of spending on student aid.

—To improve the institution's prestige and reputation. This will normally lead institutions to increase spending on research and on instruction when possible and will also lead them to provide a higher "quality" of service more generally.

Our picture, then, is of a university pursuing these broad goals under a variety of constraints, financial, legal, and other. And because different universities face different constraints, we would expect the weights attached to these goals to vary across institutions.

17. "University" here refers to colleges and universities.

18. For some private institutions, higher tuition may be seen as an indicator of higher quality and therefore may make it possible for these institutions to increase their applicant pool by raising tuition. Even for these institutions, however, such constituencies as alumni and trustees are likely to prefer lower to higher tuition.

One particular constraint, that of external funding, gives rise to this question—how will changes in the amount of funds an institution receives for a specific purpose, "earmarked funds," affect the way it allocates its resources? Although we do not ultimately endorse the notion of a simple optimizing model of university behavior, that model can provide a useful starting point for thinking through this issue of "fungibility," or the process of reorganizing internal funding when "earmarked funds" are received. Appendix C examines the issue in some detail, concluding that any increase in funds earmarked for a particular purpose will normally be "captured" by the university for other purposes. To the extent that complete fungibility exists, an increase in earmarked funding will have the same impact as an increase in unrestricted income. We would normally expect, however, that spending on the activity for which the funds were designated will increase more than if an equal increase in unrestricted income were involved. Also, spending on other nondesignated activities would increase by a smaller amount. The extent of the difference between the effects of an earmarked and an unrestricted increase in revenue is an empirical question, which we investigate with our econometric model.

Principal Issues Addressed by the Model

As we turn to a specific discussion of our empirical work, we confine ourselves to a fairly general and nontechnical description of our hypotheses and of the model's most significant results. For those who are interested in learning more about the particular, econometric nature of our model, we discuss our theoretical expectations and technical specifications in appendix D.

In the following section, we highlight the principal issues that surround federal student aid and that are addressed in our empirical model.

The impact of changes in federal student aid on changes in tuition. Other things equal, do schools that have experienced more rapid increases in federal student aid tend to have higher rates of tuition growth, as predicted by the "Bennett hypothesis" that increased aid is largely "captured" by schools through increased tuition?[19] An alternative hypothesis is that institutions that receive more revenue from student aid will, all else being equal, choose to "spend" part of the increase on

19. William Bennett, "Our Greedy Colleges," *New York Times*, February 18, 1987, p. A31.

lower tuition charges (that is, lower than they otherwise would be), since they want to be able to compete for applicants.

As for the first hypothesis, institutions might raise tuition in response to increased federal student aid for two reasons. The first is based on the simple observation that more student aid increases the purchasing power of needy students and therefore increases the demand for higher education. Depending on the degree to which the supply of higher education responds, increased demand will tend to lead to higher prices. The other hypothesis depends on institutional incentives created by the aid programs. For example, some other government subsidies are set up in such a way that higher prices automatically bring more aid—this has been true of medicare funding, for example, where the rate of compensation received by a doctor or hospital is a function of the prices charged. Such institutional arrangements obviously provide a powerful incentive for price increases.

Are existing federal student aid programs "tuition-sensitive" in this way? A close analysis of their design suggests that they are, but to a surprisingly small degree. To begin, award levels both to institutions under the campus-based programs and to individuals under the Pell program respond positively to measured student "need," with higher tuition implying higher need. However, funding levels in the campus-based programs have consistently been below the levels at which the "needs" mechanism for awarding incremental dollars kicks in. In addition, award maxima in the Pell program have been below the student charges of almost all private and many public institutions; in the case of the Pell grant, it is the family's income, rather than the tuition, that determines the award level. Thus, there are some public institutions, but almost no private institutions, at which Pell award levels are responsive to tuition increases.[20] The only federal program under which large numbers of schools in both sectors could qualify their students for more aid is the guaranteed student loan program, where the maximum amount a student may borrow is limited by the student's "remaining need" for assistance, a variable that rises with tuition. However, a significant fraction of students already borrow the maximum allowable GSL under present rules, so it is not clear that this effect is very important. Thus,

20. A further consideration is that no student may receive a Pell grant exceeding 60 percent of the cost of attendance. Therefore, schools with very low tuitions, which are generally public, may try to raise the awards for which lower-income students are eligible by raising tuition.

neither the campus-based, Pell, nor GSL program would seem able to contribute much to raising tuition, especially at private institutions.

Although the significance and magnitude of the effect of federal student aid on tuition remain empirical questions, this analysis of institutional incentives casts considerable doubt on the "Bennett hypothesis," and suggests that if any positive effect is observed it is more likely to be in the public, not the private, sector.

The impact of changes in federal student aid on changes in institutions' own spending on student aid. As with tuition, counteracting forces affect institution-based aid. On the one hand, increases in federal student aid help fund the cost of admitting "needy" students. Institutions, therefore, might simply use part of the increase in federal revenue to substitute for their own spending on student aid. On the other hand, because greater federal aid reduces the cost of admitting disadvantaged students, universities might actually use these savings to increase their own spending on aid. Thus, the net effect of changes in federal aid on changes in institutions' own spending remains an empirical question.

The impact of changes in federal student aid on changes in institutions' spending on instruction. Our theory leads us to expect that part of any increase in federal aid will go to fund increases in instructional spending, owing to the general tendency for all revenue sources to be fungible at the margin. The possible size of such an effect—indeed whether it is significantly different from zero—is important. A large, positive effect would imply that increases in federal student aid cause institutions to increase their instructional expenditures substantially. This might be viewed as a good thing if one believes that, at the margin, society would benefit from more resources' being devoted to student instruction. Yet it might be seen as a negative outcome, to the degree that it implies that university expenditures, and hence the cost to the nation of higher education, tend to be pushed up by higher student aid.

Empirical Results

As mentioned, detailed technical specification of our model and empirical findings appears in appendix D. The presentation here is limited to a summary of the basic estimation strategy, the principal empirical results, and some of their implications. We estimate behavioral relations between changes in the levels of funding from various

Table 4-3. *Estimated Effects of $100 Increase in Various Revenue Categories on Institutionally Determined Financial Variables*
U.S. dollars

Independent variable	Institutional financial aid			Gross tuition and fees			Instructional expenditures		
	Private four-year	*Public four-year*	*Public two-year*	*Private four-year*	*Public four-year*	*Public two-year*	*Private four-year*	*Public four-year*	*Public two-year*
Revenue from government									
Federal grants and contracts	11	4	8	−22	*	−10	22	13	31
State and local grants and contracts	6	*	†	−13	*	†	*	†	38
State and local appropriations	22	*	*	−86	*	†	139	30	38
Federal financial aid	20	*	*	*	50	*	*	*	*
Nongovernment income and wealth									
Gifts and endowment earnings	...	...	...	*	...	*	3	†	5
Market value of endowment	1	5	*	...	...	...	...	...	...
State income per capita	−6	*	*	26	...	3	...	...	...
Institutional pricing and aid									
Tuition and fees	23	*	49	257	139	139	31	224	*
Institutional financial aid	...	...	...	...	...	...	...	...	...

Source: Authors' calculations. See appendix D for regression results supporting this summary table. Asterisk represents effects that are not statistically significant. Dagger represents statistically significant signs that are inconsistent with theoretical expectations. Ellipsis signifies that variable has been omitted to permit consistent estimation.

sources and changes in universities' and colleges' financial behavior. In doing so, we use data for individual institutions from the two academic years 1978–79 and 1985–86. The basic variables in the analysis are changes in per student levels of various financial variables, including tuition and federal student aid.

Our analysis focuses on explaining three financial variables over which institutions have control: their spending per student on institution-based aid, their level of gross tuition and fees per student, and their level of instructional expenditures per student. Table 4-3 summarizes our essential findings concerning the influence of a number of external financing variables on these institutionally chosen variables. These external financing variables fall into three categories: revenue from government, revenue derived from private gifts and endowment income, and revenue generated by the institutions' pricing and aid policies.[21]

This last category calls for some comment. Institutions' choices about their tuition levels, spending levels on aid, and spending levels for instruction are obviously interdependent. Other things equal, an institution that can charge a higher tuition is likely to choose to spend more on instruction and on institution-based aid. At the same time, a decision to spend more on institution-based aid will tend to lead an institution to charge higher tuition. Our estimates attempt to capture this mutual dependence through the use of simultaneous-equations estimation techniques.

For most (but not all) of table 4-3, the theory described in the preceding section leads us to expect certain signs on our estimates. For example, we expect that an increase in the rate of growth in federal grant and contract awards to an institution will increase that institution's wealth and therefore lead to a slower rate of increase in tuition, more rapid growth in institution-based aid spending, and more rapid growth in instructional spending. A full treatment of the expected signs and their relation to our actual findings appears in appendix D; in summary, of the 37 statistically significant coefficients for which we had prior expectations, only 6 contradicted our theoretical expectations.

In table 4-3, we report our findings in terms of the impact that a $100 increase in a given variable would have, *holding all other variables constant*, on each of the institutionally chosen variables for each of the

---

21. As explained in appendix D, the complete model also includes the level of and the rate of change in enrollment as control variables.

three categories of institutions. We should emphasize that the numbers reported in table 4-3 are statistical estimates and are subject to error. Moreover, for the sake of clarity, table 4-3 reports only statistically significant estimates whose signs agree with theoretical expectations.[22]

The results of our estimation efforts are, we think, of considerable interest. In general, we had somewhat more success in explaining the behavior of private four-year institutions than of either public four-year or public two-year institutions, but with few exceptions the statistically significant relationships we discovered were reasonable in magnitude as well as direction.[23] Of most immediate interest are the estimated effects of changes in federal student aid on institutional behavior.

We find, interestingly, that among private four-year institutions, a $100 increase in the growth of federal aid leads to a $20 *increase* in institutional scholarship spending. Apparently, increased federal aid lowers the cost of admitting needy students sufficiently to allow private institutions to increase their own spending on aid in response to increases in federal aid. We find no evidence of the "Bennett hypothesis," that private institutions increase their tuitions when they receive more federal student aid, nor is there a significant impact of changes in federal student aid on changes in instructional spending at private institutions. It is unfortunate that data do not exist that would let us test for the influence of federal student aid on tuitions at proprietary institutions. Given the large fraction of students at proprietary schools who receive such aid, such an effect is plausible.

For public institutions, the effects of federal student aid differ in important ways. We do not find any significant relationship between federal aid and institution-based aid or instructional expenditures. We do, however, find that public four-year institutions tend to raise tuition by $50 for every $100 increase in federal student aid. This finding is consistent with the institutional facts discussed earlier: only public four-

22. A full treatment of the findings is contained in appendix D.

23. A possible explanation for this difference is that some public institutions may operate under legislative constraints that prevent them from responding "autonomously" to changes in their external financing environment. The most anomalous magnitudes concern the estimated impact of an increase in institutional financial aid on tuition and fees (we would expect the effect of a $100 increase in institutional scholarships to be an increase of less than $100 in tuition), and the effect of an increase in tuition and fees on instructional spending at public four-year institutions, where we would expect an increase of less than $100. We suspect that these results came about because we failed to control adequately for the reverse influence between the variables—the effect of tuition on institution-based aid in the first instance, and the effect of instructional spending on tuition and fees in the second instance.

year institutions can capture additional federal student aid revenue by raising their tuition levels under current arrangements. These links between federal student aid and the behavior of both public and private institutions are important factors to consider in developing proposals for reforming federal student aid.

Given the central importance of state and local appropriations for public colleges and universities, it is not surprising to find that a $100 increase in state and local appropriations leads to a $30 increase in instructional spending at public four-year institutions and a $38 increase at public two-year institutions.[24] It is perhaps more surprising that we do not find any evidence that state and local appropriation levels influence public tuition or institution-based aid levels.[25]

The findings about the impact of changes in federal grants and contract awards on institutional behavior are particularly striking. These estimates suggest that variations in these award levels (which are principally but not exclusively research awards) have impacts that extend beyond the research enterprise narrowly considered. More generous federal grant and contract funding apparently allows institutions to raise tuition more slowly, fund institution-based aid programs more generously, and increase spending on instruction more rapidly than would otherwise be the case. These relations hold up rather well across our institutional categories. Our study does not have federal research funding as a primary emphasis, and it is certainly important to pursue these relations in more depth to see if these findings are robust. They have considerable relevance for policy, since they suggest that changes in federal research (and other grant and contract) funding for higher education may have a broader institutional impact than policymakers may appreciate.

Conclusion

It is important to stress that the analysis summarized here is only a first attempt, using readily available data, to make sense of a complex

24. Because state and local appropriations to private institutions are concentrated on a few institutions, the estimated impacts of such spending at private institutions are probably statistically unreliable.

25. It is possible that the relation between state appropriations and public tuition levels is masked by differences across states. In some states, tuition is set at a fraction of the level of state spending, so that the two are positively related; in others, tuition may be adjusted up or down to balance the influence of variation in state spending on public institution budgets.

set of relationships. Nonetheless, while the results should be interpreted with caution, we feel they shed important light on a set of questions that have obvious policy implications. Some of the major results that provide insight into the multiple effects of government funds on institutions of higher learning include the following: (1) with regard to federal student aid, we find that, at private four-year institutions, increases in SEOG and Pell expenditures do not cause schools to raise tuition and fees, although increases in federal financial aid do lead to higher tuition and fees at public four-year institutions; (2) federal grants and contracts have important effects on tuition and fees, institution-based financial aid, and instructional expenditures throughout higher education—our results indicate that cutbacks in research funding would lead to higher tuitions at private four-year and public two-year institutions, lower institutional financial aid at four-year private and both four- and two-year public institutions, and lower instructional expenditures for all three groups; and (3) increases in state and local appropriations significantly increase instructional spending in all three of the institutional categories examined.

Understanding these various relationships is extremely important to lessening the chance that changes in government policy will have unanticipated, undesirable effects on the educational sector. At the same time, the results suggest that some widely discussed negative side effects of federal student aid spending do not exist. This analysis of institutional behavior influences our projections of college affordability in chapter 6 and leads us to consider the supply as well as the demand effect of government policy in our later discussion of policy alternatives.

V

Incomes, Prices, and College Choice

THIS CHAPTER uses data on the distribution of students by income background in an attempt to get at the elusive issue of "choice" in higher education.[1] As seen in chapter 1, the predominant goal of federal financial aid policy has been to improve "access": trying to ensure that everyone who wants to go to college can. Yet one outstanding feature of the American higher education system is the exceptional variety of options available to students. To the degree that all students can take advantage of this variety by choosing among a broad range of postsecondary education alternatives, the better will higher education resources be used and the better will the value of equal educational opportunity be served. Thus, in examining the overall affordability of American higher education and the role of financial aid policies in sustaining affordability, the question of *where* as well as *whether* students from various economic backgrounds can attend college is important.

Besides providing a general portrait of where various students attend college, we give special attention to two populations—one institutional, the other individual—that are especially involved with the issue of "choice." The first population comprises the "elite," high-priced, selective private colleges and universities. These institutions—symbolized by names like Harvard, Stanford, and Dartmouth—enroll a relatively trivial number of students, yet loom large in the national consciousness: as a focus of aspirations for parents and children, as entry points to the highest positions in the professions and public life, and as targets for complaints about exorbitant pricing. Are these institutions becoming bastions of economic privilege, open only to the wealthy and to the lucky few among the disadvantaged who receive generous grant awards? More specifically, we attempt to determine whether there has

1. The work in this chapter was done jointly with Larry H. Litten and Michael P. O'Malley.

75

been a differential tendency for "middle-class" students to migrate from these institutions toward less expensive alternatives. For this purpose, we equate the population of "elite" private institutions with those that are members of the Consortium for Financing Higher Education (COFHE), a group comprising many of the most selective private institutions in the nation.[2] Members of this consortium regularly survey their graduating seniors on a number of questions relating to their economic backgrounds and the financing of their education. We are able to use those data tapes to address the issues of "middle-class" enrollment and college finance.

The second population we focus on is that of exceptionally able high school students. An important social issue is whether educational opportunity is widely distributed for these young people, without regard to their economic status. By examining a group of students whose academic credentials would admit them almost anywhere, one important dimension of the "choice" issue—how and where the nation's best young students choose to educate themselves—may be made clearer. Moreover, many would argue that the nation as a whole has a particular interest in the educational destinations of these students, since it is from their ranks that many future leaders in science, industry, and government can be expected to emerge. To study these students, we draw on evidence from a sample of top high school students who graduated in 1987.

It is natural that rapid tuition increases at private "elite" institutions over the past decade have led to worries that these schools have become too expensive for certain groups of students. At COFHE schools, the median tuition increased 196 percent from 1978 to 1989, compared with a 90 percent increase in the consumer price index, while the median income of families who are headed by parents aged 45–64 (the majority of families of traditional college-age students) rose 94 percent. It is often suspected that middle-class students—not those from lower-income backgrounds—are the ones most affected by these price increases and that they are being driven away from our highly selective, highly prestigious colleges and universities. Students from lower-

2. The consortium is a research group currently containing 32 members (there were 30 members in 1978) that includes most of the institutions widely identified as the "elite" colleges and universities in the United States, including, among others, the Ivy League universities and a number of highly selective coeducational and women's colleges.

income backgrounds qualify for need-based financial aid, so tuition increases are likely to be met by similar increases in aid, lessening the chance that these students experience an affordability problem. Students from upper-income families receive a different but analogous form of financial aid—parental contributions that do not require major proportions of available annual incomes. But the situation for middle-class students is different. The real incomes of middle-class families may have leveled off recently as the previous gains realized by increasing the *number* of wage earners in a family (through the entrance into the labor force of spouses who had been homemakers) stops and salary growth moderates. Furthermore, middle-class families possess assets that reduce financial aid packages. It is usually the case that these assets (homes, family cars, retirement savings, and the like) are illiquid, so that a price squeeze may result if increases in financial aid do not keep pace with increases in tuition. Thus, when tuitions rise faster than other economic indicators, students from middle-income backgrounds may be forced to switch to less costly educational alternatives.

Some observers claim that a "melt" has already occurred. In a September 1989 *Washington Post* article, Robert Kuttner wrote, "statistics show that children from moderate-income families are indeed being driven away from private colleges."[3] Lionel Lewis and Paul Kingston point to "a small decrease in recent years in the ability of lower- and middle-income students to pay for an elite private education" and argue that in the 1980s the proportion of students from affluent families who were attending private, highly selective institutions grew at a faster rate than that proportion attending undergraduate institutions in general.[4] Thus, they argue that not only is the share of upper-income students much larger at the "elite" private institutions but the differential between these "elites" and the rest of American higher education is also growing.

By tracing the income backgrounds of students at COFHE institutions, we first show how students from middle-class backgrounds and below have weathered the recent period of marked tuition increases. We then compare shifts in the income distribution of students at "elite" institutions with those of students at other types of institutions; does it appear that students from certain income backgrounds are being priced

3. Robert Kuttner, "The Squeeze on Young Families," *Washington Post*, September 8, 1989, p. A23.
4. Lewis and Kingston (1989).

out of our most selective private institutions? We turn next to the sample of high-achieving high school students, first providing an overview of how these students are distributed across various categories of institutions by income level, and then focusing more closely on their application, admission, and matriculation rates at the "elite" institutions. We proceed to a discussion of the college destinations of top high school students who either turn down COFHE schools or never apply to any, with the familiar aim of examining how college choice is affected by price. Finally, we use the sample of top high school students to analyze how the net price of attending an elite private institution varies with income. Here, we compute income burdens—the ratio of net price to income—and ask if it is true, as the speculation holds, that middle-income families face a higher ratio at "elite" institutions than that faced by poorer or richer families. In addition, we restrict the sample to top high school students who either do not apply or are not admitted to one of the "elite" institutions and instead matriculate at a relatively low cost alternative. Do the parents of these students tend to underestimate the amount of aid available to them at "elite" institutions, particularly parents in middle-income families, thereby overestimating the net price of attending these colleges and universities?

Changes in the College Destinations of Middle-Income Students

Table 5-1 presents summary information on the income backgrounds of COFHE and other students based on student-reported data from the American Freshman Survey for 1978 and 1989. These data are derived from thirteen COFHE institutions that participated in the survey in both years.[5] We use six basic income brackets divided along constant-dollar bands. We also create two useful summary categories—below middle income, the sum of lower income and lower-middle income; and above middle income, the sum of the two upper-middle income categories and upper income. The 1989 income bands closely approximate constant-dollar equivalents for those used in 1978 (the United States experienced 90 percent inflation during this period), but they are not exact

5. Although universities predominate in COFHE (18 out of 32 members), the participants who provided the data from the American Freshman Survey are primarily colleges (9 out of 13).

adjustments because we are constrained by the response categories printed on the questionnaires. The constant-dollar income groupings from the questionnaires follow (in thousands of dollars).[6]

Income group	1978	1989
Lower	< 10	< 20
Lower-middle	10–20	20–40
Middle	20–30	40–60
Upper-middle I	30–40	60–75
Upper-middle II	40–50	75–100
Upper	> 50	> 100

To understand whether the income distribution of students in "elite" institutions has changed differentially during this period of relatively high tuition increases, we need to compare enrollments at COFHE and other schools with changes in the national income distribution. Toward this end, we first examine the national income distribution for all families headed by parents aged 45–64. We use federal government data from 1979 (1978 data are only available with income breaks that have little in common with the categories in table 5-1) and then compare these data with estimated values for 1989.[7] Over the period, we find an increase in the share of families below middle income of 8 percentage points, a decline in the middle-income share of 2 percentage points, and a decrease in the share above middle income of 6 percentage points.

When these overall trends are compared to college enrollment trends, some striking differences emerge. Data from the national norms generated by the American Freshman Survey show that in all postsecondary institutions, the share of students from below middle income fell by 2 percentage points, the middle-income share fell by 1 percentage point, and the share above middle income, therefore, rose by 3 percentage points. Thus, while the decline in the proportion of middle-income students at all institutions could be thought to reflect the decline in the

6. As indicated in table 5-1, precise inflation-adjusted categories in 1989 would break down as follows: less than $19,000, $19,000–38,000, $38,000–57,000, $57,000–76,000, $76,000–95,000, and above $95,000.

7. The most recent data are for 1987, when the national income distribution (using the 1989 income classifications) broke down as follows: lower income, 22.1 percent; lower-middle income, 31.5 percent; middle income, 24.0 percent; upper-middle income I, 9.7 percent; the sum of upper-middle income II and upper income, 12.7 percent. We look at changes in the national income distribution between 1985, 1986, and 1987, and extrapolate the 1987 figures up through 1989 to produce our 1989 estimates. Income distribution data are from U.S. Bureau of the Census (1975).

Table 5-1. *Income Backgrounds of COFHE and Other Students, Selected Data, 1978 and 1989*
Percent, unless otherwise specified

Item	Lower income	Lower-middle income	Total below middle income	Middle income	Total above middle income	Upper-middle income I	Upper-middle income II	Upper income
1978 data								
Income range, from survey (thousands of dollars)	< 10	10–20	< 20	20–30	> 30	30–40	40–50	> 50
Families with college-age children[a]	13.6	25.8	39.4	26.9	33.8	16.5	8.4	8.9
American Freshman Survey data, students enrolled at								
All institutions	16.3	33.8	50.1	26.1	23.6	12.3	4.3	7.0
Four-year private secular colleges	14.6	29.7	44.3	24.0	31.7	13.5	5.6	12.6
Four-year public colleges	18.3	33.7	52.0	27.1	21.2	12.6	3.9	4.7
Private universities	9.0	21.6	30.6	23.0	46.2	16.5	8.2	21.5
Public universities	9.8	28.9	38.7	29.0	32.4	16.7	6.4	9.3
COFHE schools[b]	5.8	15.5	21.3	22.0	56.8	17.4	9.8	29.6
Admissions testing program data[c]	13.7	39.2	52.9	26.0	21.0	...	...	...
1989 data								
Income range (thousands of dollars)								
From survey	< 20	20–40	< 40	40–60	> 60	60–75	75–100	> 100
In 1978 dollars	< 19	19–38	< 38	38–57	> 57	57–76	76–95	> 95
Families with college-age children[a]	19.9	27.3	47.2	25.2	27.8	11.5	} 16.3 {	
American Freshman Survey data, students enrolled at								
All institutions	15.9	32.3	48.2	24.6	27.3	10.8	7.2	9.3
Four-year private secular colleges	13.0	26.2	39.2	22.0	38.9	11.7	9.6	17.6
Four-year public colleges	15.9	33.0	48.9	26.9	24.2	11.5	7.1	5.6
Private universities	7.6	19.5	27.1	20.5	52.3	13.1	12.7	26.5
Public universities	11.4	27.3	38.7	25.8	35.3	13.4	9.8	12.1
COFHE schools[b]	6.3	15.1	21.4	18.2	60.2	12.9	13.6	33.7
Admissions testing program data[c]	16.8	35.7	52.5	24.9	22.7	...	...	...

Source: Authors' calculations using selected data. See text for data sources.
a. Income distribution includes only families with heads of household aged 45–64. We use 1979 values as proxies for 1978 data. See text for calculation of 1989 estimates.
b. Sample size for 1978 is 6,839; for 1989, it is 7,443.
c. In 1978 lower income is < 9, and lower-middle income is 9–20.

proportion of middle-income families in the nation, the behavior of lower- and upper-income students seems to defy national trends.[8]

The trends are somewhat different at the "elite" schools alone. At COFHE institutions, the share of middle-income students falls from 22 percent to 18 percent, while the share below middle income stays at 21 percent and the share above middle income rises from 57 percent to 60 percent.[9] A large part of the apparent "melt" of middle-income students from COFHE's entering classes can be accounted for by the disappearance of such students from college campuses in general. Comparing the decline in middle-income students at COFHE institutions with the decline at all institutions shows that 33 percent of COFHE'S loss of middle-income students reflects the decreasing number of middle-income college-bound high school seniors in the national pool.[10] The remaining 67 percent of the total drop in COFHE's middle-income students represents the true "melt" of middle-income students.[11]

8. The decline in the two middle-income figures is actually even closer. For all institutions it was 1.5 percentage points (a 5.7 percent decline) and for the national figures it was 1.7 percentage points (a 6.3 percent decline).

9. Given the considerable stability over the period in enrollments at COFHE schools and at the other institutional groups discussed later, a decline in the middle-income share represents a decrease in the absolute number of middle-income students, and a relatively more rapid percentage decline at COFHE schools signifies a decrease in the share of all middle-income students who are enrolled at COFHE schools. While, for purposes of exposition, we usually use percentage point changes in our discussion, our examination of percentage changes in income shares found that the main findings were not altered in a significant way.

Data in table 5-1 show that the combined share of students in the middle-income and upper-middle income I categories ($20,000–40,000 in 1978; $40,000–75,000 in 1989) fell substantially from 39 percent in 1978 to 31 percent in 1989. While this combined income grouping is somewhat truncated in 1989, the difference between the inflation-adjusted range ($38,000–76,000) and the actual range ($40,000–75,000) is small. This is particularly so, given the probability that a student who thinks her family's income is between $38,000 and $40,000 would round up when answering the survey and choose the $40,000–60,000 category rather than $20,000–40,000. On the other hand, the combined share of students in the upper-middle income II and upper-income categories (family income above $40,000 in 1978, and above $75,000 in 1989) rose from 39 percent in 1978 to 47 percent in 1989. Here, the change in the income category closely approximates the rate of inflation.

10. The 33 percent figure is based on a decline of 5.7 percent in the share of middle-income students at all institutions divided by the 17.3 percent decline in the middle-income share at COFHE schools.

11. Another set of student-reported national data on students' family income is the Admissions Testing Program (ATP) of the College Board. ATP data are broader in one respect than the American Freshman Survey data and narrower in another. The data come primarily from high school seniors—but also from juniors (and a few sophomores) who take the Scholastic Aptitude Tests (SATs) or the Achievement Tests—who live disproportionately on the East and West coasts. These geographic areas are precisely the markets from which COFHE institutions draw a majority

Data from the American Freshman Survey for other groups of schools indicate, however, that the "elite" COFHE institutions are not alone in losing students from middle-income backgrounds over the 1978–89 period. If "middle-income melt" had resulted from COFHE institutions' pricing themselves out of the market, the changes in the income distribution at COFHE schools should be more dramatic than at less costly alternatives, such as public universities. Yet, the experience at public universities basically mirrors that of COFHE schools: there has been a decline of 3 percentage points in the share of students from the middle-income group; a constant share of students below middle income; and a consequent increase of 3 percentage points in the share from above middle income. While it is true that COFHE students are disproportionately from upper-income families compared with students at public universities (with 60 percent of COFHE students in 1989 from above middle income compared with 35 percent at public universities), it is also true, and contrary to conventional wisdom, that the differential has been roughly stable. Specifically, the difference in the share of middle-income students at COFHE versus public universities rose only slightly from a shortfall of 7 percentage points to 8 percentage points, while the difference in the share of students above middle income held steady at 25 percentage points.[12]

While both COFHE schools and public universities lost a larger share of middle-income students than did the overall student population, the share of middle-income students at four-year public colleges was actually unchanged over the period (27 percent). The stability in the middle-income share at these latter institutions, in the face of a declining percentage of middle-income students in the general population of American freshmen, suggests a movement of middle-income students from private institutions (both COFHE and non-COFHE) and public

of their students. We have focused on the American Freshman Survey data because our COFHE data come from that source. The ATP data do show (table 5-1), however, that between 1978 and 1989, the share of SAT takers who came from families below middle income remained about constant at 53 percent (the decline was less than half a percentage point), the middle-income share fell by 1 percentage point, and the share above middle income rose by less than 2 percentage points.

12. What about comparing the more striking changes in the share of students in the middle-income and upper-middle-income I categories? Table 5-1 shows that at public universities this share fell from 46 percent to 39 percent, a bit less than the 39 to 31 percent decline at COFHE institutions. The share of students in the upper-middle-income II and upper-income categories rose from 16 percent to 22 percent at public universities, again approximating the increase from 39 percent to 47 percent at COFHE schools.

universities to public colleges. Thus, while changes in the income backgrounds of COFHE students mirror changes at public universities, a group of institutions that are much less expensive alternatives to "elite" private institutions (though, interestingly, not necessarily to public universities)—the public colleges—are gaining middle-income students' attendance.

We wondered if these findings were sensitive to either the particular years chosen or the data set used. Table 5-2 summarizes data taken from the COFHE Senior Survey on the income backgrounds of COFHE students who graduated in 1982 and in 1989. We have information from students at twenty-five COFHE institutions in 1982 and from fifteen schools in 1989.[13] The income ranges in the 1982 questionnaire dictate the constant-dollar income groups that follow (in thousands of dollars).[14]

Income group	1982	1989[15]
Lower	< 18	< 20
Lower-middle	18–30	20–40
Middle	30–50	40–60
Upper-middle I	50–75	60–100
Upper	> 75	> 100

The summary data in table 5-2 show that, in 1982, 23 percent of the

13. In addition to acting as a consistency check on income changes for all students, these data let us examine income changes for specific gender, racial, and ethnic groups at COFHE schools. Only six institutions produced representative samples in both years. Thus, differences in the two years could be the result of the participation of different institutions with different family-income distributions. We checked the data for these six institutions and the results were very similar to those we found in the larger data sets. For example, the decline in the share of middle-income students for the restricted group was 8.4 percentage points versus 8.9 percentage points in the complete data set. We use the larger set of data because the number of minority students drops too much to permit analysis by income grouping in the smaller data set. These racial and ethnic data have to be considered as only suggestive, however, because of the chance that the income distributions of the minority students in the different sets of institutions may differ independent of the effects of the "melt" phenomenon that we are investigating.

14. Inflation between 1982 and 1989 was about 29 percent, creating the following inflation-adjusted income categories for 1989: less than $23,000; $23,000–38,999; $39,000–64,999; $65,000–96,999; and greater than $97,000. The differences between the 1978 and 1982 figures derive partly from drawing data from different years, and partly from examining seniors rather than freshmen. Also, for the detailed income categories, the approximations to constant real income bands differ somewhat between years, owing to data limitations.

15. Disaggregated income categories in 1989 are identical in tables 5-1 and 5-2, except that Senior Survey data no longer allow us to divide the upper-middle-income group into two sub-groups.

Table 5-2. Income Backgrounds of COFHE and Other Students, Selected Survey Data, 1982 and 1989[a]
Percent, unless otherwise specified

Item (sample size in parentheses)	Lower income	Lower-middle income	Total below middle income	Middle income	Total above middle income	Upper-middle income	Upper income
1982 data							
Income range in thousands of dollars							
From COFHE senior survey	< 18	18–30	< 30	30–50	> 50	50–75	> 75
From freshman survey	< 20	20–30	< 30	30–50	> 50	. .	. .
Families with college-age children[b]	26.8	26.5	53.3	29.6	17.1	12.1	5.0
COFHE Senior Survey enrollment data							
COFHE total (7,546)	7.7	15.5	23.2	26.5	50.3	22.2	28.1
COFHE by gender							
Male (3,485)	7.0	15.7	22.7	27.8	49.5	20.6	28.9
Female (4,061)	8.3	15.3	23.6	25.4	51.1	23.6	27.5
COFHE by ethnic group and gender							
Asian (361)	17.2	23.0	40.2	25.5	34.3	16.3	18.0
Male (170)	15.9	21.8	37.7	28.2	34.1	15.3	18.8
Female (191)	18.3	24.1	42.4	23.0	34.6	17.3	17.3
Black (273)	18.3	26.0	44.3	31.1	24.6	16.5	8.1
Male (88)	17.0	29.5	46.5	30.7	22.7	13.6	9.1
Female (185)	18.9	24.3	43.2	31.4	25.4	17.8	7.6
Hispanic (178)	23.6	21.9	45.5	27.0	27.5	14.0	13.5
Male (105)	13.3	29.5	42.8	30.5	26.7	12.4	14.3
Female (73)	38.4	11.0	49.4	21.9	28.7	16.4	12.3
White (6,734)	6.3	14.5	20.8	26.3	52.9	23.0	29.9
Male (3,122)	6.0	14.5	20.5	27.6	51.9	21.4	30.5
Female (3,612)	6.6	14.5	21.1	25.2	53.6	24.3	29.3
American Freshman Survey, students enrolled at							
All institutions	29.7	24.7	54.4	31.1	14.6	. .	. .
Four-year private secular colleges	25.7	21.0	46.7	29.2	24.2	. .	. .
Four-year public colleges	33.7	25.5	59.2	30.7	10.2	. .	. .
Private universities	16.1	16.4	32.5	31.3	36.2	. .	. .
Public universities	20.9	21.9	42.8	36.1	21.0	. .	. .
Admissions testing program data	26.8	30.4	57.2	28.4	14.2	. .	. .

1989 data

Income range in thousands of dollars	< 20 / < 23	20–40 / 23–39	< 40 / < 39	40–60 / 39–65	> 60 / > 65	60–100 / 65–97	> 100 / > 97
From survey / In 1982 dollars							
Families with college-age children[b]	19.9	27.3	47.2	25.2	27.8	…	…
COFHE Senior Survey enrollment data							
COFHE total (7,896)	5.5	14.3	19.8	17.6	62.6	26.0	36.6
COFHE by gender							
Male (3,301)	5.1	12.6	17.7	17.6	64.6	25.8	38.8
Female (4,595)	5.8	15.5	21.3	17.5	61.1	26.1	35.0
COFHE by ethnic group and gender							
Asian (654)	8.7	17.4	26.1	17.3	56.6	24.3	32.3
Male (242)	8.7	18.2	26.9	13.6	59.5	24.8	34.7
Female (412)	8.7	17.0	25.7	19.4	54.8	24.0	30.8
Black (408)	13.7	29.7	43.4	21.6	35.0	21.8	13.2
Male (145)	17.2	26.2	43.4	18.6	37.9	23.4	14.5
Female (263)	11.8	31.6	43.4	23.2	33.4	20.9	12.5
Hispanic (268)	19.0	28.7	47.7	16.0	36.2	18.7	17.5
Male (119)	21.8	19.3	41.1	18.5	40.3	21.8	18.5
Female (149)	16.8	36.2	53.0	14.1	32.9	16.1	16.8
White (6,566)	4.2	12.4	16.6	17.4	66.0	26.7	39.3
Male (2,795)	3.5	11.2	14.7	17.9	67.5	26.2	41.3
Female (3,771)	4.6	13.4	18.0	17.1	64.9	27.1	37.8
American Freshman Survey, students enrolled at							
All institutions	15.9	32.3	48.2	24.6	27.3	18.0	9.3
Four-year private secular colleges	13.0	26.2	39.2	22.0	38.9	21.3	17.6
Four-year public colleges	15.9	33.0	48.9	26.9	24.2	18.6	5.6
Private universities	7.6	19.5	27.1	20.5	52.3	25.8	26.5
Public universities	11.4	27.3	38.7	25.8	35.3	23.2	12.1
Admissions testing program data	16.8	35.7	52.5	24.9	22.7	…	…

Source: Authors' calculations using selected survey data.

a. Survey data are from COFHE Senior Survey and American Freshman Survey.

b. Income distribution includes only families with heads of household aged 45–64. Lower income in 1982 is < 17.5, and lower-middle income is 17.5–30.

COFHE seniors responding to the survey were from families below middle income, 27 percent were from middle-income families, and 50 percent were from families above middle income. By 1989, the share below middle income fell by 3 percentage points, the middle-income share fell by 9 percentage points, and, consequently, the share above middle income rose by about 12 percentage points.

A closer look at the racial composition of the changing income distribution reveals that while the pattern for whites mirrors the overall pattern, other racial and ethnic groups had very different experiences. For Asian students, the movement in income distribution was much more dramatic than for the sample as a whole—a 14 percentage point decline in the share below middle income, a 9 percentage point decline in the middle-income share, and a 23 percentage point increase in the share above middle income. Blacks and hispanics, on the other hand, experienced virtually no changes in the shares below middle income, although the middle-income shares fell by around 10 percentage points. In sum, all racial groups experienced precipitous declines in the amount of middle-income representation between 1982 and 1989. In addition, whites lost some of their students from below-middle-income families while Asians lost a far greater number. Blacks and hispanics maintained the percentages of their students from families below middle income.[16]

Data on income distributions—both national and specifically educational—in 1982 also provide a context in which to judge the distinctiveness of the income redistribution in the "elite" institutions. Comparing federal national income figures from 1982 with our 1989 estimates, we find that the share of families below middle income fell by 6 percentage points, the middle-income share fell by 5 percentage points, and the above-middle-income share rose by 11 percentage points. In the freshman survey data for 1982 and 1989, the decline in middle-

16. Part of the apparent change may reflect the fact that the 1989 definition of middle class is more restricted than the inflation-adjusted category (we are forced to use $40,000–59,999 versus $39,000–64,999). However, the fact that the percentage of lower-middle-income students falls despite the use of an income category that is larger than the inflation-adjusted category ($20,000–39,999 versus $23,000–38,999) and that the percentage of upper-income students rises despite the use of an income category that is smaller than the inflation-adjusted category (above $100,000 versus above $97,000) implies that these changes are not a statistical aberration. It should further be noted that these data differ from the freshman data in that the observed results could be the result of interactions between income and matriculation (which is all that is captured in the freshman surveys), or between income and attrition, or both. The data do not permit disentangling these two effects.

income students at all institutions of higher education is somewhat more severe than changes in the national income distribution.[17] Table 5-2 shows a decline of approximately 7 percentage points (21 percent) in the share of middle-income students at all institutions, which compares with a decline in the share of middle-income families in the nation of about 4 percentage points (15 percent).

As far as a comparison between the COFHE experience and that at other institutions, it is unfortunate that we have data only for freshmen (rather than seniors) for the corresponding years, although they do provide some comparative perspective. Basic changes in income backgrounds between 1982 and 1989 at all institutions in the American Freshman Survey include a 6 percentage point decline in the share of students below middle income, a 7 percentage point decline in the share of middle-income students, and a 12 percentage point rise in the share of students above middle income. Comparing the decline in middle-income students at COFHE institutions with the decline at all institutions shows that almost two-thirds (62 percent) of the total loss in middle-income students reflects the disappearance of college-bound high school students in the middle-income range.[18] The remaining 38 percent of the total drop represents middle-income students who are going to non-COFHE schools.[19]

17. This difference between the national income data and the freshman survey data, and the more pronounced shifts in income distribution between the 1982 and 1989 surveys than between the 1978 and 1989 surveys, *could* reflect the way the question was worded on the respective questionnaires. Each of the survey forms has fourteen income categories, although the definition of each response category is changed over time to account for inflation. In 1978 and in 1989, the income band that we label as "middle income" is derived from two response codes—the ninth and tenth codes listed on the questionnaire; in 1982, our middle-income group comes from three response codes—the tenth, eleventh, and twelfth on the questionnaire. The reflection of these greater differences for the 1982–89 comparisons in the national income than for the 1978–89 comparisons, however, suggest that the freshman survey data are not contaminated by the change in response categories. Furthermore, to the extent that students who do not know family income tend to pick answers toward the middle of the scale (assuming that most college students think of themselves as "middle income"), the shift in the categories should have depressed our "middle-income" percentages for both COFHE and the other institutional comparisons in 1982 instead of increasing them.

18. The 62 percent figure is based on a decline of 20.9 percent in the share of middle-income students at all institutions divided by the 33.6 percent decline in the middle-income share at COFHE schools.

19. Data on the income backgrounds of SAT takers (Admissions Testing Program data) indicate significant changes during the period. Between 1982 and 1989, the share of SAT takers below middle income fell by 5 percentage points, the middle-income share fell by 4 percentage points, and the share above middle income rose by 9 percentage points.

Data from the American Freshman Survey for other types of schools once again indicate that COFHE schools are not alone in losing students from middle-income backgrounds during the 1980s. At public universities, there has been a decline of 4 percentage points in the share of students from families below middle income, a decline of 10 percentage points in the middle-income share, and a consequent increase of 14 percentage points in the share from above middle income. Hence, the difference in the shares of middle-income students between COFHE and public institutions slipped from 9 percentage points to 8 percentage points, while the difference in the percentage of students from above-middle-income families fell from 29 to 28 points. To put it another way, the substantial increase in the proportion of COFHE students from families above middle income in a period of seven years is less dramatic than the increase at public universities.[20] At four-year public colleges, on the other hand, the decline in the proportion of middle-income students was much smaller than at either COFHE schools, public universities, or for all institutions, once again indicating that these students have been migrating to that sector.[21]

Several conclusions from tables 5-1 and 5-2 are worth highlighting: (1) in 1989, students at COFHE institutions were coming from families with higher real incomes than they had been over the preceding decade; (2) students at COFHE institutions are much more affluent than those at other institutions of higher learning; (3) the differential in income between COFHE students and students at public universities has been relatively constant over the period, and may even have narrowed recently. The fact that two different sets of data covering two different periods of time have produced such similar patterns bolsters our confidence in these findings.

While the first two of the preceding conclusions are well known, the third is not. The latter clearly challenges the assertion that the increasing divergence over the past decade between sticker prices at COFHE institutions and at their most likely competitors, public universities, has

20. It should be noted that while the absolute increase in the proportion of above-middle-income students is only slightly greater at public universities than at COFHE schools, the percentage increase at COFHE schools was only 24 percent compared with a remarkable 68 percent at public universities.

21. As was true over the longer period, the decline in the middle-income share at public colleges was also less than the decline in the middle-income share in the national income distribution.

led to an exodus of middle-income students from COFHE institutions. Were this the case, we would not see declining middle-income enrollment at public universities.

We have no clear explanation for the shift of middle-income students from COFHE, other private institutions, and public universities to public colleges, though we can speculate about three forces that may have been at work.[22] First, more students may be attending four-year institutions in their home cities, either to economize on living costs or to take advantage of local labor markets. Four-year public colleges, which are more widespread geographically than public universities, are therefore more likely to enroll these students. Second, it may be that some public universities have raised their admissions thresholds in the 1980s, perhaps in response to state legislative pressures for measurable "quality" improvements. Given the correlation between income levels and measured ability in high schools, such an effort to raise the admissions threshold would tend to shift up the income distribution at these institutions. Finally, there has been some increase in the price differential between public four-year colleges and public universities.

Enrollment Destinations of High-Achieving Students

While the "elite" private institutions are not experiencing a *differential* middle-income melt relative to public universities, COFHE schools are nonetheless losing students from the middle ranks of the income distribution (compared with changes in the national income distribution and with changes at all institutions of higher learning). Another data set allows a more detailed look at how and why COFHE schools lose potential students from middle-income families: a 1987 survey of high school students with high Preliminary Scholastic Aptitude Test (PSAT) scores.[23] We have divided these students into five income groups (numbers in thousands of dollars).

22. This is a truly speculative exercise as we have no evidence that bears on the relative importance of these possible forces.

23. The survey was carried out in June 1987 by the Educational Testing Service (ETS) for Richard Spies of Princeton University, and was funded by the College Board and the Alfred P. Sloan Foundation. We thank Spies for generously providing these data. See Spies (1990).

Income group	1987
Lower	< 20
Lower-middle	20–40
Middle	40–60
Upper-middle	60–70
Upper	> 90

The top panel of table 5-3 presents destination data for 3,225 students for whom we have matriculation, family income, and standardized test score information. Of these students, 23 percent matriculated at a COFHE institution while, as indicated in the bottom panel, 41 percent of the sample with scores on the Scholastic Aptitude Test (SAT) above 1300 matriculated at a COFHE school.[24] In each case, the percentage of upper-income students going to a COFHE school is well above the average across income groups: 40 percent of all students with family income above $90,000, and 56 percent of these same students who have very high SAT scores. It is striking that, for the entire sample of top-performing high school students, COFHE institutions get more than twice as large a share of the richest students than of the lower-income, lower-middle-income, or middle-income students. Looking at the overall distribution between private and public institutions, we find that, for the entire sample, about half of all these high school students, except for those in the upper-income group, matriculated at private institutions. For those students with SAT scores above 1300, the share of students who matriculate at private institutions varies more across income groups, but the average percentage (again, excepting the upper-income group) is in the neighborhood of two-thirds. As has been mentioned, the behavior of the upper-income group for these two samples has been very different, with 72 percent of the entire sample and 78 percent of those students with very high SAT scores matriculating at private schools. The finding that the richest high school students are much more likely to matriculate at private schools, particularly "elite" private schools, than other top high school students suggests a strong link between "choice" and income.

"Choice" and Elite Private Schools

To look more closely at how income may affect "choice," we now focus on the application and enrollment patterns at "elite" institutions.

24. Although the sample was drawn on the basis of PSAT scores, ETS provided SAT data too.

Table 5-3. *Destinations of Students from 1987 Sample of High-PSAT Students*

Percent, unless otherwise specified

Item	Lower income (less than $20,000)	Lower-middle income ($20,000–40,000)	Middle income ($40,000–60,000)	Upper-middle income ($60,000–90,000)	Upper income (more than $90,000)	Total
All high-PSAT students						
Number of students	278	742	865	708	632	3,225
Destination of students						
COFHE	17.3	18.1	15.8	22.3	39.9	22.6
Other private (secular)	20.5	21.8	17.7	13.7	19.1	18.3
Other private (religious)	13.3	14.4	16.2	14.0	13.0	14.4
"Public ivys"[a]	7.6	7.5	9.7	16.8	11.9	11.0
Public "best of the rest"[a]	5.0	6.2	5.1	6.9	3.8	5.5
Other public	36.0	30.7	33.2	24.7	12.2	26.9
Military	0.4	1.2	2.3	1.6	0.2	1.3
All private	51.1	54.3	49.7	50.0	72.0	55.3
All public	49.0	45.6	50.3	50.0	28.1	44.7
Students with SATs above 1300						
Number of students	56	202	243	264	272	1,037
Destination of students						
COFHE	30.4	36.1	32.1	39.0	55.5	40.7
Other private (secular)	26.8	19.8	19.8	13.6	13.6	17.0
Other private (religious)	12.5	9.4	8.6	12.1	8.8	9.9
"Public ivys"[a]	7.1	11.4	13.6	14.4	10.3	12.2
Public "best of the rest"[a]	5.4	4.0	4.9	6.8	4.0	5.0
Other public	16.1	16.8	18.9	12.9	7.4	13.8
Military	1.8	2.5	2.1	1.1	0.4	1.4
All private	69.7	65.3	60.5	64.7	77.9	67.6
All public	30.4	34.7	39.5	35.2	22.1	32.4

Source: Author's calculations based on 1987 survey of high-ability high school students conducted by the Educational Testing Service. See Spies (1990).

a. These classifications are from Moll (1985). The "public ivys" consist of the University of California system, Miami University of Ohio, William and Mary, and the Universities of Michigan, North Carolina, Texas, Vermont, and Virginia. The "best of the rest" consist of Georgia Tech, New College of the University of South Florida, Penn State, SUNY Binghamton, and the Universities of Colorado, Illinois, Pittsburgh, Washington, and Wisconsin.

Table 5-4 shows that 27 percent of the entire sample of 3,400 students was in the middle-income group, with a total of 32 percent below middle income and 40 percent above. When one considers the distinct income distribution of those top students who elected to apply to at least one COFHE school, the percentage of applicants in the middle-income group drops to 23 percent, the percentage below middle income drops to 26 percent, and the percentage above middle income rises to 52 percent. Most striking is the large share of upper-income students (relative to their share of the entire sample) who apply to a COFHE institution. It seems clear that even the most qualified high school

Table 5-4. *Income Distribution and Rates of Application, Admission, and Matriculation, by Income Group, from 1987 Sample of High-PSAT Students*

Item	Lower income (less than $20,000)	Lower-middle income ($20,000–40,000)	Middle income ($40,000–60,000)	Upper-middle income ($60,000–90,000)	Upper income (more than $90,000)	Total
All high-PSAT students						
Total sample						
Number	306	786	924	729	655	3,400
Percentage	9	23	27	21	19	100
COFHE applicants						
Number	100	288	357	334	462	1,541
Percentage	7	19	23	22	30	100
Application rate	33	37	39	46	71	45
COFHE admits						
Number	63	188	225	236	317	1,029
Percentage	6	18	22	23	31	100
Admission rate	63	65	63	71	69	67
COFHE matriculants						
Number	48	134	141	156	252	731
Percentage	7	18	19	21	35	100
Matriculation rate	76	71	63	66	80	71
Matriculation rate of total sample	16	17	15	21	39	22
Students with SATs above 1300						
Total sample						
Number	58	210	252	270	281	1,071
Percentage	5	20	24	25	26	100
COFHE applicants						
Number	29	135	164	184	239	751
Percentage	4	18	22	25	32	100
Application rate	50	64	65	68	85	70
COFHE admits						
Number	22	97	115	140	185	559
Percentage	4	17	21	25	33	100
Admission rate	76	72	70	76	77	74
COFHE matriculants						
Number	17	73	79	103	149	421
Percentage	4	17	19	25	35	100
Matriculation rate	77	75	69	74	81	75
Matriculation rate of high-SAT sample	29	35	31	38	53	39

Source: See table 5-3.

students take income into serious account when deciding where to apply to college. Furthermore, the income distribution becomes even more skewed when the sample is restricted to those students who were admitted to at least one COFHE school. For this group, the middle-income share falls slightly more to 22 percent, the total share below middle income falls to 24 percent, and the share above middle income rises to 54 percent. Finally, the middle-income share of COFHE enrollment is only 19 percent, with the share of students below middle income being 25 percent and the share above middle income being 56 percent.

In sum, of those high-performing high school students from middle-income families, a disproportionate number (relative to other income groups) choose not to apply to a COFHE institution, a disproportionate number of the applicants are not admitted, and a disproportionate number of those admitted choose not to matriculate. The share of below-middle-income students falls at the application and admission stages, and then recovers slightly at the matriculation stage. The share of above-middle-income students rises substantially at the application stage and increases even further at the admission and matriculation stages.[25] When the sample is restricted to the most qualified students, those students with above-1300 SAT scores, the pattern is reproduced: the share of middle-income students falls at the application, admission, and matriculation stages.

Table 5-4 also describes the data in a way that may be even more illuminating—in rates of application, admission, and matriculation. Not surprisingly, the table shows that the application rates to COFHE schools increase with income. Thirty-three percent of the lower-income students apply, while 71 percent of the upper-income students and 39 percent of the middle-income students apply. The admission rate also varies with income: 71 percent of upper-middle-income students are admitted; 69 percent of upper-income students; and 65 percent of lower-middle-income students. The admission rates for middle-income and lower-income students are an even lower 63 percent. (The differences among admission rates are even more pronounced when only students with very high test scores are considered. Among students who scored above 1300 on the SAT, admission rates are decidely "U" shaped, with middle-income students at the bottom of the curve.) Finally, of those who are admitted, only 63 percent of those in the middle-income group

25. Note that these changes result from the experiences of upper-income students, not upper-middle-income students.

choose to matriculate, compared with 80 percent of the upper-income students and 76 percent of the lower-income students. In total, only 15 percent of all the middle-income students in the sample matriculate at a COFHE school: the lowest rate among the five income categories. Indeed, of this sample of top high school students, COFHE institutions get more than twice as large a share of the richest students than of those students from middle-income families and below.[26]

As described above, COFHE institutions lose middle-income students at each stage in the admissions process: they are substantially less likely than upper-income students to apply to a COFHE institution (although they are more likely than less affluent students); they are somewhat less likely to be admitted; they are much less likely to matriculate. The pattern of admission rates across income groups is interesting (it may very well reflect a lower representation of legacies—alumni children—and minority students in the middle-income group). Most striking, however, are the differences in the "yields." The yield curve—showing the fraction of admitted students who choose to attend—is "U" shaped, with middle-income students at the bottom, a pattern also true for students with very high SAT scores. Thus, in the end, we can conclude that application rates are a direct function of income, while both admission and matriculation rates are depressed for the middle of the income distribution.

Alternatives to Elite Private Institutions for High-Achieving Students

It is clear that the "elite" institutions are losing a disproportionate number of top students from the middle-income ranks. But where these students go instead—to private or public alternatives—is the question

26. An interesting question is whether income backgrounds affected application, admission, and matriculation in 1987 in the same way they did during an earlier period. To address this issue, we use data from a 1976 survey of top high school students (see Spies 1978), which are similar to the 1987 data in table 5-4. While only 1,381 observations from the 1976 sample are available, leading to rather small cell sizes (for this reason we do not separate out students with SATs above 1300), we find the income-application relationship in 1976 to be quite similar to 1987, with application rates being a positive function of income (with a significant nonlinearity at the high end of the distribution). Admission rates are "U" shaped and yield rates are highest for upper-income students. Finally, matriculation rates again are more than twice as high for upper-income students as the rates for students from families that are middle income and below.

Table 5-5. *Destinations of COFHE Nonmatriculants from a 1987 Sample of High-PSAT Students*

Item	Lower income (less than $20,000)	Lower-middle income ($20,000–40,000)	Middle income ($40,000–60,000)	Upper-middle income ($60,000–90,000)	Upper income (more than $90,000)	Total
All high-PSAT COFHE nonmatriculants						
Number of students	14	50	77	73	57	271
Destination of students (percent)						
Private (secular)	43	54	40	25	39	38
Private (religious)	21	16	17	14	14	16
"Public ivys"[a]	0	10	12	30	23	18
Public "best of the rest"[a]	7	6	5	8	9	7
Other public	29	12	18	18	12	16
Military	0	2	8	6	4	5
COFHE nonmatriculants with SATs above 1300						
Number of students	5	22	34	34	31	126
Destination of students (percent)						
Private (secular)	40	55	44	24	26	36
Private (religious)	20	9	9	21	13	14
"Public ivys"[a]	0	18	15	32	29	23
Public "best of the rest"[a]	20	5	6	12	13	10
Other public	20	9	21	9	13	14
Military	0	5	6	3	7	5

Source: See table 5-3.

a. These classifications are from Moll (1985). The "public ivys" consist of the University of California system, Miami University of Ohio, William and Mary, and the Universities of Michigan, North Carolina, Texas, Vermont, and Virginia. The "best of the rest" consist of Georgia Tech, New College of the University of South Florida, Penn State, SUNY Binghampton, and the Universities of Colorado, Illinois, Pittsburgh, Washington, and Wisconsin.

addressed in this next section. Table 5-5 looks at the matriculation decisions of students from the 1987 sample of top high school students who were admitted, but did not matriculate at a COFHE school. There were 298 such students, and we have matriculation information for 271 of them. A little over half went to a non-COFHE private institution, with the next largest segment of students going to the "public ivys."

If income was an important factor in explaining why students turn down a COFHE school to enroll elsewhere, we would also expect income to play an important role in which non-COFHE school students ultimately choose. For instance, students from middle-income-and-below backgrounds would be more likely to select top-rated public institutions than would their wealthier academic peers.

While the sample size is small, the evidence does not appear to show that income plays a large role in determining whether students turn down a COFHE school in favor of another private institution: we do not find that, among COFHE nonmatriculants, students from more affluent families are more likely than their less affluent peers to choose non-COFHE private institutions. In addition, students from less affluent backgrounds are not more likely to attend the most prestigious public institutions (the "public ivys" and "best of the rest") than other students. In fact, the income group that disproportionately selects public institutions, especially top public institutions, is the upper-middle-income group—among whom 62 percent of the students turning down a COFHE school selected a public institution (with almost two-thirds of these students enrolling in either the "public ivys" or the "best of the rest"). This is the only striking example of income appearing to matter in matriculation decisions, suggesting that, except for those students from upper-middle-income backgrounds, the relatively high price at the "elite" institutions has little effect on whether students who are accepted by a COFHE institution eventually enroll. It is possible, however, that some students are reacting to differences in net price that result from the discounting practices of non-COFHE schools, including both merit aid and need-based aid packaging.[27]

These and other financial considerations may also be involved in the matriculation decisions of those students who never even apply to a COFHE school. Table 5-6 examines matriculation decisions for 1,759 of the 1,859 students in the 1987 sample who did not apply to a COFHE institution. Only 37 percent matriculated at a non-COFHE private institution, while 43 percent chose a public institution other than a "public ivy," a "best of the rest," or a military academy. While less affluent and middle-income students do not decide disproportionately to matriculate at the most prestigious public institutions, they do select other public institutions at a disproportionately high rate. Thus, while the expense of COFHE institutions does not appear to be the prime reason that middle-income students who have been admitted to a COFHE institution do not choose to matriculate, it does appear that middle-income students are less likely to apply to a COFHE institution in the first place, and that instead they restrict their choices to less expensive institutions. When we concentrate on those students with above-1300 SAT scores, the attraction of "other public" institutions is less, but they are still a prominent destination for lower-middle-income and middle-income students. Upper-middle-income students in this

27. Very few of the COFHE schools offer merit aid (that is, financial aid that is not based on need).

Table 5-6. *Destinations of COFHE Nonapplicants from a 1987 Sample of High-PSAT Students*

Item	Lower income (less than $20,000)	Lower-middle income ($20,000– 40,000)	Middle income ($40,000– 60,000)	Upper-middle income ($60,000– 90,000)	Upper income (more than $90,000)	Total
All high-PSAT COFHE nonapplicants						
Number of students	192	472	529	381	185	1,759
Destination of students (percent)						
Private (secular)	17	20	16	13	24	18
Private (religious)	17	18	20	19	22	19
"Public ivys"[a]	8	7	9	19	15	11
Public "best of the rest"[a]	6	8	6	10	8	8
Other public	52	45	46	37	30	43
Military	1	2	3	2	1	2
COFHE nonapplicants with SATs above 1300						
Number of students	27	72	83	86	41	309
Destination of students (percent)						
Private (secular)	33	18	22	16	29	21
Private (religious)	26	17	12	23	24	19
"Public ivys"[a]	7	14	17	19	7	15
Public "best of the rest"[a]	7	6	7	14	12	9
Other public	22	40	37	27	27	32
Military	4	6	5	1	0	3

Source: See table 5-3.

a. These classifications are from Moll (1985). The "public ivys" consist of the University of California system, Miami University of Ohio, William and Mary, and the Universities of Michigan, North Carolina, Texas, Vermont, and Virginia. The "best of the rest" consist of Georgia Tech, New College of the University of South Florida, Penn State, SUNY Binghamton, and the Universities of Colorado, Illinois, Pittsburgh, Washington, and Wisconsin.

high-ability pool, as well as in the broader sample, disproportionately select prestigious public institutions as an alternative to "elite" private education. Thus, we see that college destinations among students who do not apply to a COFHE school are affected by income backgrounds— upper-middle-income students are drawn to the top public institutions while middle-income-and-below students select other public institutions in large numbers.[28]

28. Unlike the admitted applicants, whose qualified status has been certified, these nonapplicants may well include students who could not have gained admission. The disproportionate attraction of these middle-income nonapplicants to public institutions may reflect ignorance regarding costs, especially net costs after aid (an issue we explore below), relatively higher net costs than the middle-income COFHE admits due to differences in aid packages received, or some other phenomenon (perceptions of psychological or social costs involved in private college attendance).

Income and Net Price for High-Achieving Students

Information from the sample of top high school students allows us to examine the financial burden of attending a COFHE school for different income groups. One of the survey's questions asks parents how they will finance the cost of their child's freshman year in college. For students matriculating at a COFHE school, we compute the average estimate of the total cost of a freshman year (the sum of tuition and fees, room and board, travel, books, and personal expenses) for parents in each of the thirteen income categories listed in table 5-7. These resulting gross cost estimates, reported in the table, vary somewhat by income group but this variation is independent of income level for incomes below $100,000.

The column headed "Family price" in the table reports estimates of the net price to the family—gross cost less the amount of any scholarships, grants, and student loans. We then compute family price as a percentage of gross cost. The resulting ratios show that for families in the income groups below $20,000 the net price represents slightly more than a quarter of their gross cost, for students in the $30,000 to $50,000 range the net price is about half of gross cost, and for students with family incomes above $125,000 it rises to over 90 percent.[29] We then divide the net price that families report into the child's estimated contribution and the parents' net price. Because family price generally increases with income, reflecting the effects of need-based financial aid, and because a child's contribution is largely independent of income level, the parents' price also tends to increase with income.

Also in table 5-7, an examination of income burden, the family price as a percent of income, shows that the burden mostly falls as income rises: families with incomes below $10,000 pay roughly all their income, families with incomes between $10,000 and $40,000 pay a little less than 30 percent of income; families with incomes between $40,000 and $80,000 pay about 20 percent of income; the income burden falls still further for families with incomes above $80,000, with the income burden for the richest families falling to 12 percent.[30]

29. It is interesting to note that there are 40 students out of a total of 139 students from families with incomes above $125,000 who report a nonzero value of scholarships and grants. The average scholarship was a little over $3,000. Many of these students are undoubtedly bringing in scholarships from outside the institutions when they enter.

30. For each closed income category in the survey instrument, the midpoint is used in the denominator of the burden ratio. For the top category, above $150,000 a year, we use $150,000

It is obvious that we do not find evidence of the inverted "U" shape that some observers might expect, that is, the income burden does not rise from lower-income to middle-income and then decline. However, there is virtually no decline in the income burden for families in the $40,000 to $80,000 range, and there are even a few slight increases between several income brackets within this range. Nevertheless, it does not appear from these data that middle-income parents of students attending "elite" institutions are forced to pay an extraordinary percentage of family income. Why, then, does it also appear, as shown earlier, that students from families in the upper-middle-income range ($60,000 to $90,000) who do not apply to a COFHE institution are disproportionately likely to enroll at public institutions, especially the most prestigious public universities? Perhaps they *think* that they will pay dearly to attend one of the "elite" private institutions, even though this does not seem to be the case. Although the amount of scholarship aid available to families in the middle-to upper-middle-income range presumably lowers the financial burden for families in this group, it is entirely plausible that these families underestimate the amount of financial aid available to them.

A question in the 1987 survey addresses parents' potential misperceptions. Parents with a child who matriculated at a school costing less than $10,000 a year are asked the following question: if your child attended a college that costs $15,000 a year, how much do you believe that you as parents would be expected to pay toward that total?[31] We restrict our attention to those families in which the child either never applied to a COFHE school or applied but was not admitted. Thus, we eliminate families in which parents could plausibly base an answer on

---

as family income, thereby overestimating the income burden for the richest families. The number of survey respondents who provided an estimate of gross cost typically exceeds the number who provided an estimate of scholarships and grants, with the difference increasing with the income level. (For income group number one, below $10,000 a year, 93 percent of gross cost respondents provide scholarship information. For the other income groups, the percentages are 100, 90, 87, 82, 86, 86, 61, 62, 57, 37, 34, and 31, respectively.) We assume that a nonresponse for the scholarship and grant question for a parent replying to the gross cost question implies a zero value for scholarships and grants. We make the same assumption about a missing value for a child's contribution and the amount of student loans (again, the probability of a missing value increases with income level). Caution should be applied in interpreting the high income burden for the poorest families, since this figure is affected by the attribution of a zero scholarship figure for the one response out of fourteen with a missing value, the number of respondents in this income group is small, and there is a considerable gap between this number and those that follow.

31. This question was asked *only* of parents whose children matriculated at such a school.

Table 5-7. Actual and Perceived Income Burden

Income (thousands of dollars)	COFHE matriculants								COFHE nonapplicants and nonadmits			
	Number	Gross cost (dollars)	Family price[a] (dollars)	Family price/ gross cost (percent)	Child's contri- bution (dollars)	Parents' price[b] (dollars)	Family price/ income (percent)	Parents' price/ gross cost (percent)	Number	"Guess" (dollars)	"Guess"/ $15,000 gross cost (percent)	"Guess" ratio – parents' price ratio (percent)
Under 10	14	17,554	4,939	28.1	1,542	3,397	98.8	19.4	32	1,684	11.2	–8.2
10–20	33	17,149	4,478	26.1	1,499	2,979	29.9	17.4	88	3,579	23.9	6.5
20–30	61	17,847	7,428	41.6	1,452	5,976	29.7	33.5	145	6,143	41.0	7.5
30–40	71	17,999	9,511	52.8	1,986	7,525	27.2	41.8	170	6,591	43.9	2.1
40–50	57	17,980	9,507	52.9	1,882	7,625	21.1	42.4	216	8,329	55.5	13.1
50–60	79	18,008	11,928	66.2	2,091	9,837	21.7	54.6	177	9,977	66.5	11.9
60–70	64	17,268	12,156	70.4	1,993	10,163	18.7	58.9	143	11,522	76.8	17.9
70–80	57	17,725	15,202	85.8	2,071	13,131	20.3	74.1	76	12,008	80.1	6.0
80–90	34	18,188	15,117	83.1	1,859	13,258	17.8	72.9	39	11,936	79.6	6.7
90–100	44	17,367	14,402	82.9	2,238	12,164	15.2	70.0	35	12,771	85.1	15.1
100–125	63	18,299	16,315	89.2	1,542	14,773	14.5	80.7	45	13,544	90.3	9.6
125–150	41	19,013	17,786	93.5	2,083	15,703	12.9	82.6	12	13,458	89.7	7.1
Over 150	98	18,680	17,940	96.0	1,465	16,475	12.0	88.2	25	13,220	88.1	–0.1

Source: See table 5-3.
a. Family price equals gross cost less scholarships, grants, and student loans.
b. Parent's price equals family price less child's contribution.

an actual financial aid offer from a COFHE school. Table 5-7 presents the dollar value of the "guess" and also reports this value as a percentage of the $15,000 gross cost. We then compare the guess percentage with the actual percentage costs reported by the parents of COFHE matriculants.[32] The last column in the table shows the difference between the "guessed at" percentage of the gross cost of the nonapplicant-nonadmit group and the percentage reported by the parents of the COFHE matriculants. While the parents of nonapplicants and nonadmits in the very lowest and very highest income categories underestimate the parents' net price, parents in all other income groups overestimate the cost of attending a COFHE school. The degree of overestimation is fairly small for parents in the $10,000 to $40,000 range, but is considerable for parents in the $40,000 to $70,000 range. The largest overestimate of the parents' price as a percent of gross cost is found in the $60,000 to $70,000 range, where the parents of the COFHE nonapplicants and nonadmits "guess" they would pay 76.8 percent of the gross cost and the parents of COFHE matriculants in that income range actually report paying only 58.9 percent of the gross cost.[33] This overestimate of 17.9 percentage points translates into almost $3,100, given the average gross cost for that income group.[34]

Thus, while the "actual" income burden does not appear to be

32. Note that parents are asked to guess their contributions when the gross price is $15,000 a year while COFHE sticker prices were over $17,000. If parents in the $20,000–29,999 group, for example, expected to contribute around $6,100 in addition to, say, $2,000 from their children, the expected amount of financial aid would be $6,900. If we assume that the difference between $15,000 and, say, $17,000, were made up by financial aid, the parents' guess as a percentage of $17,000 would equal 0.36 ($6,100/$17,000). If we assume that none of the difference in prices were met by financial aid, the parents' guess as a percentage of $17,000 would be 0.48 ($8,100/$17,000). Instead, we assume that when parents expect to pay 41 percent of $15,000, they also expect to pay 41 percent of the actual gross cost—in other words, we assume that parents expect to pay the same percentage of any cost over $15,000 that they expect to pay of $15,000.

33. It is possible that the distribution of incomes within these bands differs across the COFHE matriculant and nonapplicant-nonadmit groups, but the band is sufficiently narrow to make any effect on net price be minimal. It should be noted that families in the two groups do not differ systematically in either number of children or value of assets.

34. The degree of overestimation is also fairly large at some of the higher-income categories, particularly at the $90,000 to $99,999 range, but these sample sizes are much smaller than the 143 families in the $60,000 to $69,999 range, implying the need for caution in interpreting the numbers for the richer families.

Notice that even if we adopt the extreme assumption that parents in the nonapplicant-nonadmit group assume that any increase in gross cost above $15,000 would be covered in full by financial aid, those in the $60,000 to $69,999 group would still overestimate the parents' price by over $1,300 ($11,522 less $10,163).

unusually high for families in the middle-income to upper-middle-income range, it does seem that parents around this range substantially underestimate the availability of financial aid at these "elite" private institutions. Quite possibly, informing these parents about the amount of financial aid for which they would be eligible at COFHE institutions could affect the application decisions of their children. Our earlier finding that so many top high school students from upper-middle-income families (especially those with SAT scores above 1300) matriculate at the top public institutions without ever even applying to the "elite" private institutions, may be explained, at least in part, by an overestimation of the net price faced by their parents.

Conclusion

The finding that students at "elite" private institutions are much more likely to be drawn from the upper reaches of the American income distribution than are students at other institutions suggests, at least at first reading, a reason for worry about the availability of a wide range of college choice for less advantaged students. However, a look at a sample of high school students with high test scores suggests that more is involved than ability to pay for college. Excepting only students from families with annual incomes over $90,000, it appears that income makes little difference to the enrollment destinations of high-achieving students—either in terms of attendance at any private institution or at the prestigious COFHE group of colleges and universities. Apparently, the uneven distribution of achievement among high school graduates by income (which is presumably the result of unequal opportunity in earlier education in and out of school) is a more important determinant than financial barriers at the time of high school graduation.

Even though upper-income students are plainly overrepresented at "elite" private institutions compared with other high-achieving students, it is clear that student aid plays a large role in extending choice to high-achieving students from less advantaged backgrounds. As seen in table 5-7, even COFHE-matriculated students with annual family incomes between $50,000 and $60,000 can expect to receive on average a little over $6,000 a year in grants and student loans, while those with incomes between $10,000 and $20,000 can expect about $12,700 in grants and student loans. A significant amount of this aid is financed by the federal government, but the bulk of the grant aid at these costly institutions is drawn from institutional resources, most of it in the form of forgone tuition revenue.[35] Middle-income families—those with annual incomes between $40,000 and $70,000—appear to seriously overestimate the price they should expect to pay at a COFHE institution, by as much as 18 percent, or over $3,000, in the case of families with incomes in the $60,000 to $70,000 range. Evidently, "elite" private higher education is somewhat more affordable for these families than they think. Indeed, the income burden on these families—19 percent of annual family income to pay for one year of an "elite" private education—seems quite reasonable when compared with an average income burden of 30 percent for families in the $10,000 to $30,000 income range and an average of 15 percent for families with incomes of about $100,000.

Although these findings provide some reassurance about the quality of the alternatives available to the very best high school students, other findings are less encouraging. First, we do find evidence that private institutions in general and "elite" private colleges and universities in particular are experiencing a "middle-class melt." A similar melt is occurring at public universities as well, where the share of upper-income students is rising. Although the commonality of this phenomenon to private institutions and public universities suggests that more is involved than sheer financial pressure, these developments are surely cause for concern about the range of college choices available to lower-middle- and middle-income students.

Second, the fact that the relative success of private institutions in attracting middle- and lower-income students seems to depend heavily on institutionally financed student aid may also be a cause for concern. Presumably, if the rapidly increasing gap in sticker prices between the "elite" private schools and their public counterparts had not been met with expanded financial aid for middle-income students at the private institutions, a "melt" from the COFHE schools to the public universities would have occurred, in a manner similar to that which took place with the public colleges.

While the "elite" and usually well-endowed private institutions have

35. Data from table 4-2 in chapter 4 show that at private institutions with endowments over $4,500 per student in 1979—a considerably broader group than COFHE—about 87 percent of all grant aid was provided from institutional funds. At the COFHE institutions, the percentage would be still higher.

thus far provided enough financial aid to mute potential enrollment effects resulting from the growing divergence between their prices and the prices at public alternatives, other private institutions may not be able to do the same. For them, a "middle-income melt" is a real possibility, as is a "lower-income melt." Data from table 4-1 show that, from the 1978–79 to the 1985–86 academic year, institutionally funded aid in private higher education grew by more than 50 percent in real terms, nearly double the growth rate of tuition revenue. Heavy discounting of tuition makes economic sense if the alternative is enrollment decline and unused capacity, but the ability of some of these institutions to continue to finance such heavy discounting is doubtful. Given recent trends in private and public prices, there is reason to think that certain students will be forced out of the private sector. Lower- and middle-income students who achieve academic excellence may continue to benefit from the huge endowments at the "elite" institutions, but other deserving students may have little chance of attending a private college or university. Recent reports that private institutions are contemplating giving up need-blind admissions suggest that students of "average" ability and with middle- or below-middle incomes may have fewer choices in the future. The ratio of private to public costs is a key to likely future trends in the general availability of private higher education, and we project this ratio for different sectors in the chapter that follows.

From the standpoint of public policy, there are obviously questions about how important it is that students of all backgrounds have access to private institutions, including that small set of "elite" private institutions on which much of this chapter has focused. In most states, state governments already provide low-priced alternatives to most students. Part of the issue then is how good are the public sector alternatives, and how wide is the range of public alternatives for students from varying backgrounds. Both the prices facing students at public institutions and the quality and range of public sector alternatives vary substantially from state to state. On a national basis, the fact is that as the share of below-middle-income families headed by parents aged 45 to 64 grew from 39 percent to 47 percent between 1978 and 1989, the share of students from below-middle-income families at public universities held constant while it actually fell at public four-year colleges. At the same time, the representation of upper-income students grew at public universities and four-year colleges. These trends imply that a larger share of state operating subsidies are going to support the education of more affluent students.

These facts underline the point that, to the extent that there is a middle-income melt at private institutions, it can be linked to the large subsidies for middle- and upper-income students at public institutions. If there is an argument for bolstering the competitive position of private institutions with regard to middle- and upper-income students, the solution might be to increase the prices facing such students at public institutions, so that more of the state subsidy dollars can be directed toward less affluent students, for whom the range of available opportunities is less.

VI

The Future Affordability
of College

MUCH OF THE public concern about the financing of colleges stems from a worry that recent trends in pricing will reduce access to college for some groups or at least severely constrain their choice of college. The purpose of this chapter is to investigate the factors that will help determine future trends in college affordability, examining both the underlying forces driving college costs and the role of government financing, including student aid, in helping families to meet those costs. These issues are addressed through the development of a simple simulation model of higher-education prices and costs. Projections of affordability—the interplay of prices, costs, and family incomes—are developed separately for four-year institutions, classified by public and private control, and two-year public institutions.

Our affordability projections fall into two groups. The first group focuses on the variability of certain external factors that have major effects on college prices and families' ability to pay. Our aims in this first exercise are twofold: to present a series of forecasts for key cost ratios representing a range of plausible variation in the higher education environment, and to determine the significance of particular cost determinants by contrasting the results of different assumptions about their rates of increase. By identifying key variables and by considering factors likely to influence them, we can determine which of these forecasts are more likely to be realized. Essentially, then, this first part of the chapter focuses on trends in affordability for the "average" family, without distinguishing between less and more affluent, or aided and nonaided, students.

For the second group of projections, we focus on differences in affordability for aided and nonaided students. To do so, we extend the treatment of our earlier simulations and add an exercise in which we simulate the effects of a structural change in the role of state and federal governments in financing undergraduate education. As seen in earlier chapters, both state and federal governments play a large role in financing higher education, but their funds are distributed differently across institutions and across income groups. In our simulations, we show the impact of a "revenue neutral" shift of funding (that is, the absolute level of funding does not change, only the source of the appropriations) from states to the federal government, and examine the effects of such a shift on the affordability of various types of colleges for both aided and nonaided students.

The Simulation Model

Our basic simulation model works from initial conditions that have been based on recent data and from which future growth rates are developed. Aware that any simulation model has embedded in it certain relationships among the variables, we have tried to create a model that is simple yet captures the main forces at work. In formulating a model of cost determination, we follow a simple accounting identity: per student, institutions' educational costs equal the sum of tuition revenue (inclusive of student aid) and nontuition educational revenue.[1] Using this formula, we project educational costs and nontuition educational revenue separately, and calculate gross tuition charges as the residual. Our model assumes that "costs of attendance" (from the student's point of view) are equal to the sum of living costs (which we assume stay constant in real terms) and gross tuition charges. We project separately per-student values for federal student aid grants, other student aid grants, and loans; we use these projected values in the calculation of a net price (with only grants deducted) and a final net price that deducts grants and loans, treating the subsidy value of loans as half the award amount.[2]

Simulations could be based on any of several models of institutional behavior.[3] For instance, our particular decision to make tuition revenue

1. This assumes that current revenue equals current expenditures and that auxiliary enterprises break even.

2. See the discussion in chapter 2 regarding the subsidy value of loans.

3. The investigation of institutional financial behavior in chapter 4 suggests several empirical relationships that could be built into a more comprehensive model for forecasting future trends

a residual, depending on the growth of other revenue and of costs, could be replaced by assuming a specified growth rate for tuition directly. With this alternative assumption, either the growth in costs or the growth in nontuition revenue would become a residual category. The approach we use does, however, provide a rough sense of the changes in affordability that would result if a specified tuition growth rate were assumed directly, since the assumptions of our model will, in each alternative scenario, imply a particular growth rate of tuition.[4] We should note that the set of assumptions we adopt is consistent with the view that college and university tuition-setting is constrained in the long run by trends in underlying costs and in nontuition revenue.

In developing our projections, we establish different initial conditions and growth rates for each of three postsecondary educational sectors: public two-year colleges, public four-year colleges and universities, and private four-year colleges and universities.[5] In calculating living costs, we treat students attending public two-year colleges as commuters, while those attending four-year institutions are considered residents. Thus, for all students, board and transportation costs are included in living costs but room charges are applied to four-year students only.

For comparative purposes we project family incomes for students at each of the three categories of institutions, with initial conditions in each sector set equal to the inflation-adjusted median family income of freshman students attending that type of institution. In our projections we track the ratio of net price to family income and the ratio of gross tuition to educational costs. This allows us to forecast two key variables—the financing "burden" borne by families and the degree to which institutions depend on tuition in meeting costs.

We use a variety of data sources in setting the initial conditions for each variable. We rely on data found in the College Board's *Annual Survey of Colleges* and *College Cost Book*, in G. Lewis's *Trends in Student Aid*, and in the Department of Education's HEGIS files, and

in college finance. Although we consider the development of such a model a worthy goal, it would unduly complicate the present modeling exercise to introduce such relationships into the simple analysis we present here. We also believe that, given the presently limited understanding of some of these behavioral relationships, one should be cautious about building them into forecasting models.

4. Later in the text, we point out ways to reinterpret some of our projection scenarios in terms of assumed tuition growth rates.

5. We do not attempt to forecast for the proprietary sector because of a lack of data.

data from the American Freshman Survey.[6] Where necessary, we adjust the values to correspond to the 1989–90 academic year.

We establish a baseline for real rates of growth in each of our variables using data from the 1978–86 period.[7] All variables are expressed on a per-student full-time-equivalent enrollment basis. These growth rates are used to provide a baseline scenario over our projection period, 1991 (referring to the academic year 1990–91) to 2010.[8] The baseline scenario is computed simply by applying 1978-86 average annual growth rates to each of the variables, and stepping the calculation forward one year at a time. It is important to note that our baseline scenario assumes a continuation of the recent past, rather than representing our "best guess" of the future. If we were to develop a "best guess" formulation, it would most plausibly be based on a considerably longer time period.

Projections of Overall Affordability

This section reports on projections of future affordability for "average" students at each institution type, with no distinction between aided and nonaided students. After describing the results of the baseline projection summarized in table 6-1, we develop alternative scenarios that examine the consequences of divergences from the baseline growth rates. In each set of scenarios, we hold the values of other variables not the focus of the exercise to their baseline trends. The specific growth rate assumptions for each of the nine alternative scenarios are presented in table 6-2. We examine the results of three broad categories of variation. The first category, group A, isolates the effect of varying the growth in federal aid support. Scenario A1 assumes no real growth in federal aid support; scenario A2 assumes growth at an annual real rate

6. College Board (1989a, 1988); Lewis (1988).

7. The choice of a baseline period for establishing historical values is somewhat arbitrary. The endpoint of the period is dictated by availability of the financial data; we chose the starting point to provide a period of adequate length—one that would capture the years during which rapid growth in college costs became an important phenomenon.

8. The tables summarizing the simulation results present information for 1990 (referring to the academic year 1989–90), which is the year before the simulation begins, as well as for 1995, 2000, 2005, and 2010. Obviously, the point forecasts for 2010 should not be taken seriously as predictions. The purpose of extending the projection period is to make trend differences more apparent.

Table 6-1. *Baseline Projections, 1990–2010*
1989–90 dollars, unless otherwise specified

Item	Education costs	Living costs	Nontuition education revenue	Costs of attendance	Pell grants	Other grants	Loans	Family income	Price net of grants	Net price	Nominal income	Nominal net price	Net price/ income (percent)	Tuition dependence (percent)
Annual growth rates														
Public (2)	1.018	...	1.015	...	1.035	1.017	1.030	1.000	...	...	...	...	...	...
Public (4)	1.020	...	1.015	...	1.035	1.016	1.030	1.000	...	...	...	...	...	...
Private	1.032	...	1.031	...	1.000	1.054	1.050	1.000	...	...	...	...	...	...
Initial values														
Public (2)	4,200	2,300	3,400	3,100	150	80	140	36,600	...	...	...	...	...	...
Public (4)	8,500	3,500	6,800	5,200	290	320	0	45,400	...	...	...	...	...	...
Private	14,600	3,800	5,800	12,600	320	1,580	1,160	56,100	...	...	...	...	...	...
Public two-year institutions														
1990	...	...	...	3,100	150	80	140	36,600	2,870	2,800	36,600	2,800	7.7	19.0
1995	...	...	...	3,229	178	87	162	36,600	2,964	2,883	46,712	3,679	7.9	20.2
2000	...	...	...	3,374	212	95	188	36,600	3,068	2,974	59,618	4,844	8.1	21.4
2005	...	...	...	3,538	251	103	218	36,600	3,184	3,074	76,089	6,392	8.4	22.6
2010	...	...	...	3,721	298	112	253	36,600	3,311	3,184	97,111	8,449	8.7	23.7
Public four-year institutions														
1990	...	...	...	5,200	290	320	640	45,400	4,590	4,270	45,400	4,270	9.4	20.0
1995	...	...	...	5,559	344	346	742	45,400	4,868	4,497	57,943	5,740	9.9	21.9
2000	...	...	...	5,970	409	375	860	45,400	5,186	4,756	73,952	7,747	10.5	23.8
2005	...	...	...	6,438	486	406	997	45,400	5,546	5,048	94,383	10,494	11.1	25.7
2010	...	...	...	6,972	577	440	1,156	45,400	5,955	5,378	120,460	14,268	11.8	27.5
Private institutions														
1990	...	...	...	12,600	320	1,580	1,160	56,100	10,700	10,120	56,100	10,120	18.0	60.3
1995	...	...	...	14,134	320	2,055	1,480	56,100	11,759	11,018	71,599	14,063	19.6	60.5
2000	...	...	...	15,935	320	2,673	1,890	56,100	12,941	11,997	91,381	19,541	21.4	60.7
2005	...	...	...	18,049	320	3,477	2,412	56,100	14,252	13,046	116,628	27,122	23.3	60.8
2010	...	...	...	20,532	320	4,523	3,078	56,100	15,688	14,149	148,850	37,542	25.2	61.0

Source: Authors' calculations based on simulation model described in text.

Table 6-2. *Annual Growth Rate Assumptions for Alternative Scenarios*
Annual growth rates

Scenario	Type of school	Educa-tion costs	Nontuition education revenue	Pell grants	Other grants	Loans	Family income
Varying federal support							
No growth (A1)	Public (2)	1.018	1.015	1.000	1.017	1.000	1.000
	Public (4)	1.020	1.015	1.000	1.016	1.000	1.000
	Private	1.032	1.031	1.000	1.054	1.000	1.000
Rapid growth (A2)	Public (2)	1.018	1.015	1.040	1.017	1.040	1.000
	Public (4)	1.020	1.015	1.040	1.016	1.040	1.000
	Private	1.032	1.031	1.040	1.054	1.040	1.000
Real decline (A3)	Public (2)	1.018	1.015	0.980	1.017	0.980	1.000
	Public (4)	1.020	1.015	0.980	1.016	0.980	1.000
	Private	1.032	1.031	0.980	1.054	0.980	1.000
Varying performance of the economy							
Strong (B1)	Public (2)	1.018	1.025	1.035	1.017	1.030	1.025
	Public (4)	1.020	1.025	1.035	1.016	1.030	1.025
	Private	1.032	1.041	1.000	1.054	1.050	1.025
Weak (B2)	Public (2)	1.018	1.005	1.035	1.017	1.030	1.000
	Public (4)	1.020	1.005	1.035	1.016	1.030	1.000
	Private	1.032	1.021	1.000	1.054	1.050	1.000
Varying rates of growth in cost and institutional aid							
High cost/high aid (C1)	Public (2)	1.028	1.015	1.035	1.017	1.030	1.000
	Public (4)	1.030	1.015	1.035	1.016	1.030	1.000
	Private	1.042	1.031	1.000	1.054	1.050	1.000
High cost/low aid (C2)	Public (2)	1.028	1.015	1.035	1.000	1.030	1.000
	Public (4)	1.030	1.015	1.035	1.000	1.030	1.000
	Private	1.042	1.031	1.000	1.000	1.050	1.000
Low cost/high aid (C3)	Public (2)	1.008	1.015	1.035	1.017	1.030	1.000
	Public (4)	1.010	1.015	1.035	1.016	1.030	1.000
	Private	1.022	1.031	1.000	1.054	1.050	1.000
Low cost/low aid (C4)	Public (2)	1.008	1.015	1.035	1.000	1.030	1.000
	Public (4)	1.010	1.015	1.035	1.000	1.030	1.000
	Private	1.022	1.031	1.000	1.000	1.050	1.000

Sources: Authors' calculations based on simulation model described in text.

of 4 percent; scenario A3 assumes a 2 percent annual real decline in support. The second category, group B, varies the performance of the national economy. Scenario B1 assumes strong economic growth, with median family income increasing at an annual real rate of 2.5 percent and nontuition revenue growing at a rate of 1 percentage point above the recent trend. Scenario B2 assumes weak economic growth, with median family income constant in real terms (a continuation of the recent trend), and nontuition revenue growing at a rate of 1 percentage point below recent trend. Note that we assume trends in real cost growth at higher education institutions are unaffected by the overall performance of the economy. Finally, group C examines the effects of various educational cost-institutional aid combinations. Scenarios C1 and C2 both assume a high rate of cost increase, equal to 1 percentage point above the recent trend. C1, however, assumes that institutional aid (which is the bulk of the "other grants" category) increases at its recent high rates of real annual growth while C2 assumes no real growth in institutional aid. Scenarios C3 and C4 assume a low rate of cost increase equal to 1 percentage point below the recent trend. The assumed growth rates for institutional aid for C3 and C4 correspond to those in C1 and C2, respectively. Thus, C3 presents a low cost growth–high aid growth scenario while C4 presents a low cost–low aid scenario. The resulting growth rate assumptions for each of the nine alternative scenarios are presented in table 6-2.

Projection Results

Having established the assumptions and the scenarios, we now return to table 6-1, which summarizes the baseline projections and reports figures for 1990, the year before the simulation begins, as well as for 1995, 2000, 2005, and 2010. We use the figures to initiate our discussion of the projection results.

We begin by examining the initial conditions and recent growth rates that underlie the baseline projection. The annual growth rates in our variables over the period 1978–86 show some interesting variation across institutional types. While there were real increases in educational costs in each of the three cases, the annual real increase was much faster at private institutions (3.2 percent) than at public four-year (2.0 percent) or public two-year (1.8 percent) schools.[9] Nontuition educational revenue shows a similar pattern.[10] On the other hand, the real rate of growth

9. Educational costs are defined as educational and general expenditures per student, based on HEGIS data. Auxiliary enterprises are excluded on the assumption that costs and revenue of auxiliary operations are equal.

10. Nontuition educational revenue is defined as per-student revenue from sources other than (gross) tuition. As discussed in chapter 4, for public institutions the main such revenue source is state operating subsidies; for private institutions it is gifts and endowment earnings. Note that student aid revenue is not included here—it is treated as revenue from students and accounted for separately. We have adjusted figures for educational costs and nontuition educational revenue to make them reconcile with both 1989–90 costs of attendance and 1985–86 ratios of nontuition educational revenue to educational costs. These numbers yield relationships that are reasonably consistent with relative costs at these categories of institutions in the 1985–86 academic year.

in Pell support was substantial at public institutions (3.5 percent at four-year and two-year schools) and nonexistent at private colleges and universities. Private institutions, however, had remarkable real growth in institutional aid (other grants), with a growth rate of 5.4 percent compared with 1.6 percent and 1.7 percent at four- and two-year public institutions. Loans also increased rapidly at private schools (5.0 percent), but increased more slowly (3.0 percent) in the public sector. Lastly, over this period there was no real growth in the median income of families headed by parents aged 45–64 (reflecting very slow productivity growth in the overall economy), leading us to adopt zero real growth rates for the family incomes of students attending each type of institution. The initial values for our variables, which serve as starting points for our simulations, are not surprising: they are generally higher at private institutions than at public four-year schools and are generally higher at public four-year schools than at public two-year schools.[11]

Forecasts using the baseline rates would give us a reasonable picture of the future if these rates persist over the next two decades. For public four-year institutions, costs of attendance would increase from $5,200 in 1990 to about $7,000 in 2010 (in 1989–90 constant dollars). The price with only grants deducted is expected to rise from $4,590 to about $6,000 and, most important, the final net price rises from $4,270 to almost $5,400. In nominal terms, then, the net price is expected to rise to around $14,300 (assuming, as we do throughout, an annual inflation rate of 5 percent). The first of our two financing ratios, the net price divided by family income, indicates that the burden borne by parents would increase from 9 percent to 12 percent over the period. At the same time, tuition dependency increases from 20 percent to 28 percent. The increase in the burden on families, of course, reflects the forecast of persistent increases in college costs in the face of constant, real

11. As indicated earlier, educational costs are computed from HEGIS data. In calculating living costs, we assume commuter status for students attending public two-year institutions. For them, living costs are limited to board and transportation costs taken from College Board (1989a). For students attending public and private four-year institutions, we assume resident status. Costs therefore include room plus board and transportation, which are also from College Board (1989a). We assume living costs grow at the rate of inflation. The calculation of nontuition educational revenue is described in note 10. Costs of attendance equal the sum of educational costs and living costs, less nontuition educational revenue. The resulting values were checked for consistency with the figures in College Board (1989a). Pell grants, other grants, and loan values were computed from information in College Board (1988). As noted before, loans are valued at a subsidy rate of 50 percent when computing net price. Finally, family income is based on data from the American Freshman Survey.

family incomes. Growth in tuition dependency reflects a slight lag in the growth of nontuition revenue relative to educational costs.

Forecasts for private institutions show the same general pattern. The real costs of attendance rise from $12,600 to about $20,500, and the real net price increases from $10,120 to about $14,100. The latter figure would be about $37,500 in nominal dollars. The ratio of net price to family income increases from 18 percent to 25 percent while tuition dependency rises from 60 percent to 61 percent. At public two-year institutions, the net price increases from $2,800 to $3,200 (around $8,400 in nominal dollars), the net price to income ratio rises from 8 percent to 9 percent, and tuition dependency increases from 19 percent to 24 percent.

The baseline projections indicate some reason to worry about the future affordability of higher education, although they do not forecast a disaster of catastrophic proportions. The increase in the burden borne by parents may have some unfortunate effects on enrollment rates. In fact, according to the estimates of the enrollment effects of financial aid presented in chapter 3, a real increase in net price of $1,672 (the average change in real net price across our baseline projections), if shared equally by all income classes, is expected to reduce enrollment rates of lower-income students by about 21 percent.[12] In addition to this general problem with affordability, it is important to note that the burden borne by parents of students attending private institutions increases relative to those with children attending four-year public colleges and universities—the private burden ratio rises by 7 percentage points to 25 percent while the public burden ratio rises by only 3 percentage points to 12 percent. The growth in the percentage of income spent on private education relative to public education may well lead to a further decline in the share of students educated at private colleges and universities, along with even larger differences in the median family incomes of these two groups of students than at present.

Alternative Scenarios

Of course, there is no reason to believe that the growth rates used in the baseline model will continue over the next two decades. By varying

12. Since the baseline scenario projects that student aid will rise more rapidly than college costs, the net price increase would be somewhat smaller for lower-income students than others in this scenario. See our projections for aided and nonaided students in the latter part of this chapter for further detail.

these rates we can produce alternative scenarios that lead to a range of affordability estimates and may also point to the importance of particular variables.

Table 6-3 shows that group A simulations produce relatively small differences in the model's projections even when wide differences in federal aid support are assumed. Keeping in mind an ultimate baseline prediction for real net price of about $14,100 for private institutions, this number rises to about $15,400 with a real decline in federal support, to $15,100 with no growth in support, and falls to $14,000 with rapid growth. The net price to income ratio for this sector, presented in table 6-4, is slightly higher with a decline in federal aid or no real growth than with either rapid growth or the baseline scenario. At public four-year institutions the net price to income ratio varies from 11 percent for the rapid growth scenario, 12 percent for the baseline scenario, 14 percent for the real decline scenario, and 13 percent for the no-growth scenario. A similar pattern results for public two-year colleges. Across sectors, the general lack of response of net price to changes in federal support makes sense given the relatively small effect this type of aid has on net price. As indicated by the initial values presented in table 6-1, Pell funds per student in the 1989–90 academic year amounted to only $150 at public two-year colleges, $290 at public four-year institutions, and $320 at private colleges and universities. Given the fact that comparable net price figures were $2,800, $4,270, and $10,120, the surprise is probably not that federal aid matters so little, but that it matters as much as it does. As we show in the next part of this chapter, variation in federal aid is more significant when aided and nonaided students are considered separately.

A look at the group B simulations shows considerable differences in real net price (table 6-3), net price to income ratios (table 6-4), and tuition dependence (table 6-5) when the performance of the economy is varied. In 2010, the baseline values for private institutions of real net price (about $14,000), of the burden ratio (25 percent), and of tuition dependence (61 percent) all rise, if the future economy is weak, to around $16,000, 29 percent, and 68 percent. For public four-year and two-year institutions, these changes are even more dramatic: net price in 2010 for four-year institutions rises from about $5,400 in the baseline scenario to about $7,000 for a weak economy, the burden ratio rises from 12 percent to 16 percent, and tuition dependence rises from 28 percent to 41 percent; for two-year colleges, these values rise from

Table 6-3. *Projections for Real Net Price, by Institutional Category, 1990–2010*
1989–90 dollars

Item	Public four-year institutions					Private institutions					Public two-year institutions				
	1990	1995	2000	2005	2010	1990	1995	2000	2005	2010	1990	1995	2000	2005	2010
Baseline	4,270	4,497	4,756	5,048	5,378	10,120	11,018	11,997	13,046	14,149	2,800	2,883	2,974	3,074	3,184
Varying federal support															
No growth (A1)	4,270	4,603	4,985	5,422	5,922	10,120	11,179	12,361	13,672	15,108	2,800	2,922	3,060	3,215	3,389
Rapid growth (A2)	4,270	4,471	4,692	4,934	5,196	10,120	10,984	11,929	12,951	14,036	2,800	2,874	2,954	3,039	3,127
Real decline (A3)	4,270	4,661	5,096	5,582	6,125	10,120	11,265	12,526	13,907	15,407	2,800	2,943	3,100	3,272	3,462
Varying performance of the economy															
Strong (B1)	4,270	4,129	3,943	3,701	3,394	10,120	10,684	11,199	11,618	11,875	2,800	2,699	2,568	2,401	2,192
Weak (B2)	4,270	4,851	5,500	6,221	7,023	10,120	11,340	12,728	14,293	16,041	2,800	3,060	3,346	3,661	4,007
Varying rates of growth in cost and institutional aid															
High cost/high aid (C1)	4,270	4,967	5,818	6,851	8,099	10,120	11,863	14,022	16,691	19,980	2,800	3,113	3,490	3,941	4,480
High cost/low aid (C2)	4,270	4,993	5,873	6,937	8,218	10,120	12,338	15,115	18,588	22,924	2,800	3,120	3,504	3,964	4,512
Low cost/high aid (C3)	4,270	4,046	3,784	3,476	3,119	10,120	10,206	10,141	9,864	9,299	2,800	2,662	2,502	2,319	2,109
Low cost/low aid (C4)	4,270	4,073	3,839	3,562	3,238	10,120	10,681	11,234	11,761	12,242	2,800	2,669	2,517	2,342	2,141

Source: Authors' calculations based on simulation model described in the text.

$3,200 in the baseline scenario to $4,000 for a weak economy, 9 percent to 11 percent, and 24 percent to 37 percent. Hence, the educational sector is vulnerable to a prolonged recession, particularly the public sector of higher education. Of course, strong economic growth would have a highly favorable effect on the future of these cost variables. Net price, the net price to income ratio, and tuition dependence fall to, respectively, $11,900, 13 percent, and 53 percent at private institutions; $3,400, 5 percent, and 12 percent at public four-year institutions; and $2,200, 4 percent, and 7 percent at public two-year colleges. The affordability implications of economic performance are rather remarkable, with the burden ratio varying from 13 percent to 29 percent at private institutions, 5 percent to 16 percent at public four-year institutions, and 4 percent to 11 percent at community colleges, depending on whether the economy is strong or weak. (Tuition dependence tells a similar story, with projections ranging from 53 percent to 68 percent at private institutions, 12 percent to 41 percent at public four-year institutions, and 7 percent to 37 percent at community colleges.)

The finding that the future of the educational sector is so strongly tied to the course of an unpredictable economy is unsettling. Our projections build in several assumptions about how variations in overall economic performance will impinge on the higher education sector. First, we assume that the growth in family income is closely related to overall economic conditions. Second, we assume that the growth of nontuition educational revenue is similarly responsive. For public institutions, this translates into an assumption that state appropriations for higher education are sensitive to economic conditions, while for private institutions we assume that endowment and gift performance are similarly sensitive to economic conditions. We should also reemphasize that we do *not* assume that college cost growth is sensitive to overall economic conditions. One could argue the reverse: that a strong economy will raise both the demand for and the real resource costs of higher education, resulting in more rapid growth in both educational costs and tuitions. This assumption could easily be incorporated in our projections. Yet it is worth noting that recent history has been different: the rapid tuition growth of the 1980s has occurred in the face of slow or no growth in productivity and incomes.

Group C simulations highlight the effects of different combinations of cost growth and increases in institutional aid. An examination of scenarios C1 and C2 shows that high rates of cost increase lead to major

Table 6-4. *Projections for Ratio of Net Price to Income, by Institutional Category, 1990–2010*
Percent

Item	Public four-year institutions					Private institutions					Public two-year institutions				
	1990	1995	2000	2005	2010	1990	1995	2000	2005	2010	1990	1995	2000	2005	2010
Baseline	9.4	9.9	10.5	11.1	11.8	18.0	19.6	21.4	23.3	25.2	7.7	7.9	8.1	8.4	8.7
Varying federal support															
No growth (A1)	9.4	10.1	11.0	11.9	13.0	18.0	19.9	22.0	24.4	26.9	7.7	8.0	8.4	8.8	9.3
Rapid growth (A2)	9.4	9.8	10.3	10.9	11.4	18.0	19.6	21.3	23.1	25.0	7.7	7.9	8.1	8.3	8.5
Real decline (A3)	9.4	10.3	11.2	12.3	13.5	18.0	20.1	22.3	24.8	27.5	7.7	8.0	8.5	8.9	9.5
Varying performance of the economy															
Strong (B1)	9.4	8.0	6.8	5.6	4.6	18.0	16.8	15.6	14.3	12.9	7.7	6.5	5.5	4.5	3.7
Weak (B2)	9.4	10.7	12.1	13.7	15.5	18.0	20.2	22.7	25.5	28.6	7.7	8.4	9.1	10.0	10.9
Varying rates of growth in cost and institutional aid															
High cost/high aid (C1)	9.4	10.9	12.8	15.1	17.8	18.0	21.1	25.0	29.8	35.6	7.7	8.5	9.5	10.8	12.2
High cost/low aid (C2)	9.4	11.0	12.9	15.3	18.1	18.0	22.0	26.9	33.1	40.9	7.7	8.5	9.6	10.8	12.3
Low cost/high aid (C3)	9.4	8.9	8.3	7.7	6.9	18.0	18.2	18.1	17.6	16.6	7.7	7.3	6.8	6.3	5.8
Low cost/low aid (C4)	9.4	9.0	8.5	7.8	7.1	18.0	19.0	20.0	21.0	21.8	7.7	7.3	5.9	6.4	5.9

Source: Authors' calculations based on simulation model described in the text.

changes from the baseline projections, with institutional aid playing a mediating role. In the worst-case scenario—high costs and low institutional aid (C2)—net price in 2010 at private institutions rises to $22,900, as opposed to $20,000 if institutional aid increases at a rapid rate (see table 6-3). In either case, this figure is well above the baseline projection of $14,100. The corresponding net price to income ratios are 41 percent and 36 percent, compared with the 25 percent baseline prediction (see table 6-4). At public four-year institutions, the high cost–low aid scenario leads to a net price of $8,200 and a burden of 18 percent, quite close to the figures for the high cost–high aid scenario ($8,100 and, again, 18 percent), both of which far exceed the baseline projections of $5,400 and 12 percent. At public two-year colleges, for both the high cost–low aid and high cost–high aid scenarios, net price is about $4,500 with a 12 percent burden, compared with $3,200 and 9 percent for the baseline. Hence, while high cost growth has a major effect on affordability in both the private and public sectors, the prominent role of institutional aid at private institutions enables these schools to reduce the effect of cost growth.

The low cost growth scenarios presented in C3 and C4 offer a much rosier view of the future. Even in the case of low institutional aid (C4), the net price for private institutions in 2010 falls to $12,200, implying a burden of 22 percent. The figures are $3,200 and 7 percent at public four-year institutions and $2,100 and 6 percent at community colleges. The combination of low cost growth and high institutional aid growth improves these numbers to $9,300 and 17 percent at private colleges and universities, $3,100 and 7 percent at public four-year institutions, and $2,100 and 6 percent at public two-year colleges. Again, it is clear that the effects of cost growth dominate those of changes in institutional aid, especially in the public sector.

It is worth noting that each of our simulations can be roughly equated to a simulation that assumes a given rate of growth in tuition, rather than computing tuition as a residual, as is done in the simulations we report. For example, the baseline assumes that educational costs at public four-year institutions will grow at 2.0 percent (over inflation), while nontuition revenue will grow at 1.5 percent. With tuition revenue accounting for only 20 percent of total educational costs in the base year, it is readily calculated that tuition must grow at an annual real rate of 3.6 percent over the twenty-year period of the simulations in order to be consistent with the growth rates assumed in this scenario.

Table 6-5. *Projections for Tuition Dependence, by Institutional Category, 1990–2010*
Percent

Item	Public four-year institutions					Private institutions					Public two-year institutions				
	1990	1995	2000	2005	2010	1990	1995	2000	2005	2010	1990	1995	2000	2005	2010
Baseline	20.0	21.9	23.8	25.7	27.5	60.3	60.5	60.7	60.8	61.0	19.0	20.2	21.4	22.6	23.7
Varying federal support															
No growth (A1)	20.0	21.9	23.8	25.7	27.5	60.3	60.5	60.7	60.8	61.0	19.0	20.2	21.4	22.6	23.7
Rapid growth (A2)	20.0	21.9	23.8	25.7	27.5	60.3	60.5	60.7	60.8	61.0	19.0	20.2	21.4	22.6	23.7
Real decline (A3)	20.0	21.9	23.8	25.7	27.5	60.3	60.5	60.7	60.8	61.0	19.0	20.2	21.4	22.6	23.7
Varying performance of the economy															
Strong (B1)	20.0	18.0	16.0	13.9	11.8	60.3	58.5	56.7	54.7	52.7	19.0	16.2	13.3	10.3	7.2
Weak (B2)	20.0	25.7	31.0	35.9	40.5	60.3	62.3	64.3	66.2	67.9	19.0	24.1	28.8	33.2	37.4
Varying rates of growth in cost and institutional aid															
High cost/high aid (C1)	20.0	25.7	30.9	35.8	40.3	60.3	62.3	64.3	66.1	67.9	19.0	24.0	28.7	33.1	37.2
High cost/low aid (C2)	20.0	25.7	30.9	35.8	40.3	60.3	62.3	64.3	66.1	67.9	19.0	24.0	28.7	33.1	37.2
Low cost/high aid (C3)	20.0	18.0	16.0	13.8	11.7	60.3	58.5	56.6	54.7	52.7	19.0	16.2	13.2	10.2	7.0
Low cost/low aid (C4)	20.0	18.0	16.0	13.8	11.7	60.3	58.5	56.6	54.7	52.7	19.0	16.2	13.2	10.2	7.0

Source: Authors' calculations based on simulation model described in the text.

At private institutions, the annual real growth rate of educational costs in the baseline scenario is 3.2 percent and that of nontuition revenue is 3.1 percent. To reconcile these, the model implicitly assumes that tuition must grow at 3.2 percent in real terms. The implied tuition growth rate for public two-year institutions in the baseline scenario is 2.9 percent. Similar tuition-equivalent growth rates can be calculated for all the scenarios reported here.

The various scenarios above describe very different pictures of the future affordability of higher education. Do some of these scenarios seem more likely than others? To address that question, we start by focusing on the most important factor in the scenarios—the economic performance of the nation. Our most favorable scenarios—sustained high rates of economic growth—appears unlikely for at least two reasons. For one, we have completed the longest peacetime economic expansion in history and to assume that this steady growth will be followed by another two decades of economic progress is probably overoptimistic. Further, current national policies, including large government deficits and low national investment rates, do not bode well for future growth.

If growth performance is poor, the prospects for avoiding a college affordability problem are not good. In the face of slow or no growth in family incomes, the burden on families of paying for college will probably rise unless one of three things happens: the underlying costs of providing a college education do not grow; nontuition sources of educational revenue grow steadily; or student financial aid, presumably mainly from the federal government, grows steadily. Since most observers predict shortages in faculty labor markets, shortages that are likely to make college costs grow, it is difficult to see how existing levels of educational costs could be held down without eroding the quality of college education. Few observers would feel satisfied with a solution that led to declining college quality. The other two alternatives—steady growth in either nontuition revenue or federal aid support—are themselves likely to depend on a healthy economy. Thus, a promising future for college affordability appears to depend critically on good economic performance in the coming decades.

That said, what other factors will crucially impinge on future affordability? It is clear from our simulations that the next most important factor (after overall economic performance) is the behavior of the educational costs of institutions. Over the twenty years of the simulation, the burden on families differs by a factor of around two or more depending on whether college costs move a percentage point above or below the trend established in the 1978–85 period. As noted earlier, college costs have tended to grow more rapidly than inflation over the last fifty years. The reasons for this long-run tendency are fundamental, having to do with the slow rate of technical progress in this industry compared to the economy as a whole. What was distinctive about the 1980s, however, was a pattern of rapid real cost growth in colleges during a period when productivity was fairly stagnant in the rest of the economy. Beginning in the mid–1990s, growth in the population of young people is likely to lead to increases in college enrollment (although not as much as in the 1960s). The resulting growth in demand may lead to cost increases as colleges attempt to expand facilities and faculty in response. On the other hand, the intensity of competitive recruiting efforts at the most expensive colleges will likely abate, and this may reduce cost pressures at these highly visible institutions. In our best judgment, the most likely future has college costs growing ahead of inflation, but probably less rapidly than in the 1980s. Thus, the future probably lies somewhere between the baseline and the "low cost–high institutional aid" scenario.

Future Affordability for Aided and Nonaided Students

This first round of simulations highlights some of the crucial factors impinging on the future affordability of higher education for all income groups. We turn now to a set of simulations designed to shed light on the relative affordability of college for students who receive student aid compared with those who pay the full sticker price. Most of the factors considered in our first set of simulations above, such as rates of growth in college costs and of the economy, are likely to have an impact on all income groups, whereas the most important factor influencing the relative affordability of college for different income groups is the level and the form of government financing of colleges.

We therefore begin our analysis by simulating the effects of federal student aid policy on aided and nonaided students. Table 6-6 reproduces the baseline model reported in table 6-1, but with effects on aided and nonaided students shown separately. We have simplified the presentation somewhat by combining the amount of Pell grants and the subsidy value of federal loans into a single variable called "federal subsidy." We have also, in presenting the simulation results, added a separate line for "nontuition revenue" to help keep track of the fiscal implications of alternative policies. The important innovation in the table is the presentation of separate net prices, incomes, and affordability ratios for aided and nonaided students.

The net price for nonaided students is simply the "sticker price," reported here as the cost of attendance. For aided students we estimate the net price by drawing on data from the Department of Education, which reports the percentage of students at each category of institution receiving any financial aid, and which assumes that all aid (both federal subsidy and other grants) is distributed over this group of students.[13] To compare these net prices to the ability to pay, we have developed estimates of median incomes for aided and nonaided students at each institutional category.[14] In general, as the initial conditions for table 6-6 show, annual median incomes are about $30,000 to $45,000 higher for nonaided than for aided students. As a result, in all three sectors we examine, aided students on average pay a larger fraction of family income than do nonaided students. Averaging over sectors, the family of the median, nonaided student pays about 12 percent of its income for college, while the family of the median, aided student pays about 22 percent. The baseline scenario shows that a continuation of recent trends would result in the burden of college costs rising for both aided and nonaided students over the next twenty years. (Recall that the baseline scenario projects a continuation of zero growth in median family income.) The gap between the burden facing aided and nonaided students is projected to shrink by a tiny amount over this period—a result of the fact that the baseline scenario projects federal student aid to rise a little faster than educational costs over the period. The projected increase in the real net price facing aided students over the period is

13. We used data from the NPSAS survey, as reported in Korb and others (1988).

14. Information contained in Korb and others (1988, table 5-7, p. 66) was used to develop estimates of the median income of dependent, aided students in the fall of 1986. The NPSAS data on income distribution of aided students were combined with American Freshman Survey data for all dependent freshmen in fall 1986 to develop estimates of the income distribution of nonaided students. The estimated medians were adjusted for inflation between 1986 and 1990 using the consumer price index. Because the NPSAS table reports the income distribution only of students receiving federal aid, we have probably underestimated the median income of aid recipients and overestimated the median income of nonrecipients. The income figures used to report ratios of net price to income averaged over institution types are enrollment-weighted averages of these medians.

Table 6-6. *Baseline Projections for Aided and*
1989–90 dollars

Item	Educa-tion costs	Living costs	Non-tuition educa-tion revenue	Costs of attend-ance	Pell grants	Other grants	Loans	Federal subsidy
Annual growth rates								
Public (2)	1.018	. . .	1.015	. . .	1.035	1.017	1.030	1.033
Public (4)	1.020	. . .	1.015	. . .	1.035	1.016	1.030	1.032
Private	1.032	. . .	1.031	. . .	1.000	1.054	1.050	1.032
Initial values								
Public (2)	4,200	2,300	3,400	3,100	150	80	140	220
Public (4)	8,500	3,500	6,800	5,200	290	320	640	610
Private	14,600	3,800	5,800	12,600	320	1,580	1,160	900
Public two-year institutions								
1990	. . .	. . .	3,400	3,100	. . .	80	. . .	220
1995	. . .	. . .	3,663	3,229	. . .	87	. . .	259
2000	. . .	. . .	3,946	3,374	. . .	95	. . .	306
2005	. . .	. . .	4,251	3,538	. . .	103	. . .	360
2010	. . .	. . .	4,579	3,721	. . .	112	. . .	424
Public four-year institutions								
1990	. . .	. . .	6,800	5,200	. . .	320	. . .	610
1995	. . .	. . .	7,326	5,559	. . .	346	. . .	715
2000	. . .	. . .	7,892	5,970	. . .	375	. . .	839
2005	. . .	. . .	8,502	6,438	. . .	406	. . .	984
2010	. . .	. . .	9,159	6,972	. . .	440	. . .	1,154
Private institutions								
1990	. . .	. . .	5,800	12,600	. . .	1,580	. . .	900
1995	. . .	. . .	6,756	14,134	. . .	2,055	. . .	1,055
2000	. . .	. . .	7,871	15,935	. . .	2,673	. . .	1,236
2005	. . .	. . .	9,169	18,049	. . .	3,477	. . .	1,448
2010	. . .	. . .	10,681	20,532	. . .	4,523	. . .	1,697

Source: Authors' calculations based on simulation model in the text.

about $700. Our estimates of enrollment elasticity in chapter 3 suggest that this increase in price would reduce lower-income enrollment by about 9 percent.

The impact of variations in federal student aid on relative affordability is suggested by a comparison of table 6-6 with table 6-7, which examines the implications of the "no-growth-in-federal-support" scenario (A1) for aided and nonaided students separately. With no growth in federal aid, the burden on aided families would rise substantially relative to the baseline scenario and relative to the projection for non-aided families in the A1 scenario. At public four-year institutions, for example, the "no-federal-growth" scenario forecasts that the burden on nonaided families would rise from 9 percent of income to 12 percent, while the burden on aided families would rise from 17 percent of income to 25 percent by 2010. In the baseline scenario the burden on aided families goes from 17 percent to just 19 percent over the same

Nonaided Students, 1990–2010

Family income	Family income, aided	Family income, non-aided	Students receiving aid (percent)	Average net price	Net price, no aid	Net price/ income, no aid	Net price, aided	Net price/ income, aided	Tuition dependence (percent)
1.000	...	...	...	...	...	...	...	...	...
1.000	...	...	...	...	...	...	...	...	...
1.000	...	...	...	...	...	...	...	...	...
...	15,500	43,000	29.2	...	...	...	...	...	...
...	19,000	56,000	47.0	...	...	...	...	...	...
...	26,000	71,000	65.4	...	...	...	...	...	...
...	...	...	...	2,800	3,100	0.07	2,073	0.13	19.0
...	...	...	...	2,883	3,229	0.08	2,043	0.13	20.2
...	...	...	...	2,974	3,374	0.08	2,004	0.13	21.4
...	...	...	...	3,075	3,538	0.08	1,952	0.13	22.6
...	...	...	...	3,185	3,721	0.09	1,884	0.12	23.7
...	...	...	...	4,270	5,200	0.09	3,221	0.17	20.0
...	...	...	...	4,497	5,559	0.10	3,300	0.17	21.9
...	...	...	...	4,756	5,970	0.11	3,387	0.18	23.8
...	...	...	...	5,048	6,438	0.11	3,481	0.18	25.7
...	...	...	...	5,379	6,972	0.12	3,582	0.19	27.5
...	...	...	...	10,120	12,600	0.18	8,808	0.34	60.3
...	...	...	...	11,024	14,134	0.20	9,379	0.36	60.5
...	...	...	...	12,026	15,935	0.22	9,957	0.38	60.7
...	...	...	...	13,123	18,049	0.25	10,518	0.40	60.8
...	...	...	...	14,311	20,532	0.29	11,020	0.42	61.0

period. Averaging over educational sectors, a policy of no growth in federal aid is projected to cause the burden on aided families to rise from 22 percent to 31 percent over twenty years, compared with a rise from 22 percent to 26 percent if recent growth in federal support continues.

The implications of such a change in federal policy are not trivial. The average net price facing aided students would be about $1,050 higher in 2010 if federal aid did not grow than if it grew at the baseline rate. According to the estimates we developed in chapter 3, such an increase would reduce the lower-income enrollment rate by about 13 percent.

The substantial impact on lower-income students of even this moderate variation in federal aid makes it interesting to consider what the impact of a much larger change in federal financing would be. Unlike the incremental changes we have considered so far, it is unreasonable

Table 6-7. *No Growth in Federal Student Aid: Projections for Aided*
1989–90 dollars

Item	Education costs	Living costs	Non-tuition education revenue	Costs of attendance	Pell grants	Other grants	Loans	Federal Subsidy
Annual growth rates								
Public (2)	1.018	. . .	1.015	. . .	1.000	1.017	1.000	1.000
Public (4)	1.020	. . .	1.015	. . .	1.000	1.016	1.000	1.000
Private	1.032	. . .	1.031	. . .	1.000	1.054	1.000	1.000
Initial values								
Public (2)	4,200	2,300	3,400	3,100	150	80	140	220
Public (4)	8,500	3,500	6,800	5,200	290	320	640	610
Private	14,600	3,800	5,800	12,600	320	1,580	1,160	900
Public two-year institutions								
1990	. . .	. . .	3,400	3,100	. . .	80	. . .	220
1995	. . .	. . .	3,663	3,229	. . .	87	. . .	220
2000	. . .	. . .	3,946	3,374	. . .	95	. . .	220
2005	. . .	. . .	4,251	3,538	. . .	103	. . .	220
2010	. . .	. . .	4,579	3,721	. . .	112	. . .	220
Public four-year institutions								
1990	. . .	. . .	6,800	5,200	. . .	320	. . .	610
1995	. . .	. . .	7,326	5,559	. . .	346	. . .	610
2000	. . .	. . .	7,892	5,970	. . .	375	. . .	610
2005	. . .	. . .	8,502	6,438	. . .	406	. . .	610
2010	. . .	. . .	9,159	6,972	. . .	440	. . .	610
Private institutions								
1990	. . .	. . .	5,800	12,600	. . .	1,580	. . .	900
1995	. . .	. . .	6,756	14,134	. . .	2,055	. . .	900
2000	. . .	. . .	7,871	15,935	. . .	2,673	. . .	900
2005	. . .	. . .	9,169	18,049	. . .	3,477	. . .	900
2010	. . .	. . .	10,681	20,532	. . .	4,523	. . .	900

Source: Authors' calculations based on simulation model in text.

to consider a massive change in federal responsibility without some treatment of how it would be financed. We have therefore found it useful to examine the implications of a "revenue neutral" swap of federal and state financing of higher education. The following analysis shows the implications of a modeling exercise in which federal student aid rises substantially, while at the same time states withdraw part of their direct institutional support from public colleges and universities. This would in effect be a kind of exercise in "fiscal federalism," with the federal government relieving state governments of part of the burden of financing the education of lower-income students.

A "swap" of this kind would be in some measure a natural conse-quence of substantial increases in the size of federal student aid grant awards. Most states would have to raise tuition significantly in order for their students to benefit from such increases, and would also have substantial incentives to do so. The resulting higher tuitions could then substitute for state operating subsidies in financing public higher

and Nonaided Students, 1990–2010

Family income	Family income, aided	Family income, non-aided	Students receiving aid (percent)	Average net price	Net price, no aid	Net price/ income, no aid	Net price, aided	Net price/ income, aided	Tuition dependence (percent)
1.000	. . .	. . .	. . .	. . .	. . .	. . .	. . .	. . .	. . .
1.000	. . .	. . .	. . .	. . .	. . .	. . .	. . .	. . .	. . .
1.000	. . .	. . .	. . .	. . .	. . .	. . .	. . .	. . .	. . .
. . .	15,500	43,000	29.2	. . .	. . .	. . .	. . .	. . .	. . .
. . .	19,000	56,000	47.0	. . .	. . .	. . .	. . .	. . .	. . .
. . .	26,000	71,000	65.4	. . .	. . .	. . .	. . .	. . .	. . .
. . .	. . .	. . .	. . .	2,800	3,100	0.07	2,073	0.13	19.1
. . .	. . .	. . .	. . .	2,922	3,229	0.08	2,178	0.14	20.2
. . .	. . .	. . .	. . .	3,060	3,374	0.08	2,297	0.15	21.4
. . .	. . .	. . .	. . .	3,215	3,538	0.08	2,432	0.16	22.6
. . .	. . .	. . .	. . .	3,389	3,721	0.09	2,584	0.17	23.7
. . .	. . .	. . .	. . .	4,270	5,200	0.09	3,221	0.17	20.0
. . .	. . .	. . .	. . .	4,603	5,559	0.10	3,524	0.19	21.9
. . .	. . .	. . .	. . .	4,985	5,970	0.11	3,874	0.20	23.8
. . .	. . .	. . .	. . .	5,422	6,438	0.11	4,277	0.23	25.7
. . .	. . .	. . .	. . .	5,922	6,972	0.12	4,739	0.25	27.5
. . .	. . .	. . .	. . .	10,120	12,600	0.18	8,808	0.34	60.3
. . .	. . .	. . .	. . .	11,179	14,134	0.20	9,615	0.37	60.5
. . .	. . .	. . .	. . .	12,361	15,935	0.22	10,471	0.40	60.7
. . .	. . .	. . .	. . .	13,672	18,049	0.25	11,356	0.44	60.9
. . .	. . .	. . .	. . .	15,108	20,532	0.29	12,239	0.47	61.0

education. There is, of course, no reason to suppose that in reality this mechanism would produce a dollar-for-dollar substitution of federal for state support.[15] Moreover, in a realistic forecast of the consequences of a major change in federal funding, a number of additional behavioral responses of institutions in both the public and the private sectors should be considered. Chapter 4, in fact, provides some econometric evidence on what some of those responses might be.[16] Still, for purposes of

15. States could wind up reducing their support by more than a dollar for every dollar increase in federal aid if they were induced to raise tuition enough to capture a substantial fraction of the "rents" accruing to full-tuition payers. On the other hand, states might return part of their increased revenue to higher education, either by providing financial aid to middle- and upper-middle-income students who would not receive federal support, or by increasing educational expenditures at state-run institutions. Note that the regressions in chapter 4 do not detect any measurable tendency for state institutions to raise instructional spending when student aid rises, but they do indicate that state institutions raise gross tuition by about 50 cents for every dollar increase they receive in federal student aid.

16. The preceding footnote mentions possible state responses. Higher federal student aid levels might also lead private institutions to adjust their own funding of student aid, to change

Table 6-8. *Projections of Consequences of Federal-State*
1989–90 dollars

Item	Education costs	Living costs	Non-tuition education revenue	Costs of attendance	Pell grants	Other grants	Growth in share of aid (percentage points)	Loans	Federal subsidy
Annual growth rates									
Public (2)	1.02	...	1.02	...	...	1.02	2.00[a]	...	1.25[b]
Public (4)	1.02	...	1.02	...	...	1.02	0.25[a]	...	1.15[b]
Private	1.03	...	1.03	...	...	1.05	0.00	...	1.11[b]
Initial values									
Public (2)	4,200	2,300	3,400	3,100	150	80	...	140	220
Public (4)	8,500	3,500	6,800	5,200	290	320	...	640	610
Private	14,600	3,800	5,800	12,600	320	1,580	...	1,160	900
Public two-year institutions									
1990	...	...	3,400	3,100	...	80	...	...	220
1995	...	...	2,896	3,995	...	87	...	...	661
2000	...	...	1,558	5,762	...	95	...	...	1,987
2005	...	...	1,358	6,430	...	103	...	...	2,303
2010	...	...	1,101	7,200	...	112	...	...	2,670
Public four-year institutions									
1990	...	...	6,800	5,200	...	320	...	...	610
1995	...	...	6,559	6,326	...	346	...	...	1,204
2000	...	...	5,504	8,357	...	375	...	...	2,377
2005	...	...	5,609	9,331	...	406	...	...	2,755
2010	...	...	5,680	10,450	...	440	...	...	3,194
Private institutions									
1990	...	...	5,800	12,600	...	1,580	...	...	900
1995	...	...	6,756	14,134	...	2,055	...	...	1,549
2000	...	...	7,871	15,935	...	2,673	...	...	2,667
2005	...	...	9,169	18,049	...	3,477	...	...	3,091
2010	...	...	10,681	20,532	...	4,523	...	...	3,584

Source: Authors' calculations based on simulation model in the text.
a. Growth falls to zero after the year 2000.
b. Subsidy growth equals 1.03 after the year 2000.

bringing out the differential impacts of state and federal funding, we believe the following simplified exercise is justified.

Table 6-8 shows the results of a simulation in which federal student aid grows at 15 percent a year (in real terms) for ten years, and then resumes its recent trend of growth of 3 percent a year. In every year, we assume that state appropriations for public higher education are reduced by exactly the amount of the increase in federal spending. Thus, the projection examines the consequences of partially replacing state operating subsidies for institutions with federal student aid.

We assume that the 15 percent annual increase in federal aid will be apportioned across sectors so that the absolute dollar increase in federal

their tuition levels, or to change their levels of spending on instruction. Although actual responses would depend on the form of the change in the federal grant programs, the regressions in chapter 4 indicate that private institutions would raise their own spending on student aid and that tuition and spending on instruction would be unaffected.

Funding Swap, 1990–2010

Family income	Family income, aided	Family income, non-aided	Students receiving aid (percent)	Average net price	Net price, no aid	Net price/income, aided	Net price, aided	Net price/income, aided	Tuition dependence (percent)	Share of aid
1.00	...	...	...	...	...	...	...	...	...	...
1.00	...	...	...	...	...	...	...	...	...	...
1.00	...	...	...	...	...	...	...	...	...	...
...	15,500	43,000	29.2	...	...	...	...	...	...	...
...	19,000	56,000	47.0	...	...	...	...	...	...	...
...	26,000	71,000	65.4	...	...	...	...	...	...	...
...	...	...	...	2,800	3,100	0.07	2,073	0.13	19.0	0.29
...	...	...	...	3,247	3,995	0.09	2,087	0.13	36.9	0.39
...	...	...	...	3,680	5,762	0.13	1,531	0.10	69.0	0.49
...	...	...	...	4,024	6,430	0.15	1,540	0.10	75.3	0.49
...	...	...	...	4,418	7,200	0.17	1,545	0.10	81.6	0.49
...	...	...	...	4,270	5,200	0.09	3,221	0.17	20.0	0.47
...	...	...	...	4,775	6,326	0.11	3,112	0.16	30.1	0.48
...	...	...	...	5,605	8,357	0.15	2,798	0.15	46.9	0.50
...	...	...	...	6,170	9,331	0.17	2,944	0.15	51.0	0.50
...	...	...	...	6,816	10,450	0.19	3,109	0.16	55.0	0.50
...	...	...	...	10,120	12,600	0.18	8,808	0.34	60.3	0.65
...	...	...	...	10,529	14,134	0.20	8,622	0.33	60.5	0.65
...	...	...	...	10,595	15,935	0.22	7,769	0.30	60.7	0.65
...	...	...	...	11,480	18,049	0.25	8,005	0.31	60.8	0.65
...	...	...	...	12,424	20,532	0.29	8,135	0.31	61.0	0.65

aid over the ten-year period is the same in each sector. This implies growth rates of 25 percent, 15 percent, and 11 percent for public two-year colleges, public four-year institutions, and private four-year institutions, respectively. One further refinement of the model should be noted. Rapid increases in federal aid would increase the share of students qualifying for such aid, especially at lower-cost institutions. We allow for this tendency by permitting the share of students receiving aid to grow by 2 percentage points a year at public two-year institutions and by 0.25 percentage point a year at public four-year institutions until 2000. This growth rate brings the percent aided to roughly 50 percent in each of these sectors by 2000.

The consequences of such a federal-state funding swap are striking. The net price facing the average aided student falls in real terms under the swap, instead of rising as it does under both the baseline and "no-federal-increase" scenarios. Averaging across sectors, the net price to income ratio for these students falls from 22 percent in 1990 to 21 percent in 2010, instead of rising to 26 percent or 31 percent as it does in the baseline and "no-federal-increase" scenarios. The counterpart to reduced prices for lower-income students, in this revenue-neutral scenario, is higher net prices for nonaided students. By the year 2000, the net price to income ratio for nonaided students rises from 12 percent to 17 percent, and rises further to 22 percent by 2010, winding up 1 percentage point higher than the ratio for aided students. The burden ratio for this group winds up at 17 percent in the other scenarios.

This change in relative net prices for aided and nonaided students emerges most sharply at public institutions. Thus with no federal increase (table 6-7), the burden for nonaided students at public four year institutions rises from 9 percent to 12 percent over the period, while that for aided students rises from 17 percent to 25 percent. With the federal-state swap (table 6-8), the burden for nonaided students rises to 19 percent by the end of the projection period, while that for aided students falls to 16 percent.[17] At public two-year institutions, aided students under the "swap" would experience a drop in the burden ratio over the period from 13 percent to 10 percent instead of a rise under the "no-federal-increase" scenario from 13 percent to 17 percent. The swap would cause the burden ratio for nonaided students to rise from 7 percent to 17 percent, instead of from 7 percent to 9 percent.

Along with this change in relative prices for aided and nonaided students at public institutions goes an important change in their financing. Substantially more public institution revenue would come from tuition payments under the swap than is true now or would be true under the other scenarios.[18] In the baseline scenario, tuition dependency is projected to rise from 20 percent to 28 percent at public four-year institutions over the period and from 19 percent to 24 percent at public two-year institutions. With an expanded federal aid role substituting for state operating subsidies, these increases would be much more dramatic—rising from 20 percent to 55 percent at public four-year institutions and from 19 percent to 82 percent at public two-year institutions.

Under the assumptions of our projection model, at private institutions

17. Because the share of students receiving aid at public institutions is projected to rise with rapid growth in federal aid, their average income levels would presumably be somewhat higher. Thus the actual burden ratio might be somewhat lower than these figures suggest.

18. These are *gross* tuition payments, so they include revenue from federal student aid.

neither tuition dependence nor the net price facing nonaided students would be affected by the federal-state financing swap. However, the increase in federal student aid funding would have a considerable effect on the financing burden facing aided families. Under the "no-federal-increase" scenario, the burden ratio for aided families at private institutions rises from 34 percent to 47 percent over the projection period. Under the federal-state swap, the ratio for this group is instead projected to fall from 34 percent to 31 percent.

Finally, for nonaided students the federal-state swap has significant implications for the relative prices of different types of colleges. Under the "no-federal-increase" scenario, the ratio of net costs for nonaided students at public two-year, public four-year, and private institutions in 2010 is projected to be approximately 1:1.9:5.5. With the federal-state swap these ratios change to 1:1.5:2.9. That is to say, rather than private colleges' costing nonaided students more than five times what community colleges do, they would cost slightly less than three times as much. And comparing public four-year to private institutions, the relative cost would drop from about three to one to about two to one.[19] This reflects the fact that each institution type under this scenario would wind up financing the majority of its costs from tuition revenue.

In sum, the most striking point that emerges in examining affordability projections for aided and nonaided students separately is the degree to which federal financing contributes to reducing the net costs facing lower-income students. At present, the fraction of income represented by net college costs (less student aid) is higher for aided than for nonaided students at every category of institution, and this trend is expected to continue in the baseline scenario and modest variations around it. If federal aid fails to grow (as in table 6-7), the ratio of net price to income for aided students is projected to rise significantly in all higher education sectors in the years ahead. One way of reversing that increase, without adding to the taxpayers' costs, would be to increase federal student aid funding at the expense of reducing state operating support for public institutions. The favorable effect on afford-

19. Under the assumptions that we have imposed about how the increase in federal aid would be distributed, the federal-state swap would have little impact on the relative prices of different institution types for typical aided students. Under the "no-federal-increase" scenario, the ratio of net costs for aided students at public two-year, public four-year, and private institutions in 2010 is projected to be approximately 1:1.8:4.7. With the federal-state swap these ratios change to 1:2:5.3. Thus, although affordability of more costly alternatives improves for aided students under this scenario, the relative prices of different options are not much affected.

ability for lower-income students results because federal aid is targeted on such students while state operating subsidies reduce costs for all public sector students regardless of income.[20]

Conclusion

Affordability of higher education is a major national concern, influencing prospects both for economic growth and economic justice. In this chapter, we have used projections to examine likely future trends in affordability for higher education as a whole, and for aided and nonaided students separately.

By examining a variety of scenarios regarding factors affecting future trends in affordability, we have produced a range of alternatives that may reasonably be thought to bracket likely future developments concerning college costs and family ability to pay, as well as an analysis of the principal factors that will influence these future trends. Our analysis by no means supports the view that we are facing an immediate "crisis" in college affordability. Nonetheless, we have identified some worrisome trends. Perhaps the point of broadest interest is the great dependence of future college affordability on favorable growth performance for the economy as a whole. Higher education, although it benefits from particular governmental programs, has a strong stake in the sound management of the economy. We also note that a number of scenarios point to a tendency for private college prices to rise relative to those at public institutions—a development that could potentially threaten the future of America's dual higher education system.

In examining future affordability trends for students who receive student aid and those who pay the full price, our projections emphasize the importance of federal student aid to aided students. Given the large differences in the way federal and state higher-education subsidies are targeted, we show that an increasing relative role of federal support would tend to improve affordability for aided students and reduce the gap between public institution and private institution tuitions for nonaided students.

20. As sketched here, this scenario is highly abstract and simplified. Its policy implications are discussed in chapter 9.

VII

The Targeting of Student Aid

IN THE PRECEDING chapters, we presented evidence concerning the role of government spending in the finance of undergraduate education in the United States. In this and the final two chapters, we turn from these empirical analyses to a discussion of the policy issues and alternatives for American higher education.

As seen in previous chapters, in the United States a system of undergraduate higher-education finance has evolved that combines important roles for the government at both the state and national levels with substantial contributions from institutions' own resources and from parents and students. As a result, the questions of who pays for college, of who receives governmental or private assistance in paying, and of how payments are financed are tangled ones.

The financial aid provided to students is therefore just one element in this complex system. Because of that, an understanding of the aid system must depend in part on an appreciation of how aid figures into these overall financing patterns. On the one hand, aid may serve to balance or redress some otherwise undesirable features of the existing system—for example, by reducing the tuition gap between private and public institutions. On the other hand, the aid system itself may set up incentives that produce unfortunate effects elsewhere in the system— for example, some observers allege that the methods used for calculating family ability to pay have the unintended side-effect of discouraging families from saving for college.

This chapter examines some distributive dilemmas facing the undergraduate financing system. Do the programs reach the right people? Do they support an appropriate set of institutions and activities? We consider a variety of issues: whether federal aid should take into account the cost of the institution a student attends, how aid fits into the relations between public and private higher education, how vocational and technical education are treated, how adult and independent students are handled in a system that was basically designed for young high school

133

graduates, and how students who demonstrate special academic "merit" should be treated. Throughout, we emphasize the need to consider how these programs fit into the overall scheme for financing higher education in the United States. Putting aid, and in particular federal aid, into context, is an essential element in evaluating reform proposals for the student aid system.

Needs Testing and Income Testing

When a number of private colleges and universities developed the principles of need-based student aid in the 1950s, a guiding principle was that students' choice of college should be based on educational, rather than financial, considerations. In principle, therefore, one goal of need-based student aid was to make the price a student and his or her family paid independent of the choice of institution.

As federal student aid has evolved, the design of its programs has been heavily influenced by the principles of need-based student aid. Currently, for example, Stafford loan eligibility is determined by the same needs-analysis methodology as applies to institutions allocating their own aid funds. The Pell methodology is different, but in its broad principles conforms to the basic structure of needs analysis—including the provision of larger awards to students attending more expensive institutions. In practice, as noted in chapter 4, this "tuition sensitivity" is largely inoperative, because the maxima on Pell awards have been too low to make the costs of attendance the binding constraint on individual awards.[1]

However, such tuition sensitivity is present for Stafford loans and would be present for Pell grants if award levels rose sufficiently. Clearly, making the amount of aid sensitive to the cost of the institution as well as to family resources is a sensible policy for the institutions

1. The Pell grant system says in effect that a student is entitled to a grant that meets his or her need (as determined by the cost of attendance and the family's resources) up to a maximum also determined by the level of family resources. This maximum for any student is a function of the family's resources and of the maximum grant for a student with no resources—$2,300 in the 1989–90 academic year. Thus, the only time a student's award can be increased by her choice of a more expensive institution is when her full need is met by a Pell grant at the more expensive institution. (Otherwise she will receive the maximum Pell allowed for someone at her income level, and will not receive more by going to a more expensive school.) Few institutions, especially private institutions, have a price low enough for a Pell grant to meet a student's full need.

that must compete for students through price and aid packages, but for the government and its programs of student support, this arrangement has two obvious drawbacks. First, tuition-sensitive federal aid provides an incentive for institutions to raise prices. Suppose, for example, that 30 percent of an institution's students are receiving tuition-sensitive federal grants, and that half of them are receiving less than the maximum award for which they qualify. For that 15 percent of the student body, any increase in tuition will be paid for by the federal government, at least up to each student's maximum award level. For public institutions, such a tuition increase would largely represent a transfer of resources from federal to state governments—that is, as long as states reduce their spending on higher education as tuitions are allowed to rise. For public institutions, such a "swap" of federal for state support might well be a good thing, as we argue in chapter 9. In private higher education, however, higher tuitions would presumably translate into higher institutional spending, and therefore into greater resource use in higher education. In light of recent concerns about cost inflation in private higher education, introducing incentives to increase prices in that sector seems clearly undesirable.

A second concern is the important element of discretionary choice in determining how much a student's education will cost, and therefore how much that student's "need" will be. Generally, when government programs respond to "need" rather than simply to income, the level of need is seen as something largely involuntary—as in aid for disabled people, or the sensitivity of medical care payments to the costs of different procedures. We do not, on the other hand, give more food stamps to a family that prefers steak to macaroni.[2] To the extent that schools differ in tuition because they differ in the amount of resources they spend per student, it is not at all clear that the federal government should stand ready to make up the difference. This judgment is also complicated by the presence of substantial state government operating subsidies to public institutions. Indeed, the main reason private colleges cost more than public colleges is not that they use more resources per student, but that they do not receive state operating subsidies. To the extent that federal aid works to "close the gap" between public and private tuitions, the federal government is really providing a subsidy to private higher education that tends to reduce the difference in public

2. The example is from Finn (1978, p. 55).

subsidies between the two sectors. Thus, the issue of income-testing versus needs-testing of aid is closely connected to the issue of maintaining a "dual" system of higher education.

Student Aid in a Mixed Public-Private Higher Education System

A key institutional feature of American higher education is the large-scale presence of both state-run and independent, nonprofit institutions. This dual system raises several important questions regarding the role of financial aid. First, regarding public higher education, states, as was seen in chapter 1, devote most of their educational appropriations to general institutional subsidies, which have the effect of lowering the tuition paid by all students. One set of questions is how desirable this form of subsidy is compared with alternatives such as converting state operating subsidies into student financial aid.[3] A distinct but related question, taking the low-tuition strategy in public higher education as a given, is whether state operating subsidies adequately support the less affluent students at public institutions, or whether their families need more help, federal or other.

Most state-run schools have low tuition for in-state students and offer little other financial aid from their own resources. The low level of tuition implies that federal need-based aid must go to students from families with low or modest incomes (others will not be able to demonstrate need), and the paucity of institution-based funds means that for most such students the bulk of their aid will come from the federal government. Thus in public higher education, federal need-based aid acts as a *supplement* to the low-tuition strategy by helping keep down the costs facing lower-income families. Whether federal aid going to public institutions promotes distributive "fairness" depends on whether one believes that some income-sensitive aid should be introduced into the pattern of public subsidies in that sector, beyond that provided by

3. Early proponents of the notion that states should reorient their funding from operating subsidies to student aid were Hansen and Weisbrod (1971). Among the many contributions to the resulting controversy, Bowen (1974) and Breneman and Finn (1978, chap. 10) are especially worth attention.

the small amount of needs-tested aid states already finance.[4] Because federal aid introduces an element of income sensitivity into what is otherwise a fairly regressive pattern of subsidy in public higher education, it seems fair to say that it has a favorable effect on the overall equity of the financing system.[5]

Regarding private higher education, federal student aid programs go some distance toward reducing the tuition gap between private and public institutions (for those students who receive aid). In addition, institutions' own expenditures on aid, in the form of tuition remissions or direct grants or loans, add further to this gap-closing. How much of an impact do these two sets of programs have on the tuition gap? Is it reasonable for the federal government to use its resources to try to help private institutions compete with their state-subsidized counterparts? Should private institutions be using their own resources for this purpose?

To start, private institutions spend a fair amount of their own resources on need-based grants and price discounts—partly owing to the pressure to compete with low-cost public institutions. Thus, even without federal intervention, subsidy policies in private higher education are already rather income sensitive. Therefore, federal aid directed to private colleges does two things. First, as discussed in chapter 4, it federalizes some of the costs of aid policies that colleges would, within the limits of their resources, assume anyway. (This is clearest with the campus-based programs, which pay money directly into schools' financial aid budgets, but it also applies indirectly to the Pell and GSL programs.) Second, as our empirical analysis in chapter 4 indicates, federal aid tends to increase private institutions' spending on need-based aid and, presumably, focuses more of that spending on higher-need, lower-income students than the colleges would have been able to do on their own.[6]

4. Of total state government expenditures of $30 billion in the 1985–86 academic year, about $1.3 billion took the form of student aid grants. See National Center for Education Statistics (1989, table 269, p. 292) and College Board (1989b).

5. "Regressive" is used here in the sense of tax policy. A regressive tax policy increases taxes more slowly than income rises; a regressive subsidy policy reduces benefits more slowly than income rises.

6. The regressions in chapter 4 indicate that increased federal aid causes institutions to increase their own expenditures on aid—federal and institution-based aid are complements rather than substitutes. The most plausible explanation for this is that increased federal aid makes it more feasible for the institution to enroll lower-income students–hence the presumption that the avail-

Thus, whether federal contributions promote fairness in private higher education depends on judgments about whether the federal government should bear part of the costs of "choice"—of sharing with families and with private colleges the burden of making these institutions available to needy students. It is important to stress that the federal government does not come anywhere near to picking up all these costs. Federal student aid pays only about a third of the costs lower-income students face at private institutions and about a quarter of the costs facing middle-income students at these institutions.[7] In total, federal student aid provides about half of total student aid at private institutions; institution-based aid provides more than a third.[8] As figures 2-7 and 2-8 in chapter 2 indicate, the net effect of this aid is that, on average, for families with incomes below $20,000 (in 1990 dollars), the net price at private four-year institutions is still about 75 percent more than at public four-year institutions. The issue, then, given current funding levels, is not whether the federal government should stand ready to underwrite the full costs of an expensive private higher education for needy students, for it could not, but whether in the cause of fairness it should at least assume *part* of the burden. It seems fairly clear to us that it should.

If existing federal aid programs help improve the balance between the financing of public and private higher education, would expansion of those programs make things even better? Presumably, the effects of such an expansion would depend heavily on the form that expansion took and the ways in which state governments and both public and private institutions reacted to it. Suppose, for example, that federal support were increased by making more middle- and upper-middle-income students eligible for aid (say, by reducing the "taxing rate" in the formula for distributing Pell grants). In public higher education, such a change would do little to affect the distribution of subsidies, since these students already receive substantial state subsidies in the form of low tuitions, which would leave them qualified for relatively

---

ability of federal aid causes schools to target more total aid at lower-income students than they would otherwise.

7. See Miller and Hexter (1985a, p. 23; 1985b).

8. According to results of the National Postsecondary Student Aid Study (NPSAS) survey, in the fall of 1986, 46 percent of aid revenue at private institutions was from the federal government and 30 percent was from institutional funds. The comparable figures for public institutions are 68 percent federal and 10 percent institution-based. See Korb and others (1988, tables 4.1 and 4.2, pp. 24 and 25).

small amounts of aid. At the same time, because private institutions already provide substantial amounts of aid to middle-income students, a federal increase would probably cause institutions to substitute federal resources for their own. Indeed, if a change in federal formulas in favor of middle-income students were made so that the formulas were more tuition-sensitive, the effect might be to encourage private institutions to raise their prices.

On the other hand, a federal policy change that involved raising support for lower-income students without substantially increasing the aid eligibility of middle- and upper-middle-income students would probably have quite different effects. In public higher education, it would give states the incentive to raise tuition in order to capture more federal aid, thus making the net price students pay in public higher education more income sensitive. In private higher education, such a policy change might or might not induce tuition increases, depending on how it was designed. If it avoided tuition increases, such a change would tend to reduce the net price facing lower-income students, thus increasing the attractiveness of their private sector options. We pursue this kind of policy change further in chapter 9.

Vocational Education

As noted in chapter 2, a substantial fraction of federal student assistance is now provided to students attending nondegree, vocational programs. One important segment of this market consists of proprietary vocational-technical institutions, which in the 1987–88 academic year received more than a quarter of all Pell funds—a larger share than was received by private institutions or public two-year institutions.[9] In addition, a significant fraction of the students attending public two-year colleges are enrolled in nondegree vocational programs.

The remarkable growth of the proprietary vocational sector in the 1970s and 1980s is almost certainly linked to the expanded role of federal student aid. Although reliable historical data on enrollments in this sector are not available, the fact that their share of Pell funds grew from 10.5 percent in 1979–80 to 26.6 percent in 1987–88 is testimony

9. See table 2-5.

to their rapid growth.[10] It is particularly remarkable that students at proprietary institutions received more than a quarter of all Pell grant funds while constituting fewer than 7 percent of undergraduate postsecondary enrollment. Evidence suggests that a large fraction of the costs at these institutions is financed through federal grants and loans. In the 1986–87 academic year, fully 80 percent of students enrolled at proprietary postsecondary institutions received some form of federal student aid, compared with 48 percent at private nonprofit institutions and 29 percent at public institutions. Forty-seven percent of proprietary school students received Pell grants, compared with 17 percent at private nonprofit institutions, and 16 percent at public institutions. Sixty-seven percent of proprietary school students received guaranteed student loans, compared with 35 percent at private nonprofit institutions, and 14 percent at public institutions.

The striking competitive success of this sector—surely an unintended consequence of expanded federal student aid—raises important issues for postsecondary education policy. One obvious question is why this sector has managed so well in the face of competition from public sector suppliers that are even more heavily subsidized, typically through direct appropriations from state and local governments. Part of the answer is that the proprietary institutions make great efforts to economize on student time: training programs that take one or two years at community colleges are often completed within six months at proprietary schools.[11] Proprietary schools, being heavily dependent for their financing on attracting students with portable aid dollars, also have incentives to provide programs with strong student appeal. These incentives are presumably muted at public institutions because they must appeal to state and local governments for much of their revenue.[12]

Some observers have added less favorable explanations. There is concern that some proprietary institutions make misleading claims about the employment prospects for their graduates, fail to emphasize

10. See table 2-5. The remaining figures in this paragraph are from the NPSAS survey, as reported in National Center for Education Statistics (1989).

11. According to the NPSAS survey, as reported in National Center for Education Statistics (1989), 63 percent of proprietary school students were enrolled in programs of less than two years, while this was true of less than 2 percent of all other students. Only 11 percent of students were enrolled in public institution programs of two years or less.

12. Public subsidies are often linked to enrollment; this linkage gives institutions an incentive to attract students. However, to the degree that the subsidies are linked to the length of time students are enrolled in the program, institutions have an incentive to lengthen programs.

to students their obligation to repay loans, and do not deliver educational services commensurate with their costs.[13] Of course, nonprofit or state-run institutions can also engage in deceptive practices.

To the extent that deceptive practices are a problem for postsecondary vocational training, part of the answer may simply lie in more effective regulation at the federal level. At present, federal efforts to assess the adequacy of providers and to define the range of supportable educational activities are minimal. The regulations largely delegate the job of screening the educational providers to the states, which have little incentive to do so rigorously. To the extent that the providers are making false claims about job placement or failing to deliver services, a more effective regulatory presence can obviously help.

More difficult questions, however, must be faced. Does the nation have the same social interest in investing in purely vocational training that it has in subsidizing traditional collegiate education? To whatever degree the nation decides to subsidize postsecondary vocational training, should the same subsidy mechanisms apply to both collegiate and vocational education? At least part of the justification for subsidizing college education is a perception that it generates significant externalities, in the form of greater political participation, better understanding of public issues, and so on. The size of these benefits is difficult to measure, but that some such benefits exist seems plausible, and it also seems plausible that they are larger for a broad "liberal arts" education than for a narrowly focused vocational training. Insofar as vocational training simply provides private benefits, by giving individuals access to better jobs, the social interest might be discharged by simply ensuring that credit, rather than grant money, is available for these programs on fair terms. Indeed, from the standpoint of social efficiency, real distortions may be introduced by subsidizing "in-school" vocational alternatives while leaving various kinds of on-the-job training unsubsidized.

This argument by itself, however, neglects the distributive concerns that help motivate the current subsidies for postsecondary vocational training. Increasing the earning capacity of socially disadvantaged citizens, thereby combating income inequality and promoting more equal employment opportunity, is an important social goal. To the extent that

13. See, for example, "Taking Aim at Trade Schools," *Time*, February 22, 1988, p. 61, and Jason DeParle, "Trade Schools: Defaults and Broken Promises," *New York Times*, August 8, 1990, p. B6.

vocational training programs are effective in reaching disadvantaged groups and in providing useful skills, these services make them worthy of government subsidy.

The fact is that we have very little systematic knowledge about the operation or performance of proprietary vocational-technical institutions. As we have noted, the sector has grown up rapidly. The Department of Education reports that in the 1987–88 academic year there were 6,229 noncollegiate proprietary institutions offering postsecondary education. The total number of colleges and universities in that year (including community colleges) was 3,587.[14] Only within the last several years have the proprietary institutions been incorporated in the Department of Education's statistical data bases, and most of these data are not yet available for analysis. Journalistic accounts have highlighted scandals at particular proprietary schools, but these do not provide any meaningful basis for judging the performance of the sector as a whole. Neither are we well informed about the performance of the vocational programs at public community colleges. Federally maintained data do not clearly distinguish the academic and vocational aspects of community colleges. Even simple indicators like program completion rates and job placement rates are unavailable on a national basis for either proprietary or community college vocational programs. It is extremely difficult to consider appropriate policies for this sector in the presence of such an information vacuum.

Whatever one concludes about the quality of these programs, it is not clear that support for them should be incorporated into the same system that subsidizes college education, for several reasons. First, the requirement of high school graduation, which seems appropriate for traditional postsecondary education, has no obvious relevance for qualifying for a vocational program. Second, many vocational programs are short term, often running six months or less, while the financing system for postsecondary education is geared to programs running at least a year, and typically two years or more. Third, the range of suitable programs and providers may be quite wide, including not only "schools" but programs run by labor unions, community groups, and employers. These programs may fit poorly with a financing mechanism that is built around a core conception of full-time attendance at an educational institution. Finally, student aid programs for postsecondary vocational

14. National Center for Education Statistics (1989, pp. 324 and 219).

education overlap considerably with training programs operated by the Department of Labor as well as with other vocational programs operated in the Department of Education, some of them within schools and some in other kinds of institutions. For instance, in addition to regular student aid, in the 1989–90 academic year the federal government spent over $4 billion through the Job Training Partnership Act for the vocational training of disadvantaged youth and adults, and the Education Department spent over a billion dollars more on vocational education programs. The lack of integration among these rather substantial efforts is a serious issue.

One can distinguish two broad reforms that would improve the current, awkward hybrid of collegiate and vocational support. One would be to draw a sharp distinction between degree-oriented collegiate instruction and short-term vocational instruction, establishing separate programs and funding sources for each. There would plainly be some difficulty about defining the two programs, but definitions based on program content and duration could presumably be made workable. Some version of traditional student aid would then continue to apply to collegiate programs, while short-term vocational training would be supported by an alternative mechanism, perhaps overseen by the Department of Labor rather than the Department of Education. An advantage of the latter arrangement is that it would permit greater integration with other training programs currently financed through the Labor Department. One possible version for the mechanism would be financing short-term vocational training through contracts with the providers, who would be screened and paid directly by the federal government rather than through portable payments to students.

A sharply different reform proposal would obliterate the distinction between collegiate and other forms of educational investment altogether. Henry Levin has proposed that existing financial aid programs be replaced by a single federal entitlement program, which would provide every young person with an account that could be drawn on throughout his or her lifetime.[15] Levin has suggested that differences in family circumstances could be allowed for by apportioning the account differently between grants and loans, with a greater share of grants in the accounts of disadvantaged citizens. These accounts would replace not only existing federal student aid but also the state operating

15. Levin (1983).

subsidies to public colleges and universities. Students would be free to invest in postsecondary education at any point in their lives and to distribute their investments among traditional colleges, other sorts of training institutes, on-the-job training experiences offered by employers and unions, and others. The federal government would require the supported programs to provide accurate information about what they offer, but would only minimally screen program content and objectives.

Levin's program responds to the issues raised by the financing of adult students as well as those raised by nontraditional forms of education. The program's neutrality among alternative forms of investment has some attractive features, including that of substantially equalizing the subsidies available to students pursuing different kinds of educational alternatives. It also has at least two potential disadvantages (aside from considerable worries about its political feasibility). One is that this entitlement approach may substantially underestimate the regulatory challenge for the federal government. Experience with the Pell program suggests that the government has had considerable difficulty in screening even a relatively limited set of educational providers supported by a relatively straightforward financing scheme. In extending support over a lifetime and extending the range of potential providers, these problems would multiply. The second concern is that this system would make student choice in the market the sole governance for higher education; that is because all government support for undergraduate education would be channeled through students. Although there are good arguments for increasing the role of the market in the governance of the college and university system, there may also be some reasons unique to higher education for also preserving some significant, non-market support.[16] In chapter 9 we discuss a proposal that expands the role of the market but stops short of exclusive use of student entitlement support.

Adult and Nontraditional Students

Our current college financing system is based on the presumption that parents bear the greatest responsibility for college costs, but plainly

16. See Bowen (1974) for arguments that the institutional autonomy of higher education is bolstered by support from a mixture of sources. See Gutmann (1987, chap. 7) for arguments that public tuition should be higher than it is currently, but should not be raised to cover the full cost of attendance.

there are some important groups whose financing needs are not tied to their parents' circumstances. This is the group of "independent" or "emancipated" students, most of whom are adults no longer living at home.

The relative importance of this group grew substantially during the 1970s and 1980s. In 1975, about 37 percent of all students (including graduate and professional students) were over 25 years of age. By 1986 this percentage had grown to 43 percent.[17] Much of this change can be explained by demographics—enrollment rates by age have in fact been fairly steady, with most of the "action" occurring because baby boomers have moved into the later stages of postsecondary education.[18]

Federal support for the education of adult students has grown much more rapidly than their representation in the college-going population. As we reported in table 2-5, the proportion of Pell recipients classified as independent students grew from 30 percent in the 1975–76 academic year to 58 percent in 1987–88. Although data are not available for every year, in the years for which comparative award levels for dependent and independent students are available, the average awards for dependent and independent students are similar, with some evidence that awards going to independent students are growing relative to those to dependent students, suggesting that a rapidly increasing share of Pell funding has migrated from dependent to independent students.[19] Although good data are not available about the distribution of federally guaranteed loans, it is reasonable to believe that a similar shift toward independent students has occurred for these as well.

This general shift toward independent students is related to the shift of federal support toward vocational education, since adult students are substantially more likely than others to be enrolled in vocational programs, typically at community colleges or at proprietary vocational institutions. According to the Department of Education, in 1982, 70 percent of postsecondary students aged 16 to 24 were engaged in academic programs, while only 33 percent of those aged over 24 were

17. National Center for Education Statistics (1989, p. 169).

18. See O'Keefe (1985) and Hodgkinson (1985).

19. College Board (1986, pp. 8–9) reports data for the 1979–80 and 1983–84 academic years. The figures for dependent and independent students, respectively, in 1984 dollars follow—1979–80, $1,174 and $1,172; 1983–84, $1,015 and $1,023. According to the NPSAS survey, the average federal grant award to independent undergraduates in 1986–87 was $1,842 (in 1986 dollars), while the average federal grant to dependent undergraduates was $1,448.

so engaged.[20] Since apparently something close to half of the academic enrollment of these older students was in postbaccalaureate graduate or professional programs, the evidence is that only about one-sixth of students over age 25 are involved in degree-oriented undergraduate programs.[21]

As seen in chapter 2, with the slow growth in federal student aid in the 1980s, the effect of this shift toward adult and vocational enrollment has been to reduce real levels of federal grant support for dependent students during this period. In fact, the real level of Pell support for dependent students went from $1.9 billion in the 1980–81 academic year to $1.6 billion in 1987–88 (both values are expressed in 1988 constant dollars)—a decrease of 16 percent. Meanwhile, support for independent students rose from $1.3 billion to $2.2 billion.[22] Plainly, these facts raise a difficult dilemma. The nation has permitted the range of students and programs receiving federal student aid to grow, but has not supported commensurate increases in federal funding. Choices must be made, either to expand funding levels to serve a broader range of students, to set priorities among the groups, or to continue spreading available resources more thinly across a growing array of eligible students and programs.

Unfortunately, our knowledge of the relative private and social returns to educational investments for adult and "college-age" students is meager, as is our knowledge of the socioeconomic characteristics of adult student-aid recipients. Most of the available information about the social and economic backgrounds of adult students derives from information provided in their financial aid applications. In some ways, however, this information may provide a misleading picture of their economic status. The existing needs-analysis system for independent students is a modified version of the parental assessment system for dependent students. It is driven by the *current* income and assets of

20. Nonacademic programs include both vocational programs and "continuing education"—noncredit courses for job improvement, personal development, or social and recreational purposes. See National Center for Education Statistics (1989, p. 318).

21. In 1987, 1.4 million students aged 25 and over were enrolled in graduate or professional degree programs out of a total of 1.7 million students in such programs. In 1982, 3.0 million students in that age group were enrolled in academic programs. Over the 1982–87 period, graduate and professional enrollments (which are predominantly from this age group) grew by less than 10 percent. See National Center for Education Statistics (1989, pp. 170 and 179).

22. Calculated from data in College Board (1989b, pp. 7 and 12). This calculation assumes that average Pell grants to dependent and independent students are equal. As noted earlier, this probably understates the shift in funding that has occurred.

the student (and spouse). Moreover, under the current congressional methodology, married students and students with dependent children are "taxed" on the same basis as the parents of dependent students, but unmarried independent students without dependents are taxed more heavily.[23]

As with parents, no systematic attempt is made to gather information on the long-term economic status of the applicant. This omission is, however, even more important in the case of independent students than of parents of dependents. An adult going to college (or graduate school) full time will most likely have a low *current* income, simply because he or she will not usually work full time while in school. The existing system partly compensates for this by assessing payment capacity from the actual income earned in the year the student applies for assistance (the so-called "base-year income") rather than on the estimated income for the following year, during which aid will be awarded ("award-year income").[24] However, this distinction between base year and award year is only meaningful in the first year of attendance, since after that the applicant will display a student income profile.

It would be valuable to know more about the longer-term income profiles of independent students. For example, what percentage of older adults who receive Pell grants would have been eligible for such grants had they applied at an age when they were still dependent on their parents? This is a relevant question to the extent that a major purpose of student aid is to offset inequalities in opportunity resulting from inequalities in parental income. Similarly, we do not know what the typical economic condition of adult students was over, say, the three years before their decision to return to school. This might be a more meaningful index of their ability to pay than the measures that are collected under the existing needs-analysis system.

Although it is difficult to judge the *average* economic status of independent Pell grant recipients relative to their dependent counterparts, it seems safe to say that needs analysis for this group is less reliable, simply because the decision to attend school itself has such a sharp impact on short-term measured income. Students with very differ-

23. College Scholarship Service (1990b, pp. 1–6).
24. A report from the College Scholarship Service states that in the fall of 1989, average award-year earnings for undergraduates were 26 percent less than average base-year earnings— $8,765 versus $11,769. No doubt there is a great deal of variation hidden in these averages. See College Scholarship Service (1990b, p. 7).

ent underlying capacities to pay are likely to appear quite similar under the needs-analysis system for independent students.

It is probably not the case that "tinkering" with the independent-student needs analysis can make it more reliable. The information needed to determine a student's long-term capacity to pay is considerable. It is interesting to note that Henry Levin's proposal for "lifetime entitlements" offers a radical response to this difficulty. Levin would determine a person's eligibility for lifetime assistance at a fixed point in time, roughly at his or her graduation from high school. This makes the link between grant assistance and parental income clear, and makes it independent of when a person chooses to attend school. This has obvious attractions from the standpoint of "horizontal equity," or treating people in similar circumstances similarly.

Levin's proposal also has some drawbacks. Fixing lifetime eligibility at a single point in time overlooks the fact that personal circumstances can change over time. On the one hand, a person's parents may strike it rich when she is twenty-five, but because they were poor when she was seventeen, she will still qualify for generous assistance. On the other hand, a person with affluent parents may suffer adversity in later life, making him a plausible candidate for grant assistance. A different kind of drawback is the long time lag between the implementation of a lifetime system and its relevance for the existing generation of adults. At a minimum, policymakers who wished to introduce such a system would need to devise a transitional program for the current adult population, whose entitlement levels had not been assessed at the time they graduated from high school.

A different approach to putting independent and dependent students on the same footing would be to expect both groups to finance their educations themselves, through loans. Levin's entitlement approach treats adults and "children" symmetrically by linking the awards to both groups to parental income at some fixed point in time. Proposals for financing education through student loans alone—often with an income contingency feature—introduce a comparable symmetry by making parental resources irrelevant to all students. Because this sort of proposal will receive further discussion in the following chapter, we will only note here that the equity of such a proposal depends critically on the assumption that most parents, including affluent ones, will indeed refrain from financing their children's education, and will expect their children to do it themselves through loans. If affluent parents continue to pay for their children's education while lower-income students must borrow heavily, considerable inequalities of educational opportunity can be expected to persist.

A final approach to the finance of education for independent students would be to develop a separate financing system for their education. It would, however, seem both implausible and offensive to base such a distinction purely on age or independent economic status: it is an obvious violation of the principles of equal treatment to deny a person access to a federal program simply because of age or personal characteristics not relevant to the program's purposes. However, as we noted earlier, there is a very high correlation between age and enrollment in nondegree programs, which are often vocational in nature. We estimate that over 80 percent of undergraduate students aged over 25 fall into this category.[25] Thus, if it seemed advisable for other reasons to reorganize the federal support for vocational and continuing education into a separate program, a byproduct of that decision would be to place most support for independent undergraduates into this program as well.

Merit Aid

Much of the history of student aid policy in private higher education has been a struggle between the desire of individual institutions to attract strong students through the offer of "merit scholarships" and an attempt by the financial aid community, for a variety of motives, to get institutions to award aid strictly on the basis of financial need. Federal efforts to support undergraduate education have been much more consistently targeted at need than at merit, but proposals periodically surface that have the federal government offering additional scholarship support to exceptionally able undergraduates. Currently, only one small-scale program of federal merit aid exists, and its impact is largely symbolic. It is, however, an important question whether educational quality, and perhaps too the principle of rewarding excellence, would be served by expanded efforts at offering merit aid, either through institutions or through the federal government.

Discussion of this issue is often marred by a failure to appreciate how much "reward for merit" already exists in the current higher

25. See the earlier discussion in this section.

education system. Although the most selective colleges and universities are generally the most determined to limit the role of merit scholarships in their aid-award decisions, the overall effect of a selective admissions system is to provide substantial rewards for merit. The most highly selective colleges and universities, which are typically the most expensive and the best endowed, confer a highly prized reward when they grant admission to meritorious students. Even those who do not qualify for any financial aid in effect receive a substantial subsidy for the educational resources they are provided, since a substantial fraction of the costs at these institutions is borne by the endowment.

In most state higher education systems, a somewhat analogous mechanism operates. In general, the "flagship" institutions of the state system have more rigorous admission standards and higher per-student subsidies than other institutions in the state system. Thus, even without any explicit merit aid, access to these wealthier institutions confers a benefit on those students whose high school credentials warrant admission. In addition, an increasing number of states do offer explicit merit scholarships to state institutions in an attempt to keep some of their strongest students in their home state for college.

Added to this is the fact that a great many private institutions offer merit scholarships, and an even larger number adjust the mix of grant and loan funds in response to a needy student's academic merit. According to a recent survey of private institutions, 23 percent of institution-based aid in the 1987–88 academic year was non-need-based merit aid, up from 15 percent in 1970–71.[26]

In light of these facts, it is not apparent what social purpose would be served by an expanded role for merit scholarships in federal aid policy. In fact, federal aid is essentially the only component of the undergraduate financing system that does not respond strongly to merit.

What about the role of merit scholarships in the financial aid policies of individual institutions, especially private institutions, where the bulk of institutionally provided financial aid originates? There is a general, and powerful, argument in favor of the "needs" principle in awarding institution-based student aid. That argument is essentially that the competition between institutions to attract "good" students through merit aid dissipates institutional resources without providing any benefits to

---

26. National Institute of Independent Colleges and Universities (1990).

the system as a whole. A collective agreement among colleges and universities to stick to need-based aid avoids what amounts to a "zero-sum" competition for highly qualified students. Moreover, it can be argued that since these students already benefit from their superior talent and training, and from access to exceptionally good higher education, they are not "short-changed" by practices that restrict merit awards.

Although this argument has considerable force, and in our view provides a rationale for schools to cooperate in limiting merit aid competition, there are other considerations, too. First, since the wealthiest institutions tend to enroll the most "meritorious" students, and to provide the largest subsidies owing to their large endowments, an agreement to restrict all aid to students with demonstrated need may give an advantage to the "elite" institutions. If, for example, Harvard University and Boston College agree that the net cost facing a particular student should be $6,000, Harvard has an enormous competitive advantage in recruiting that student because it can offer many thousands more in educational subsidy from its endowment.

A further strand of the merit aid argument considers the consequent distribution of talented students across institutions.[27] There is some evidence that highly talented students, at least in the right circumstances, confer educational benefits on their fellow students. There is also some, more tenuous, evidence that these learning externalities are larger for less bright students.[28] To the extent that this relationship holds, there are net educational benefits from distributing exceptionally bright students across a range of colleges and universities, rather than concentrating them in the "best" institutions.

Merit scholarships offered by nonelite institutions may, then, have a social purpose. It may be useful to offer a merit scholarship to a student at a less prestigious institution as a "payment" for an educational service that student can perform: namely, conferring educational benefits on other students at this less prestigious institution. A regime, then, in which the most prestigious institutions abjure merit scholarships but accept the use of such scholarships by less prestigious institutions may have some significant educational benefits.

If this bit of analysis is persuasive, it justifies some limited amount

27. For a more extended treatment of this problem, see McPherson and Schapiro (1990).
28. The evidence, such as it is, is reviewed in McPherson and Schapiro (1990).

of merit scholarship competition at the institutional level.[29] But note that the same benefits could not be achieved by a federal merit scholarship program. If such scholarships were made portable across institutions, and were awarded to the most highly qualified students, almost all of the award winners would wind up at the most prestigious institutions.[30] The ironic effect is that it would become even more difficult for less prestigious institutions to attract some of these students to their campuses.

Conclusion

This survey of financial aid issues points to a number of difficulties and problems in the way student support is distributed in the United States. Yet these problems, although real enough, should not be allowed to obscure the fact that this system has some genuine strengths. The basic idea of apportioning substantial amounts of student support, and especially federal student aid, according to family ability to pay is a sound one, and for the core cases that the system was designed to treat—dependent students at traditional colleges and universities—it works reasonably well. Many of the problems arise in trying to stretch principles tailored for this relatively simple group of students to cover other groups. Thus, while vocational and adult students could be handled better, it is important to recognize that any financing system will produce awkward and difficult cases, a reality that should not condemn the whole system. Finally, we believe that it is possible for the system to improve relations between the finance of public and private colleges and universities. However, as we argue in chapter 9, the way to accomplish this is not by shunning the principle of need-based aid, but by embracing it more vigorously.

29. A number of qualifications and other dimensions of the problem are examined at length in McPherson and Schapiro (1990).

30. This is exactly what happens with competitive federal graduate fellowships, such as the National Science Foundation awards.

VIII

Higher Education as an Investment

FOR BOTH society and the individual, higher education should be viewed as an investment in search of future returns.[1] Indeed, when such an investment occurs, it involves a considerable opportunity cost to public and private parties, in terms of direct expenditure and forgone earnings, while the returns to undergraduate education accrue over a lifetime.[2] This investment principle is an important one, and many issues in student finance revolve around it. Two fundamental ones are whether the returns to investment in higher education exceed the costs, both from the point of view of the individual and from that of society, and whether capital markets function adequately in the financing of such "human capital" investments. In this chapter, we intend to explore these issues, with the following two sections briefly reviewing the evidence on the returns to college investment and the issue of capital market imperfections in American higher education.

This chapter also considers the workings and limitations of the Stafford program of guaranteed student loans—the principal vehicle for combating capital market imperfections—as well as some possible alternatives to it. Following this, the perspective shifts from student borrowing to the role that parents play in the financing of college. In the United States, parents have traditionally held a central role in the financing of their children's higher education; in this chapter we con-

1. Plainly, education has a significant consumption value for some students: they may value the time spent at school independent of any future monetary payoff. It is also true that part of the investment return accrues in nonmonetary terms—through improved enjoyment of leisure, better performance of civic duties, and the like. Although these latter returns are difficult to measure, in principle they should be seen as part of the investment return from higher education.

2. The time pattern of educational returns is difficult to measure, but most studies focusing on questions of human capital indicate that the earnings differentials attained by college-educated workers persist throughout their working lives, and suggest that these differences should be attributed to educational differences.

153

sider some of the financial and educational considerations that arise from such cross-generational subsidies compared with those that arise from putting each generation "on its own nickel" by having students rely on loans to finance college.

A final set of issues concerns the relation between student aid and the labor market. Much of the return to higher education comes in the form of higher wages (and presumably higher productivity) for college-educated workers. Thus we ask how does and how should the financing system for higher education influence the occupational choices of workers. We consider in that section the degree to which student aid might help correct labor market imbalances, as well as the issue of whether high debt burdens discourage students from pursuing certain kinds of socially valuable careers.

Returns to Higher Education

Since the advent in about 1960 of the "human capital" revolution in economics, a great many studies have attempted to estimate the returns to education in general and to college education in particular. In method, these studies have tried first to identify that portion of people's earnings that can be attributed to the differences in their levels of schooling, and then to relate the resulting stream of earnings differentials to the costs of education: in other words, they compare the costs of education to the future earnings that an education creates. Such calculations of social returns compare pretax rather than post-tax earnings differentials, and consider the social rather than the individual costs of schooling.[3] A number of controversies bedevil these efforts, perhaps the most persistent being the difficulty of distinguishing between earnings differentials that are caused by schooling and those that result from the preexisting characteristics of people with different amounts of schooling.

Despite these difficulties, a wide variety of studies, using different data and sundry statistical techniques, have arrived at fairly similar estimates of the private rates of return to college: at reasonable discount rates, private returns exceed the costs of the investment and social

3. In principle, the calculation of both social and individual returns should include nonmoney returns to the individual. In addition, the calculation of social return should include "external" benefits (or costs) that an individual with added schooling provides to (or inflicts on) others. In practice, these dimensions have largely eluded measurement.

returns are usually found to equal or exceed private returns.[4] Although returns have generally been found to exceed costs, the size of the net return to college investments has apparently fluctuated in recent decades. A simple measure of how well the labor market rewards college educations is the wage of college graduates relative to that of high school graduates for people of comparable age or labor market experience. As Richard Freeman demonstrated in his influential book *The Overeducated American*, the gap between college and high school wages grew quite rapidly in the 1960s and then shrank fairly dramatically in the 1970s.

Larry Katz and Kevin Murphy have recently provided a comprehensive analysis of these college–high school wage differentials for the post–World War II period.[5] Their analysis shows that, in the strong labor market of the 1960s, wages for both high school and college graduates grew substantially, but the growth in real college wages (25.5 percent from 1963 to 1971) outpaced that for high school graduates (16.7 percent over the same period). From 1971 to 1979, however, the real wages of high school graduates held steady (rising by only 1.4 percent), while the real wages of college graduates fell by 10.1 percent. Over the 1979–87 period this pattern again reversed, with high school graduate wages falling by 4.0 percent in real terms while college graduate wages grew by 7.7 percent. The 1980s experience is even more dramatic when attention is focused on new entrants into the labor

4. For valuable surveys of the literature on private returns, see Leslie and Brinkman (1988) and Psacharopoulos (1981). Leslie and Brinkman (1988, p. 47) review forty-three studies that yield a mean estimate of the private rate of return of approximately 12 percent. In comparing estimates for cohorts graduating in different years between 1939 and 1980, they find mean estimates of returns varying between 11 and 17 percent.

Judgments about the social rate of return relative to the private rate are sensitive to theoretical views about how labor markets work and why education confers a labor market advantage. According to the familiar human capital view, education makes workers more productive, and all the gains to individual workers are therefore part of the social gain from investments in education. According to the "screening" view, part of the gain an individual obtains from education is certification of preexisting talents. According to the latter view, the difference between earnings of more and less educated workers is no longer a good measure of their productivity differences. It can be shown that on a variety of plausible assumptions, these earnings differences will overestimate the social returns to education. On the other hand, most estimates of social return omit positive externalities from the calculation, which leads to underestimates of the social rate of return. Leslie and Brinkman (1988, chap. 5) find that thirty studies of the social rate of return yield a mean return of approximately 12 percent. See also Bowen (1977) for a discussion of the nature and the magnitude of higher education's social benefits.

5. Katz and Murphy (1990).

market—those who had been in the labor market fewer than six years. High school graduates in that category experienced a real wage drop of 19.8 percent from 1979 to 1987, while new entrants to the college graduate labor market experienced a 10.8 percent rise. Thus, the net effect for the 1980s has been a dramatic increase in the returns to an investment in college.[6] These data underline the importance of a college education in providing more equal employment opportunity in today's labor market.

Much less is known about the *comparative* returns to alternative postsecondary investments. It would plainly be of enormous value both for public policy and for guiding the investment decisions of college students if reliable information were available about the relative impact, both on future earnings and on nonmonetary effects of college, of attending, say, a liberal arts college versus a university, a public versus a private institution, a small versus a large institution. One obstacle to learning more about this has been the paucity of information about where an individual attended school and about his or her subsequent experiences. Such data are, however, becoming available as a result of longitudinal studies begun by the Department of Education in the 1970s.[7] Unfortunately, there is still little systematic quantitative evidence to help guide personal or social choice among postsecondary alternatives.

Capital Market Imperfections

But why, if the returns to college consistently exceed the costs to individuals, is public intervention in the market necessary at all? At most, it might seem, governments need only ensure that prospective students are well informed about the available returns, to make sure that students rationally invest their own resources. Yet, this argument neglects a familiar but important feature of markets for "human capital":

6. In general, the experiences of people with less than four years of college fall between those of high school and college graduates, according to the Katz and Murphy data.

7. For a preliminary attempt to use these data, in particular the National Longitudinal Survey of the High School Class of 1972, see James and others (1989). The authors find that institutional selectivity and size have positive effects on earnings, and that students from private universities in the East earn more than others. Expenditures per student do not seem to matter. However, these institutional characteristics are relatively unimportant compared with variables that depend largely on student choice, such as grade point average, major, and number of math credits.

it is extremely difficult to "collateralize" debt incurred to invest in human capital; unlike a car or a business, an education cannot be repossessed by a bank in the event of default.

This feature of capital markets alone provides a basic reason for government involvement in higher-education finance, independent of any external social benefits that may accrue from such investments and distinct as well from equity arguments for subsidizing the educational investments of the disadvantaged. In the absence of adequate private credit markets, those who do not have access to sufficient personal resources will fail to invest in a college education that would more than pay for itself; as a result, some socially worthwhile investments will not be undertaken, and the productivity of the economy as a whole will suffer. Although this is an efficiency rather than an equity argument, it is worth noting that these obstacles to investment will be more severe for students from lower-income families, since those from more affluent families may be able to rely on their parents' assets to gain credit.[8]

A related problem touching on the "collateral" issue is that of pooling the risks associated with educational investments. Although on average the returns to education are high enough to warrant investment, there is evidence of considerable variation around those average returns.[9] A person who incurred substantial debt but got a poor return on his or her education would have a tough time repaying the loans. For business debt, devices such as limited liability allow a group of individuals to share the cost of an investment as well as the resulting gain or loss. But, for the same reasons that it is difficult for banks to "repossess" an education, it is difficult for a person to sell "equity" shares in his or her educational investment, and thereby mete out the risk.[10]

Thus, government intervention can bolster the market for college credit in two ways. First, governments can step in either directly to provide loans on fair market terms or indirectly to provide insurance to private lenders for educational debt they accept. In the United States, both these options exist at the federal level, through the relatively small Perkins loan program, which provides institutions with the capital to lend to students, and through the much larger set of guaranteed loan programs, which provide federal guarantees of unsecured loans to students and parents. These programs deal with the problem of access

8. For an illuminating analytical treatment of this issue, see Becker (1975, app.).
9. See Thurow (1975, chap. 3).
10. For an early and illuminating discussion, see Friedman (1962).

to credit markets, but not directly with the issue of risk sharing for educational investors. It has been repeatedly proposed that governments might help to pool the risk of educational investments by providing, or encouraging the market to provide, so-called income-contingent loans, whose repayments are dependent on the borrower's future income. Such a program would provide borrowers with a form of insurance, or risk sharing, for their educational investments: those whose investments were unusually successful would provide excess payments that compensated for the losses incurred on less successful students. The federal government currently funds a small pilot program that has some income-contingency features, but such loans have not been offered by the federal government on a large scale.

It is crucial to note that none of these "market-perfecting" efforts need involve direct government subsidy of the interest rates paid by borrowers. Borrowers can be charged a market interest rate, matched to the rate on other investments with comparable repayment periods. Even the expected costs of default could be built into an insurance fee charged to all borrowers. Income-contingent loan plans could also be designed to break even, by matching the "premiums" charged to exceptionally successful borrowers to the anticipated losses from others.[11]

Actual federal loan programs have tended to combine "guarantee" or "insurance" components with subsidy components. This has been a source of confusion in policy analysis, since a family's "need" for credit may be quite different from its "need" for subsidies. The main purpose of federal subsidies, presumably, is to redress inequalities in opportunity that result from differences in family resources. But even families with assets adequate to finance college may lack liquidity and encounter difficulties in converting their future earning power into debt. Thus a

11. Income-contingent loans give rise to several problems, which are also common to insurance programs. The most important problem is "adverse selection": unless students are compelled to participate in the program, those students who are relatively more likely to succeed in the labor market will choose not to participate, thus reducing the funds available to compensate for the lower repayments made by less successful borrowers. To allow for this, the plan would need to raise the repayment rate for everyone, causing still more defections. There may also be worries about "moral hazard": knowing that their repayment is contingent on income, some graduates may choose relatively nonremunerative careers, or even withdraw from the labor market. On the other hand, some low-paying careers are judged to have high social value—for example, teaching and various forms of public service. It is sometimes argued that an advantage of income-contingent loans is that it would make such career choices more feasible than regular loan finance does. For a recent discussion of these and other problems, see Byron (1989) and Reischauer (1989).

program that combines subsidies and loan guarantees into one "loan" is almost bound to either deny credit to some people who need it (to avoid giving them subsidies) or to provide subsidies to some people who do not need them (to give them access to credit). Most likely, such programs will do some of each. A further problem is that the subsidy elements in existing loan programs—especially the guaranteed student loan program—have been difficult to measure, making it hard for Congress and policy analysts to weigh this use of subsidy dollars against alternatives.

Market Incentives and Federal Loan Guarantees: An Economic Appraisal

The choice about what share of educational costs should be borne by students through debt compared with the share that should be borne by parents, governments, and others is a broad social issue that should turn largely on judgments about the educational and social consequences of different financing regimes. At any given level of loan finance, however, the question of how loans are best provided turns largely on more technical questions about the performance of lending institutions and the proper role for the federal government in supporting the credit market. In this section, we consider some features of the major federal loan program—the Stafford, or guaranteed student loan, program—and some possible alternatives from an economic point of view.[12]

As just noted, the predominant form of federal credit assistance to students is that of guarantees of private loans arranged with banks. The use of the private banking system makes the Stafford loan program appear to be a market-driven, and presumably efficient, way to help students finance college. The reality, as we see it, is somewhat different. Although the GSL program makes heavy use of the nation's private credit system, the private banks in the program act not as sellers in a

---

12. Currently the federal government uses a guarantee mechanism not only to finance subsidized loans to undergraduate and graduate students through the Stafford loan program, but also to finance less heavily subsidized loans both to parents of undergraduates through the parental loans to undergraduate students (PLUS) program and to independent students through the supplemental loans to students (SLS) program. Stafford loans are by the far the largest of these programs, and they are the focus of our discussion.

market system but as administrative agents in a centralized bureaucracy. Indeed, while the government appears to be intervening in the GSL program only modestly, to perfect the private credit markets, it is in fact subsidizing participants in the system substantially, and in ways that seriously impede congressional assessment of the costs of the program.

This is not to say that there is an easy alternative solution. In some respects, the conflict between guaranteeing loans and relying on market principles runs fairly deep. Thus, while the difficulties of properly accounting for the costs of the loan subsidies in the federal budget are not intrinsically difficult, they would call for reform of the whole of the federal credit accounting system, not just of the GSL program. This is an issue that we return to later in this chapter.

The Uses of Private Credit Markets

Governmental regulation sharply constrains the role of the market in shaping the terms of guaranteed student loans. The real advantages of relying on private credit markets involve the incentives these markets create for borrowers and lenders alike to find the most favorable possible deal and to see to its enforcement. This is actually a special case of the more general economic insight that the greatest strength of markets lies in their ability to coordinate decentralized information and to cope with uncertainty.[13]

The informational problems that credit markets need to solve are particularly subtle ones. Consider first the problem of determining what sort of contract best meets borrowers' and lenders' needs. Borrowers will want to weigh the prospective returns on an investment. They will also weigh their own attitudes about risk and about future repayment commitments. They may compare the advantages, for example, of paying off a loan faster, in larger chunks, against those of stretching out the loan period and making smaller payments. Lenders will want to consider how long they want to tie up their funds, and will also need to judge the creditworthiness of the borrower. Both borrowers and lenders will need to think about the future course of interest rates and inflation and consider different ways of defining the loan contract (as

13. Helpful treatments of these issues include Arrow (1974), Williamson (1975), and Hayek (1945).

in the relatively novel device of variable rates) in order to mete out the risks of those developments.

When loan markets are working well, we have some reason to think that borrowers and lenders work out agreements that serve their respective interests. Indeed, because not all borrowers and lenders share the same interests and perceptions, markets often generate a menu of alternative loan agreements. Automobile purchasers can "shop around" for their preferred combination of interest rate, down payment, and repayment period; home buyers can accept some risk of rising interest rates by arranging a variable-rate mortgage or can "pay" a bank to assume that risk by agreeing to a higher rate for a fixed-rate mortgage.

Lenders in a competitive market also have incentives to innovate. Some of their ideas will catch on; others will fail to find a market and fade away. This innovation allows the market to respond actively to changes in economic conditions and in borrowers' and lenders' needs. The resulting pattern of agreements contains information that is itself valuable to economists and policymakers: if markets are competitive, the difference between the interest rates on variable- and fixed-rate mortgages of equal length approximates the banks' best estimate of future inflation risk; the difference between the interest rates on two-year and four-year car loans shows what consumers (at the margin) are willing to pay for stretched-out payments and what lenders (at the margin) require to keep their funds tied up longer; and the difference between what banks charge on a loan of a certain type and what banks must pay to acquire those loan funds measures the administrative cost to the bank of that kind of loan.

Market incentives are also useful in dealing with the problem of enforcing contracts; enforcement, too, is at root an informational problem. To collect a loan, the lender must stay informed about where the borrower is and about his or her capacity to repay. Market arrangements urge lenders to spend the resources necessary to track borrowers and to take further steps to enforce the agreements when necessary.[14]

Nevertheless, it is important not to idealize the workings of real credit markets in any of the above respects. To the extent that markets are imperfect or slow to adjust, interest rates may not accurately reflect the valuations of different lenders and borrowers. Also, private credit

14. Collection problems also lead lenders to screen borrowers in advance, either denying loans to poor credit risks or charging high-risk borrowers a higher interest rate. This latter feature of credit markets is one that loan guarantee programs aim to eliminate.

markets will not always do a good job of introducing desirable financial innovations. Individual banks may feel that such experiments are too risky, especially because much of the gain from successful innovation can be captured by other banks that imitate the leader but that assume much less risk. Moreover, some experiments, in order to work, may have to be tried on a scale too large for a single bank. For example, some observers have suggested that, in the 1930s, government leadership was essential to the development of the long-term, self-amortizing home mortgage.[15]

Finally, the incentives that private markets create to enforce loan contracts have their drawbacks. Lenders will try to minimize their default risks not only by spending resources to collect loans but also by prescreening borrowers to weed out poor risks. In general, this has the desirable social function of directing investment toward the most promising projects. But for student loans—which must be secured by the personal credit of the borrower or cosigners, rather than by tangible investment assets—the incentive to minimize default risk will lead private lenders to screen loans on the basis of personal attributes that we believe should be ignored, such as family income or even the racial and social backgrounds of applicants.

Markets and the Guaranteed Student Loan

The trick, obviously, to improving the credit market for students, is to preserve or even strengthen the desirable features of the current market arrangements while eliminating or attenuating the undesirable ones. Yet, while a seemingly simple task, it is not an easy one.

How well has the GSL program managed to improve the working of private credit markets while neutralizing their undesirable features? We can identify four key criteria for measuring its success:

1. Making credit widely available without regard to family background and personal characteristics.

2. Using competitive forces to shape loan contracts and to establish costs to borrowers and rates of return to lenders.

3. Encouraging experimentation and financial innovation.

4. Creating incentives for discouraging default and for pursuing the collection of defaulted loans.

15. Bosworth, Carron, and Rhyne (1987).

On criterion 1, it is clear that after a shaky start, the GSL program is now a resounding success.[16] Banks across the country make student loans, and students from all kinds of institutions and a wide variety of backgrounds participate in the program. Indeed, the often-expressed concern that students from disadvantaged backgrounds may be participating too heavily in the program is backhanded testimony to this achievement.

Performance on criterion 2 is much less satisfactory. As noted, the main features of the loan agreement—length of repayment period, repayment schedules, fixed versus adjustable rates, and so on—are determined by the legislation authorizing the program. Over the years, there has been considerable discussion about whether these arrangements are the most desirable ones for educational loans, and some changes have been introduced (notably, arrangements to consolidate and refinance loans).[17] But the fact is that the highly centralized stipulation of the loan terms has meant that we have not learned much about the relative desirability of other arrangements.

The same is true about testing the costs to borrowers and the rates of return to lenders in the marketplace. The government has got itself into the remarkable situation of fixing both the rate of interest paid by borrowers and the gross returns received by lenders in this program. Even more remarkable, it pegs the interest rate to a fixed rate—protecting borrowers against future interest rate rises—and pegs the rate of return to lenders to a variable rate–insuring them, too, against losses from rising interest rates. Given the pegging of both these rates, there simply is no primary market for student loans.[18]

Are the returns, then, that banks are guaranteed in the GSL program excessive? Debate on this question has been endless, and some attempts have been made to answer it by closely examining the accounts of the banks and of the Student Loan Marketing Association ("Sallie Mae"). But without a market test, it is nearly impossible to answer the question satisfactorily. How much is it worth to banks, for example, to have a

16. For a discussion of the history of the GSL program in this context, see McPherson (1989).

17. The most commonly discussed feature has been the length of the repayment period, or the term. Many economists have argued that the term of the loans should be matched to the lifetime of the investment, which in the case of higher education is typically thirty years or more. Others have suggested, partly on the basis of survey results, that students would be reluctant to borrow on such long terms. If one could observe in the market the relative success of loans of different terms, surely some useful evidence on this question would emerge.

18. Resale of loans in the secondary market does provide some market test of the costs.

long-term asset that is fully insured against interest rate fluctuations? We simply do not know.

Regarding criterion 3, it should be clear that the GSL apparatus has not encouraged experimentation and innovation in the development of student loan instruments. Banks have very little leeway in writing student loan contracts. State guarantee agencies, even ones that originate loans, are bound by the same restrictions. Federal involvement in the program is limited to writing the checks and keeping the necessary records. There is no locus of innovation at the federal level. Any innovation, then, occurs nationally and uniformly when the law is periodically reauthorized. In general, this means that alternative loan instruments will be available in the market sequentially rather than simultaneously, with the result that one does not learn much about how borrowers and lenders judge the alternatives. It is true that Congress can legislate an experiment, as it has done recently with income-contingent repayments. But congressional experiments are infrequent, and the accompanying legislative parameters sharply reduce their flexibility.

Finally, there is criterion 4—the questions of reducing default and of collecting loans. The GSL program is the only major federal credit program that offers a 100 percent guarantee to lenders.[19] Because banks and state guarantee agencies are largely insured against losses from default, they have no real market incentive to identify bad risks or to collect loans. Moreover, federal rules severely restrict the ability of lenders to reject loans. The government has sought to cope with these problems by creating regulatory and bureaucratic procedures—lenders must follow a well-defined series of steps known as "due diligence" requirements. These requirements are modeled on the procedures that banks themselves use in collecting uninsured loans, but some lenders seem to exercise their diligence more "duly" than others when collecting GSLs. This lack of diligence results from the lenders' incentive under the 100 percent GSL guarantee to be procedurally correct rather than to be effective; lenders do not profit from collecting a loan from the borrower rather than from the government. Similarly, lenders have no financial incentive at the outset of the process to reject high-risk loans. This important function of private credit markets is blocked by the

19. Guarantee agencies whose default rates exceed certain percentages receive a reduced rate of guarantee on their loans. In the worst case, the guarantee may fall as low as 80 percent.

fundamental aim of the GSL program: creating access to loans for people who would not normally get them.

In sum, the GSL program appears to make extensive use of the attributes of private credit markets. But in reality, the program has succeeded in largely destroying all market incentives involved. Indeed, the main achievement of the program—the widespread availability of guaranteed student loans without regard to the creditworthiness of the borrower—has been accomplished chiefly through the circumvention of the market.

Could the loan program do better? After all, the whole point of the GSL program has been to reform a credit market that failed to provide student loans. Thus, at least some of the undesirable loss of market incentives must be considered an inescapable by-product of the effort to correct that market failure. Yet the loss of market incentives in the present program suggests two possible directions for further reform. First, we consider a market-oriented reform of the GSL program, aimed at reintroducing market incentives to the present program without undoing the good work of making credit widely available. Second, we could simply accept the fact that the GSL program is not market oriented and consider ways of replacing the role of the private credit system with a government entity.

Market-Oriented Reform of the GSL Program

In principle, three steps could be taken to bring market incentives into the existing GSL program. None is without its drawbacks. The first market-oriented reform would be to stop pegging the returns to both sides of the GSL market, borrowers and lenders. Suppose the federal government simply offered to pay banks a certain annual fee for each GSL loan they carried, proportioned to the size of the loan, and then allowed banks to negotiate the loan's interest rate with the student borrowers directly. The annual fee might be fixed at some average value of the "special allowance," the federal contribution to the costs of the loans that banks have been receiving in recent years, or it might be allowed to vary with some selected interest rate, such as the rate on three-month Treasury bills, as the existing special allowance does. To the degree that the banking industry is competitive, any excess of the new fee over the costs to the banks of making the loans would be reflected in lower interest rates to student borrowers. Or, to put it another way, the sum of the interest paid by students and the allowance paid by the federal government should accurately reflect the costs to the banks of making these loans.

A related, but perhaps preferable, approach would be for the government to continue pegging the interest rate paid by students, and invite banks to bid for federal contracts to provide student loans. In effect, the government could use an auction mechanism to set the "special allowance" at a competitive level. Competition among banks would lead them to bid at levels that reflected the costs of providing that service. (Large banks would be likely to make contracts with the federal government and to subcontract with smaller banks for making loans.) Again, the sum of student interest payments and federal contract fees should reflect the costs to the banks of making these loans.

The most obvious drawback of these first market-oriented proposals is the possibility that anticompetitive behavior by banks would allow them to earn an excess return in this environment. However, it can be said in the banks' favor, first, that the consumer banking industry, especially in the present era of deregulation, is marked by active competition, and, second, that anticompetitive behavior, if it exists, will still infect the present attempts to calculate the special allowances that banks now receive.

Another difficulty is that if banks are allowed to negotiate interest rates with customers, individual banks might discriminate in the prices they charge to different classes of students. In addition, banks in different localities might wind up charging different interest rates. Avoidance of these kinds of discrimination is an important advantage of the second alternative—that of letting the fee paid to banks, rather than the interest rate charged to students, be set by the market.

A second market-oriented innovation would be to expand the range of student loan instruments that the federal government would guarantee. This step would be a natural accompaniment to the other competitive, market-oriented changes in the loan program already discussed and should help ameliorate the lack of financial innovation in the current program's loan structure. As we have suggested, banks have little incentive to innovate if the returns they can earn are rigidly fixed, as they now are. Of course, federal regulation would place some limits on the range of instruments the government was willing to guarantee.

Some federal entity may be needed to make discretionary judgments about the range of agreements—maturities, interest rates, fixed versus variable interest rates, and so on—that the government would guarantee. Some of this discretionary authority could also be delegated to state guarantee agencies.

An obstacle to introducing such flexibility into student loan arrangements is that GSLs provide subsidies to borrowers as well as guarantees to lenders. Some of the rigidity in the present system–involving regulations on loan eligibility, maximum loan amounts, and interest rates–is designed to ration these subsidies fairly.[20] Thus, while it might still be possible to scrutinize alternative loan arrangements in order to guard against an adverse effect on the pattern of subsidies, this practice will make the introduction of new innovative loan arrangements much more complicated.

A final possible reform for the GSL system would give lenders financial incentives to discourage default and to collect loans. The obvious way to do that is to make lenders and state guarantee agencies bear a significant share of the default costs. This could be accomplished in a relatively straightforward way by guaranteeing less than 100 percent of the value of a student loan. In fact, under current regulations, guarantee agencies with excessively high rates of default are required to accept less-than-full guarantees. But to influence lender behavior significantly, the government would have to reduce the insurance substantially. Other federal guarantors, such as the Federal Housing Administration and the Small Business Administration, have usually operated on 90 percent guarantees. At these rates, a bank that succeeded in collecting an extra dollar of student loan repayment would earn only ten cents, which may not be enough to induce much collection effort.

There is a risk, however, to lowering the guarantee percentage further. If the percentage were reduced more substantially, the underlying market imperfections, which the guarantee aimed to overcome, would reemerge. Some banks would become reluctant to make student loans, and all banks would become more cautious about making loans

---

20. For example, as long as interest rates to borrowers are pegged below market rates, it is in the interest of borrowers to repay their loans as slowly as possible. To the degree that the annual "special allowance" to lenders exceeds the cost to them of extending credit, lenders will also have an incentive to extend the repayment period. Thus, as long as these arrangements hold, one cannot leave the length of the repayment period to be negotiated between borrower and lender.

to students who were perceived as higher risks. There is an inescapable trade-off between giving banks an incentive to make risky loans and giving them an incentive to keep defaults down.

Alternatives to Guaranteed Student Loans

The capacities of the existing GSL program to draw on the strengths of private credit markets are limited, and there are obstacles to improving the program. It is natural to consider, then, whether a program that actually made less use of private credit markets might be able to "mimic" some of the desirable features of private markets more successfully than the present hybrid program does.

The most plausible structural alternative to reforming the GSL program would be to create a new federal lending entity—a student loan "bank"—that might use colleges and the existing state guarantee agencies as intermediaries in providing loans. Could such an institution disseminate loans widely, establish costs and rates of return efficiently, encourage financial innovation, and discourage default?

With regard to the dissemination of loans, colleges and other postsecondary institutions as agents of a federal student loan bank would need to generate the loans, a task that is now assigned to banks. The main obstacle here would be that some schools might be unwilling to participate. Presumably, colleges would need to be compensated for their administrative costs in handling the loans, as banks are now, and that would raise some of the same problems about establishing appropriate ways of measuring those costs. But if colleges served only to generate loans and were required neither to raise capital nor to service loans, establishing fair compensation rates would be considerably simpler than it is under the current program. What about the cost of the federal entity itself? Would the cost be any easier to identify than it is now? And what are the actual costs of raising loan capital and of providing lender services? Presumably, a federal student loan bank would raise money as a federal borrower and would contract with private agencies for loan servicing and collection.

The accounting practices under which the federal government operated until late 1990 tended to exaggerate the federal costs of direct lending activity and to understate the costs of federal loan guarantees.[21]

21. These practices counted the full amount of direct loans as a budgetary cost, not recognizing the future revenue stream resulting from repayment of direct loans. At the same time, they failed to recognize the future costs of loan guarantees, in the form of interest subsidies and default costs.

The budget agreement of the fall of 1990 reformed these practices, bringing the accounted costs of these two forms of federal support for loans closer to their true economic costs.

Accounting obscurities aside, the main difficulty in assessing the cost of the GSL program is that it is hard to know whether the current special allowance payments reflect the minimum cost to the banking system of providing these services—that is, of knowing whether part of the GSL subsidy is going to bank profits rather than to reduced loan costs to borrowers. Whether this ambiguity would persist under a federalized system would depend principally on whether the federal bank could purchase loan servicing and collection services from the private sector at minimum cost and whether hidden subsidies were passed along in those payments. Competitive bidding for servicing and collection should minimize these worries. A federal bank could probably do about as well as the GSL program could as long as banks were forced to compete with one another in providing services to the federal government.

Perhaps a federal bank could do better as a source of financial innovation. There would be no obvious need to bind a federal bank to a narrowly defined loan instrument; the bank could be permitted by statute to experiment with different maturities, repayment patterns, and the like—even with income-contingent repayment. Other federal lending agencies, notably the Federal Housing Administration, have played an analogous role in other credit markets.

The substantial subsidies in federal student loans complicate this picture. If a federal loan bank were obligated to run on an unsubsidized basis, the ground rules for its experiments would be fairly clear; they would be largely determined by the market. The bank, however, would not be run this way. Thus, the problem of rationing the total federal subsidy provided through student loans and distributing it fairly among borrowers hinders the creation of a menu of loan alternatives and makes innovation more difficult.

Last is the question of defaults on and collections of loans. The main advantage a federal entity might have here is that it could make the deployment of federal resources more nearly a first rather than a last resort in collecting delinquent loans. As we have said, the basic decision to federally guarantee student loans removes the market incentive to collect those loans and makes collection a federal problem. The corresponding advantage is that the federal government has powerful resources to draw on, if it decides to use them, in collecting loans. Even short of the "ultimate weapon" of using the Internal Revenue Service (IRS) as a collection agency, the federal government is positioned to locate and track borrowers and to use its powers to enforce collection agreements. Although it makes sense to decentralize the creation of student loans—either through the banking system, as in the GSL program, or through educational institutions, as a federal loan bank might do—it has never seemed to make much sense to decentralize the collection of these loans, particularly in an environment where the borrowers are highly mobile and the lenders have no financial incentive to collect.

Income-Contingent Loans

A federal loan bank might go further and develop a more radical alternative to traditional student loans through the provision of income-contingent loans. On a national scale, a full-blown income-contingent system is administratively ambitious: each person's repayment in any given year would be a function of his or her income in that year and those earnings records would need to be systematically checked. By far the easiest way to do this is to involve either the IRS or the social security system in both record keeping and loan collecting. Modern computers probably make this a fairly straightforward matter, but IRS officials have consistently expressed worries about an erosion of the core functions of the IRS, which the officials believe would undermine citizens' inclination to comply with IRS regulations by complicating them with functions that are essentially independent of tax collection. Instead of using the IRS, there is perhaps a better argument for income-contingent repayment's being seen as a kind of social insurance program, which logically leads to such loans' being integrated with the social security system's already extensive tracking, collection, and payment apparatus.

As we discussed earlier and pursue further in the following section, the appeal of income-contingent loans is probably greatest when they are considered not as alternatives to existing federal loan programs but as substitutes for other, more specific elements of the current financing system, including state operating subsidies to institutions and parental contributions to college support. Simply as a replacement for existing programs, however, income-contingency seems less appealing. There is little evidence that existing levels of debt burden are insupportable for most students. Moreover, the apparatus surrounding income-contingency would be complex and unfamiliar for students. Much of the purpose of income-contingency could be accomplished in a simpler fashion if the federal government simply included "lower-income insurance" as a provision of the existing federally guaranteed or direct loans.[22] The government would simply assure borrowers that their repayments would not exceed a stipulated fraction of their family income, and that if they did, the government would pay the difference, upon application from the student.[23] The costs to the government of these payments could either be included as a worthwhile subsidy element in the program or be incorporated into an insurance fee charged in advance to all borrowers.[24]

Federal Credit Reform and the GSL Program

One persistent source of difficulty in operating the GSL program, as we have suggested, is combining loan insurance (or guarantees) and subsidy elements in the same loan. These problems have been compounded by the fact that until recently the subsidy elements were poorly measured in the federal budget and were also measured differently depending on details of the lending program.[25] Federal credit accounting was reformed under the Budget Enforcement Act passed in November 1990, and the reformed practices are much more satisfactory.[26] Since the reformed procedures are quite new, and could conceivably be rescinded in future legislation, it may be worth explaining the difficulties caused by the earlier procedures.

Under the procedures in place before the Budget Enforcement Act, Congress appropriated funds every year to meet the current costs of

22. See Hauptman (1989).

23. Under the existing GSL regulations, borrowers can defer their payment obligations for up to two years if they are unemployed. The proposal described in the text is analogous to, but broader and more systematic than, this provision.

24. This form of subsidy would be much better targeted and much easier to measure than the existing subsidies, which benefit all borrowers.

25. Loan insurance and loan guarantees are sometimes distinguished on the basis that the former refers to protection against default, the cost of which is fully reflected in the cost of the loan, whereas the latter means that a guaranteeing entity assumes the costs of defaults. In that sense, a guarantee already contains a subsidy. The discussion in the text focuses on subsidies additional to those implicit in the guarantee.

26. For a summary of the relevant part of the legislation, see *Congressional Quarterly Weekly Reports*, December 1, 1990, p. 4036.

outstanding loans; the costs consisted mainly of special-allowance and in-school interest payments to banks and of the purchases of defaulted loans. Thus, in any year, budget outlays almost entirely reflected the cost of *past* loan activity. New loans, although they embodied a contractual commitment to spend money in the future, cost very little on the budget in the year they were generated under these procedures.

If, instead, loans were provided by a federal entity, the procedures in place before the reform would count the full amount of the new loans as expenditures on the federal budget, and repayment of outstanding debt would be recorded as a federal receipt. Consequently, the budgetary cost in any year would be the amount of new loan volume created less the amount of debt repayments—a figure that would show high net costs, or expenditures, in the early years of a new lending program. Because no repayment occurs in the first year of a loan, the net cost on the budget of a new loan under these procedures is equal to the amount lent, just as if it were a grant.

Obviously, neither of these treatments is economically correct. The true cost to the federal government of guaranteeing a new loan is the value of the stream of subsidy payments to which the government is committing itself (taking into account the probability of default), discounted at an appropriate interest rate, perhaps the cost of funds to the federal government. For a loan made by a federal entity directly, the cost is the discounted value of the difference between the initial loan outlay and the expected stream of repayments. For loans subsidized to the same degree, the costs should be equal between the two loan systems.

The credit accounting procedures introduced with the Budget Enforcement Act mandate this economically correct treatment for all federally generated or guaranteed loans. The essential idea is to require Congress, at the time a new loan is created, to appropriate a "loss reserve" that reflects a fair estimate of the cost to the federal government of the loan over its lifetime.[27] Such appropriations are required for loans generated under most federal credit programs beginning with fiscal year 1992, but an exception has been provided for entitlement credit programs, including the guaranteed student loan program. However, although an appropriation is not required for student loans, beginning

27. For an extensive treatment, see Bosworth, Carron, and Rhyne (1987).

in fiscal 1992 the new accounting rules will be used to determine the budgetary impact of student loan activity.

Adopting these reformed procedures should have several important advantages for developing desirable policy toward federal student loans. First, it puts loan guarantees, direct lending, and the use of a federal loan bank on an equal footing. Although each of these loan systems is roughly comparable in real costs when interest charges to students are kept roughly equal, under the old procedures Congress was presented with an optical illusion that made loan guarantees appear much cheaper in the short run, Congress's usual time horizon.

It may be worth noting that the confusion between accounting and economic costs has contributed to the idea that it is economically more desirable to have banks raise money for student loans in private capital markets than to have the federal government do it more directly—either through direct federal lending or through a federal loan bank. Yet, the real cost of funds devoted to student loans is the amount of alternative investment activity that those funds could otherwise support. In an economy with well-developed financial markets, those costs will be essentially the same whether funds are raised through private sources or through government borrowing. Whether these borrowings show up on the government's books is a matter of accounting practice, not of economics.

A second advantage of proper accounting is to give Congress a much more accurate picture of the relative costs of loans and other forms of federal subsidy to higher education. Before these reforms, it was impossible for Congress to achieve substantial short-run budget savings by curtailing GSLs, whereas it is easy to do so by curtailing Pell grants. At the same time, the expanded role for GSLs, which this asymmetry has encouraged, has tended to contribute to higher outlays in future years as the subsidy costs of old loans come onto the budget. The higher outlays in turn have added to the pressure to limit grant expenditures. It seems likely that these quirks of accounting played a role in Congress's decisions to increase the loan limits in the GSL program much more than the maxima in the Pell program.

Finally, a clear accounting of the subsidies in the GSL program might encourage Congress to rethink the practice of combining loan guarantees and subsidy elements in a single loan program. We have noted that this "hybridization" causes Congress to limit access to credit to those who need subsidies, even though these groups need not be the same. At the same time, the need to ration subsidies is one source of the rigidity in the loan agreements the federal government will guarantee. This rigidity discourages the search for more suitable instruments for financing college education. Indeed, even if the government continues to combine subsidies and guarantees in a single credit program, better accounting of the subsidies might make it easier for Congress to extend guarantees to a wider range of loan instruments, provided that their subsidies were of comparable value.

College Finance as an Intergenerational Compact

As the costs as well as the benefits of a college education come to be spread over a larger fraction of people's lifetimes, the value of thinking about college finance in explicitly intergenerational terms is likely to become more apparent. Just as it is profitable to view issues about pensions and social security, federal budget deficits, and long-term health care for the elderly through the lens of appropriate burden-sharing among successive generations, so it is likely to be profitable to bring the same sort of framework to bear on higher-education finance.

In the same way that the politics and economics of social security are shaped by the fact that today's workers will be tomorrow's recipients of social security, so our thinking about college finance should be shaped by the knowledge that every parent was once a "college-age" young person and most current college-age people will someday be parents. In principle, a stable system of family finance of higher education could be run by having each generation either pay for its own education or pay for that of its successor generation (or some combination)—just as publicly funded pensions can be financed on a "pay-as-you-go" basis or by having each generation save for its own future pensions.[28]

The symmetry between own-generation and next-generation payment holds so long as each generation agrees to perpetuate the chain. Any one generation can get off scot-free by accepting its parents'

28. See the classic article by Samuelson (1958) for an exposition of the basic model of intergenerational pension finance. For further discussion of the application to higher education, see McPherson and Skinner (1986).

largesse and refusing to help its own children. This possibility raises two important points. The first is that if, at any time, a society wishes to move in the direction of having its children pay for more of their own education through student loans—as there is some reason to think our society is beginning to do—there is an awkward problem of managing the transition fairly.

The second point is that, in any society that wants to sustain a particular pattern of intergenerational transfers, the decisions about making those transfers cannot be viewed as purely private ones. Governmental coercion need not be involved, but social norms and expectations must encourage members of each generation to uphold the terms of the intergenerational compact. This point applies not only to higher-education finance but to a wide range of intergenerational financial issues, including care for the elderly and management of governmental budget deficits.

Currently, some important policy alternatives for the financing of undergraduate education are connected to intergenerational options. As already noted, there has been recurrent interest in the idea of placing the burden of college costs directly on students through the use of income-contingent loans. In the eyes of some analysts, such loans might substitute for some or all of the current financing mechanisms, including parental subsidies to students, government operating support of institutions, and federal student aid.[29] An alternative to greater student responsibility is offered by those who would prefer to see the parental role strengthened through some device that would encourage parental saving for college. In this vein, several proposals have been advanced for permitting parents to prepay their children's tuition, or to purchase special college savings instruments that would provide tax advantages.

Debate about such reforms is often absorbed in technical details about how to make the programs work, sometimes at the expense of focusing on the fundamental question of whether each generation should pay for itself or should pay for its successor. What are the merits of own-generation versus cross-generation finance in higher education: how should we compare the advantages of having students pay for their own education to those of having each generation of parents pay for its children's education? Brought down to the level of the individual, this

29. See Reischauer (1989) and Byron (1989).

can be expressed in the form of two questions: would you prefer to pay for your own or for your children's education? And, *when* in your life would you prefer to pay?

Clearly, shifting the "hot potato" of college finance does not make it disappear. Part of the current interest in encouraging parents to save for college rests on the belief that their doing so will help relieve young people of the burden of paying back student loans. This is a myopic view: the students' future debt burden is relieved only at the expense of loading that same generation with an obligation to save for *its* children's education. Similarly, shifting the burden forward to students through loan finance relieves the present generation of parents, but no future generation. Freed of an obligation to pay for their children's education, future generations will instead be paying off their own debts.

From a macroeconomic or a financial point of view, there is little to distinguish these different temporal patterns of payment as long as they are reliably fulfilled and managed in institutionally feasible ways. Notice, in particular, that from the point of view of the economy as a whole, the "saving" inherent in paying for college is in fact the human capital investment that occurs when a student attends college; whether this is paid for by consumption reduction before the event (as it would be if parents save) or afterward (through the repayment of student loans) is a second-order consideration macroeconomically.

However, the social and educational consequences of these alternative financing mechanisms may be anything but second-order considerations. From an educational point of view, a key question is how young people's choices about where to attend school and their orientation toward the educational programs in which they enroll may be influenced by how that education is financed. Although there may be a general argument that the prime beneficiary of an investment should bear its costs and decide the disposition of those funds, this is not so clear in the case of higher education.

Decisions about college investments are made by young, inexperienced people who must weigh choices, the consequences of which they know very little about. Under existing arrangements, a significant fraction of educational costs, especially for students from upper- and upper-middle-income families who attend private institutions, is financed by "grants" from parents to students. For other families, a significant fraction of costs is borne by grants from government to students. A financing environment in which students are not immediately responsible for the cost may give them more freedom to experiment with new ideas and to develop a taste for learning for its own sake.

From this perspective, a shift in the payment burden toward greater student responsibility might cause these young people to make their choices about college and future occupation on narrow economic grounds. This is, in fact, a worry expressed by some observers about even the current regime, where borrowing for most undergraduates covers only a modest fraction of college costs. Part of the alarm about "rising debt burdens" is that these burdens will push young people further into a "careerist" orientation. As we explain below, while no one has yet succeeded in detecting such an effect, at least at the undergraduate level, existing debt burdens are rather modest. It does seem reasonable, therefore, to be concerned that a dramatic shift away from parental and governmental responsibility for financing college might have substantial, and possibly adverse, consequences for young people's educational choices. On balance, a reasonable argument can be made for a system that, like our present one, includes a limited component of student financial responsibility with a substantial component of parental responsibility for those who can afford to pay.

Parental Saving

To the degree that a strong parental role in student finance is seen as socially desirable, there may even be some justification for governmental incentives to encourage parents to contribute to their children's education. It can even be argued that the existing student aid system actually discourages parental saving for college, because those parents who have accumulated savings are assessed as having a greater ability to pay than others. As a result, their children may not be eligible for as much student aid as if their parents had saved less.

In an earlier study, one of the authors of this book collaborated on an effort to assess the quantitative importance of these saving disincentives under existing needs-analysis systems.[30] Two of that study's conclusions deserve emphasis. First, there is little reason to suspect that the Pell program, the principal federal grant program, produces significant saving disincentives: the implicit marginal tax rates on savings in that

30. Case and McPherson (1986).

program are low, and the targeted population does not have high enough incomes to save much anyway. Thus, if there are policy issues raised by saving disincentives, they apply much more to institutions' use of funds in need-based student aid than to federal grant awards. Second, the study further concluded that, given reasonable estimates of the magnitude of individual responses to saving disincentives, it is unlikely that the effect of the needs-analysis system on saving behavior is quantitatively important. Indeed, it is even possible that, for some families, student aid may increase saving by bringing otherwise unattainable targets within reach.

The effect on families' judgments about the *fairness* of the system may, however, be more important, since a relatively small number of upper-middle-income families, whose children attend expensive schools, could conceivably receive considerable aid by following a deliberate policy of not saving for college. Several reforms might help ameliorate this inequity. One step would be to use information on parents' occupation and work history to impute a "savings expectation" for all families. Under such a reform, a family that "should" have been able to save, but elected not to, might remain eligible for unsubsidized loans but would not receive grant aid.[31] A second reform would be to revise the principles of needs analysis so that parents, even needy parents, are expected to pay more if their children attend a more expensive school. In principle, under the existing needs-analysis methodology, a family that qualifies for aid pays the same no matter where the child goes to school. In other words, parents need make no additional effort to improve their children's college opportunities: there is no saving incentive. An incentive analysis does show, however, that even a modest expectation of payment at the margin has substantial effects on restoring the incentive to save among parents who are eligible for aid.[32]

31. The main difficulty with this proposal is that of getting sufficiently good information on which to base a reasonable savings expectation. Mistakes in inferring past earnings would introduce inequities of their own. Whether these inequities would be worse than those of the present system depends on how reliably information on current occupation and a limited amount of information on work history can be used to infer savings opportunities in the past.

32. In practice, as we have shown in earlier chapters, even aid-eligible families do pay more for attendance at more expensive schools. The current needs-analysis system, however, tends to obscure that fact and thus to blunt incentives to save. For further discussion of these and other policy alternatives, see Case and McPherson (1986), including the accompanying technical report.

Rather than, or in addition to, reforming needs analysis to reduce saving disincentives, there has been increasing interest in providing direct governmental subsidies to parental saving for college. Most such proposals, both at the state and federal levels, have involved providing some form of federal tax preference for saving that is devoted to college expenditure.[33] Although, in principle, a concern for strengthening the "intergenerational compact" might justify some form of subsidy, there are serious difficulties in developing an attractive public policy for this purpose. First, important general considerations argue against using the tax system to subsidize preferred activities. Such subsidies are harder to account for in the federal budget than are direct expenditures, and therefore are less likely to be carefully traded off against alternatives. Moreover, tax subsidies, especially when they take the form of deductions from taxable income rather than tax credit, tend to provide the majority of their benefits to relatively upper-income people, who face higher marginal tax rates. (This exacerbates the general problem that programs to subsidize saving tend to subsidize upper-income people, since they are much more likely to save than are lower-income people.) Thus, if there is to be significant federal subsidy for college saving, it would be much better in the form of a direct spending program than in a tax subsidy.[34] A second general problem with programs to encourage saving for particular purposes is that it is hard to make them effective at the margin. People with substantial assets can often simply "earmark" a portion of those assets for the intended purpose, thus taking advantage of the subsidy without adding at all to their net saving. Finally, any program, including nontax-oriented ones, that reduces the cost of investing in higher education at the margin will encourage people to spend more of their resources on higher education and will therefore tend to some degree to encourage them to save for it. On balance, it

33. Beginning in 1990, families with annual income below $60,000 ($40,000 for single parents) can purchase EE savings bonds and avoid all federal income tax on the proceeds if the bonds are used to fund certain college expenses. The benefit is phased out for families with incomes above that level and disappears entirely at $90,000 for couples and $55,000 for single parents. See Sullivan (1990, pp. 18–39). State programs often involve conferring a federal tax benefit by making bonds available that are not subject to federal tax; to be eligible for the tax benefit, families would have to earmark the bonds for college saving. See McGuinness and Paulson (1990).

34. For example, special accounts could be set up under which families would have their contributions to a college saving fund matched by federal dollars, perhaps at a declining rate with income.

seems much more sensible to support directly those higher-education activities that seem worthy of subsidy than to support them through indirect saving incentives.

Student Aid and the Labor Market

Concerns about how various financing mechanisms of undergraduate education could affect the labor market have several important dimensions. First, it is possible to use student aid policy to "fine-tune" labor market responses by providing added incentives to attract students to "shortage" areas of the economy, or by creating disincentives for students to enroll in subject areas of labor market surplus. A second issue, which is easily confused with the first, is that of designing student aid policies that will correct long-term or structural defects in the labor market—specifically a concern that some socially valuable occupations are "underpaid." Closely related to this second issue is a concern that debt finance of higher education imposes such onerous repayment obligations on students as to cause them to place too much weight on future income in developing their career goals. Finally, the large fraction of federal support that is currently absorbed in short-term vocational training raises some special issues about the value and effectiveness of this training.

Fine-tuning the Labor Market

Although concerns about labor market shortages and surpluses have been an important consideration in federal policies toward postgraduate education, they have been a rather secondary consideration in the policies toward undergraduate education. For the most part, the federal philosophy toward student assistance has been that postsecondary educational investments are socially worthwhile regardless of the field of concentration and that the choice of occupational goals should be left to students and their families.

Some student aid efforts, however, have been partly rationalized by a goal of redirecting students' occupational plans to those areas of temporary labor market shortage. The loan-forgiveness provisions of the original National Defense Education Act (NDEA), for example, were aimed at increasing the nation's supply of teachers for the baby boom period. Current concerns about encouraging students to pursue graduate study in anticipation of a shortage of college teachers in the late 1990s are similar. Some European countries have much more extensive programs to anticipate labor market needs, and control students' educational plans accordingly.

Both economic theory of and economic experience with fine-tuning at the postgraduate level suggest that there are a number of obstacles to managing labor markets in this way.[35] First, the government must be able to forecast labor demand far enough in advance to intervene effectively: there is a considerable lag between undergraduate choice of major and eventual labor market outcomes. Second, in targeting the supply of new workers to a shortage area, these programs overlook the possible reallocation of experienced workers who may be qualified to work in the shortage field. For example, as the market for elementary and secondary schoolteachers has improved in recent years, the majority of persons entering the teacher market are not newly minted teachers but reentrants, who had withdrawn during the downturn of the 1970s. Finally, the government needs to find forms of student aid that reliably induce students to pursue the "right" career. Since the choice of undergraduate major is not strongly determinative of eventual career destination, simply rewarding students for preparing in a certain area is likely to prove inadequate. Even loan-forgiveness programs, like the NDEA program of the 1960s, appear to have had little lasting effect on career choice.[36]

The obvious alternative to incentive-laden financial aid programs is to allow the labor market to direct students and others into shortage areas. There is considerable evidence that students do respond to changes in relative rewards when choosing their occupational goals, although generally with a lag.[37] Such marketwide incentives have the advantage of working on experienced workers as well as new trainees. Moreover, governments might be able to reduce the lags in student response by disseminating reliable information on future labor market trends.

35. For a compelling critique of federal efforts to manage postgraduate educational choices in this way, see Freeman and Breneman (1974).

36. See Arfin (1986).

37. Freeman (1971) and Murnane and Olsen (1989) show that such relative rewards influence the supply of labor to the teaching profession.

Subsidizing "Underpaid" Occupations

A different matter is the attempt to use student aid to attract students into labor market areas that are in "permanent" shortage, presumably because the social value of these occupations exceeds their market rewards. The obvious question here is why these occupations are underpaid: for example, a natural response to an inadequate supply of qualified teachers would simply be to pay teachers better.[38] This solution is certainly one that policymakers should consider: it is a rather straightforward way to improve supply conditions.[39]

Yet, at times, there may be serious political or institutional obstacles to such direct intervention. In those cases, the offering of subsidized education to those preparing for such socially valued careers deserves consideration. Probably the longest lasting and most effective such program at the undergraduate level is the Reserve Officer Training Corps. ROTC offers to pay undergraduate tuition in exchange for participation in some military training during college and a binding commitment to serve in the military after college. A study of this and other similar programs concluded that this "service-payback" model is more effective than alternatives such as loan forgiveness or scholarships, which simply reward the pursuit of a certain course of study.[40] In addition, income-contingent loans, as noted earlier, also make the choice of a relatively low-paying profession easier for students.

Debt Burden and Occupational Choice

While there is relatively little enthusiasm for using more federal student aid to direct students toward particular professions, there is substantially more interest in addressing the somewhat more diffuse problem of avoiding a financing regime that actively discourages students from pursuing low-paying but socially rewarding professions.

38. Murnane and Olsen (1989) present evidence that more able teachers (as measured by test scores) are more likely to leave the teaching profession in favor of better paid alternatives than are others.

39. It is worth noting that policies which subsidize the preparation of people to enter "underserved" occupations tend to suppress wages in those professions by adding to the supply. Thus they tend to sustain the underlying condition that leads to the policy in the first place, and they tend to shift the costs of employment from the employers to those who provide the subsidies.

40. Arfin (1986).

The clearest model of such concern is again at the postgraduate level. Students pursuing medical or legal education sometimes incur quite substantial debt. Their willingness to do so reflects the relatively high salaries doctors and lawyers can expect to receive. Yet some career paths, even those associated with a medical or legal education, are much less rewarding financially, although they are at least as valuable socially in the eyes of most observers. Medical research, rural medical service, legal aid work, and work in public defenders' or prosecutors' offices are examples. The chronic shortage of professionals in these relatively low-paying alternatives might be explained in a number of ways, but one obvious concern is that high-debt burdens compel doctors and lawyers to pursue "conventional" careers in order to repay their debts. Some prominent professional schools have recently instituted programs that forgive some or all of the debt incurred by students who pursue lower-paying or public-service-oriented careers.

Does a similar problem exist for career choice at the undergraduate level? The answer turns partly on how widespread high-debt levels are, or are likely to become, and partly on the influence debt has on career choice. Perhaps the most commonly voiced worry is that students are discouraged from pursuing academic graduate study by fear of adding to the already substantial debt burdens they carry after completing undergraduate work.

In assessing these concerns, it is important not to exaggerate the degree of *undergraduate* indebtedness. In the 1986–87 academic year, only 23 percent of undergraduates incurred any federal indebtedness. The average amount borrowed for those who did was $2,425 for full-time full-year undergraduates, and $2,121 for all other undergraduates. Thus, an undergraduate who attended four years and borrowed the average amount in every year would wind up borrowing almost $10,000, a substantial sum. However, since in any year more than three-quarters of all undergraduates do not borrow at all, a heavily indebted undergraduate is relatively rare. Further, in the 1986–87 academic year, 30 percent of all federal borrowers were enrolled in programs lasting two years or less, so that for them the accumulated debt burden would be smaller still.

This is not to deny that excessive debt burdens are a problem for some undergraduates. Observers have noted that much of the growth in indebtedness in the 1980s has occurred among the lowest-income students.[41] There is also evidence that default—the most obvious symptom of excessive debt burden—is concentrated in the lower-income population.[42] Default, however, does not seem to result mainly from high levels of indebtedness. Rather, defaults are most common among students who attend postsecondary institutions for only a year or two (often in vocational programs at proprietary institutions or community colleges). These students have relatively low levels of indebtedness, but also tend to have relatively low future earnings.[43]

Several attempts to detect the impact of high undergraduate debt on the behavior of those repaying the debt have found little evidence of an effect. One of the authors of this book recently collaborated on a study of the propensity of students from highly selective colleges and universities to attend graduate school in the arts and sciences; the study found no effects for graduating seniors in the classes of 1982, 1984, and 1989.[44] A survey of studies of the effects of student indebtedness on a variety of personal choices, such as marrying and purchasing homes, reports that few significant effects have been discovered.[45] The same survey notes that two studies, which report a positive correlation between high levels of indebtedness and choice of a high-paying career, fail to control for the likely reverse causation: students who expect to pursue high-paying careers are willing to incur more debt.[46]

Existing studies are by no means definitive. Because borrowing has increased rapidly, historical evidence may not adequately forecast the experience of current students. Note, however, that the study by Schapiro and others included students who graduated as recently as 1989. Moreover, there may be subpopulations—an example might be disadvantaged minority students—where important effects exist but are hard to detect owing to small sample sizes. Still, there seems little reason to believe that indebtedness has a large effect on career choices. Of course, the picture might change sharply if proposals to radically increase the role of debt finance in higher education were enacted. If this occurred,

41. Mortenson (1990) cites data from the Pennsylvania Higher Education Assistance Authority showing that debt levels grew for lower-income families and fell for upper-income families over the 1980s.

42. Mortenson (1990).

43. See Hansen (1987).

44. Schapiro, O'Malley, and Litten (1991).

45. Hansen (1987).

46. Hansen (1987, p. 19).

income-contingent loans would become attractive options because they would tend to reduce the impact on career choice.

Conclusion

Although this survey of issues surrounding investment aspects of student finance has turned up a number of issues on which our empirical knowledge is poor—for example, we know little about the comparative returns to different types of postsecondary education or about the implications for educational choice of parental versus student financing of college expenses—we have arrived at some illuminating analytical insights and some reliable empirical findings concerning higher-education policy. First, consistent findings of positive net private and social returns to higher-education investments suggest that public programs to encourage higher enrollments tend to be economically justified. Since, as we showed in chapter 3, spending that is targeted on lower-income students tends to have the largest enrollment impact, the findings here tend to support targeting of student aid on lower-income students. At the same time, the fact that spending on middle- and upper-middle-income students apparently has little enrollment effect, together with the fact that any plausible program for subsidizing saving would benefit students from the middle class and above, provides a strong argument against public investment in such programs.

We also addressed the following question—should the current mixed system of college finance, which combines elements of public and parental subsidy with elements of student finance through borrowing, be replaced with one that puts the principal burden on students, since they are the main beneficiaries of educational investments? The most theoretically elegant way of doing this would be through a comprehensive federal program of income-contingent loans, a program that has many strengths. We have tried to suggest, however, that the educational consequences of moving away from the present system, in which parental contributions to college costs give parents an influential voice in college choice, in favor of one that puts the burden of payment and the weight of decisions directly on young people, may be serious. In our view, such consequences are more important than the purely financial considerations that weigh on such a choice.

Finally, our analysis of the federal guaranteed student loan program suggests that the inclusion of both credit and subsidy elements in a single package makes it difficult to target the program effectively. Moreover, current federal accounting practices lead Congress to greatly underestimate the real costs of federal guaranteed lending. These concerns about the present lending program figure in our policy proposals, to which we turn in the next, concluding chapter.

IX

Toward Improved Public Policy for Higher-Education Finance

THIS BOOK has aimed to provide the reader with analytical and empirical information about the workings of the financing system for undergraduate higher education in the United States, with a special emphasis on the role of student aid in promoting wide access to college. We have also aimed, in the last two chapters, to review some of the major considerations involved in formulating intelligent policies toward student finance. Although different observers might well use the accumulated evidence to draw different conclusions about the appropriate direction for policy, we believe the evidence paints a revealing picture of the strengths and weaknesses of the existing financing system, and points to at least one conception of a reformed financing system that has substantial merit.

In this chapter we pull together our assessment of the financing system, and present a concrete proposal for reform in the structure of the government's financing of undergraduate education. Our proposal would increase the role of "ability-to-pay" financing of educational costs, by expanding the role of income-tested federal student aid. At the same time, it would reduce the size of the "across-the-board" subsidies that states now provide to public colleges and universities by increasing these institutions' reliance on tuition. This proposal represents, in our view, a desirable goal for long-run structural reform of

This chapter benefited greatly from a series of forums on issues surrounding the reauthorization of the Higher Education Act. The forums were organized by Robert Atwell and Arthur Hauptman. Neither the conveners nor any of the participants in these seminars should be held responsible for the views expressed here.

the financing of undergraduate education. Moreover, the proposal helps point up the consequences of reforms less sweeping than ours.

Strengths and Weaknesses of the Existing Student Finance System

In chapter 1, we identified three broad standards against which the effectiveness of the undergraduate financing system could be judged— those of promoting educational opportunity, safeguarding institutional health and effectiveness, and distributing higher-education costs fairly. With regard to these standards, evidence from other chapters points to some distinctive strengths and weaknesses of the existing system.

Educational Opportunity

We consider under this head both the issue of accessibility for lower-income students and the overall distribution of subsidies by income class.

ACCESS FOR LOWER-INCOME STUDENTS. On the plus side, the combination of state institutional subsidies and federal student aid makes *some* form of postsecondary education financially accessible to a wide range of Americans. Although it would be an exaggeration to claim that the problem of "access" is completely solved, it is important to stress the considerable success of the American system in enabling many students with lower-income backgrounds to continue their education beyond high school.

Yet the existing financing system may be much less successful in providing a *suitable* postsecondary experience for many disadvantaged students. Under existing arrangements, the range of alternatives available to students is sharply constrained by their incomes. As seen in chapter 2, in most states community colleges provide the cheapest and most accessible form of education for lower-income students, a fact that is reflected in their disproportionate representation in these institutions. Our examination of student distribution in chapter 5 shows that while about half of all freshmen are from families with incomes below $40,000, only about one in five freshmen at the "elite" COFHE institutions are from that income group, and slightly less than 40 percent of freshmen at public universities are. The differences are even sharper for more disadvantaged students: the lowest-income students (those with family incomes below $20,000) represent 16 percent of all freshmen, but only 6 percent of COFHE freshmen and 11 percent of public university freshmen. Although the issue of "choice" is often expressed in terms of public versus private alternatives, the opportunity to attend a flagship public university or indeed any four-year public institution is frequently and significantly constrained by income.

The highest-ability students are something of an exception to these generalizations. Evidence indicates that for lower-income students of exceptionally high ability the opportunity to attend a range of institutions is quite broad. Partly because elite private institutions devote substantial resources to financial aid for lower-income, high-ability students, they are about as well represented at those institutions as middle-income and even upper-middle-income students. They are similarly well represented at public flagship universities, presumably owing at least in part to merit scholarships and active recruiting efforts.

DISTRIBUTION OF SUBSIDIES BY INCOME. Evidence on the enrollment effects of student aid suggests that enrollment responds to student aid in a way that is inversely proportional to income; that is, lower-income students are more responsive to student aid than others. Thus, if an objective of student aid is to encourage investment in college, then efficiency in attaining that objective argues for targeting subsidies on lower-income students. This efficiency argument complements the argument that the promotion of equal opportunity requires the targeting of subsidies on lower-income students.

How well does the current system of college finance perform from the standpoint of targeting subsidies on lower-income students? The picture is mixed. On the one hand, the importance of financial need as a criterion in allocating a large portion of student aid introduces a significant measure of income sensitivity into the financing system— even though relatively affluent students may qualify as "needy" at high-priced private institutions. On the other hand, most state funding, which is a quite important component of the overall financing system, is not income sensitive. Indeed, because community colleges are less costly than most public four-year colleges and universities, state subsidies going to students in public higher education tend to be positively related to income—high-income attendees (most of whom enroll at four-year schools) receive, on average, higher subsidies from state operating revenue than do those with lower income (many of whom attend two-year schools). An analysis of the distribution of subsidies from all sources (including federal, state, and institutional) shows that they are only modestly related to income, with somewhat higher subsidies for lower-income students.[1]

Institutional Impacts of the Financing System

Our analysis of the impact of external funding on institutional financial behavior shows that most forms of external support have broad effects on institutional behavior. Thus, for example, increases in federal research support, which might seem closely targeted on a limited range of institutional activities, actually appear to increase an institution's instructional and student aid expenditures and to reduce tuition growth below what it would otherwise be. Increases in federal student aid also induce institutional responses: there is evidence that when federal aid increases, private institutions increase their own provision of aid, while public four-year institutions increase their tuitions. Changes in state and local appropriations for public institutions have substantial effects on instructional spending at those institutions.

An important policy implication of this widespread interdependence of funding and spending activities is that substantial changes in any source of funding for colleges and universities may have significant indirect consequences. A further general implication of this interdependence is that policymakers really need to think about the financing system as a whole when shaping intelligent policies—a point that is reflected in our own long-run reform proposal below.

We can also note some more specific consequences of the existing set of government financing arrangements. As noted in chapter 1, some observers have worried that federal need-based student aid is counterproductive because it induces colleges to raise their prices and overall spending. Our analysis indicates, however, that this potential weakness of federal student aid policy does not exist under current policies. There is no evidence that private institutions whose federal financial aid receipts have grown more rapidly have raised their tuitions faster as a result. In public higher education, we do find such an effect, but the interpretation is different. Since a large fraction of costs at public institutions is borne by state governments, the increases in

1. Lee (1987).

tuition that accompany more rapid increases in federal student aid in that sector are best seen as a set of transfer payments: more federal subsidies for lower-income students result in somewhat smaller state subsidies for upper-income students (whose tuition charges rise) and perhaps somewhat smaller state appropriations for higher education.

Distributive Fairness

As we argued in chapter 1, concerns about fairness in the overall distribution of student aid and other forms of funding for colleges are politically and socially important. We have already discussed the distribution of subsidies by income, which has an important fairness dimension. We want also to consider the strengths and weaknesses of the existing financing system with regard to horizontal equity, access to credit markets, and the reliability and simplicity of the financing system.

HORIZONTAL EQUITY. Are students in equal or comparable circumstances treated similarly? Ensuring horizontal equity is a principal goal of the "needs analysis" on which the distribution of student aid is based. As noted in chapter 8, existing needs-analysis systems are not without difficulties regarding horizontal equity, especially in regard to treatment of saving and other "intertemporal" concerns. Yet the distribution of need-based aid does reflect a conscientious effort to make aid awards responsive to relevant differences in circumstances.

Perhaps a more important source of horizontal inequity in the financing system is the difference in circumstances confronting students in different states. The price of in-state enrollment at public four-year institutions varies considerably across states, ranging in the 1986–87 academic year from a high of $6,357 a year for tuition, room, and board in Vermont to a low of $2,793 in Arkansas.[2] Just as important, the range and quality of public alternatives also vary significantly across states. Many states have extensive community college systems, which provide both geographical and financial access to most students, but some states have much more limited systems. Similarly, student costs of attending an internationally prestigious public flagship university are low for the residents of states that operate such institutions but may be

2. National Center for Education Statistics (1989, table 259, p. 283).

192

KEEPING COLLEGE AFFORDABLE

high for students who can attend such an institution only by enrolling out of state. These differences are relatively more important for students from lower-income families.

READY ACCESS TO CREDIT MARKETS ON FAIR TERMS. As we argued in chapter 8, there are strong reasons why private markets will not make capital available for student loans on terms that reflect the expected returns on investment in education. An effective student aid system should correct this market imperfection by making loans available to students at interest rates that fairly reflect the opportunity cost of this use of funds. The Stafford program of guaranteed student loans aims to do that, but it is hampered in this role by the fact that it combines a substantial interest rate subsidy with access to credit. Access to Stafford loans must then be rationed to ensure fair distribution of the subsidies. This problem is ameliorated to some degree by the availability of unsubsidized loans to parents and to independent students who do not qualify for Stafford loans under the needs test, or who have borrowed all they are eligible for under that program.

RELIABILITY AND SIMPLICITY OF THE FINANCING SYSTEM. An important goal of the student aid system is to provide a stable basis for students to plan effectively and early for postsecondary study. For students to make sensible choices about "precollege" high school curricula, and for families to make realistic financial plans for helping with college expenses, students must be able to form a reasonable judgment about their financial capacity to attend college. Indeed, an important rationale for the development of the basic educational opportunity grant, or BEOG, program in the early 1970s was to provide this sort of reliable foundation for college financing.

Things have not exactly worked out that way. Regarding reliability, there have been considerable fluctuations in the funding of the federal student aid programs. Table 9-1 shows how the maximum grant level in the BEOG (Pell) program, taken as a fraction of average college costs of attendance, has fluctuated over the 1976–88 period, reaching a peak in the 1979–80 academic year at 64 percent of costs and falling by 1987–88 to 38 percent of costs. Beyond the actual fluctuations, which have plainly been substantial, during much of the 1980s students trying to make college plans must have found the headlines about federal policy highly unsettling. For several years running, the Reagan administration launched efforts to cut student aid substantially. Although these efforts were blunted by Congress, they did create the

Table 9-1. *Maximum Pell Grant Award as a Percentage of College Costs, Academic Years 1976–88*

Year	Maximum Pell award (dollars)	Total tuition, room and board (dollars)	Maximum Pell award as percentage of total tuition, room, and board
1976–77	1,400	2,275	61.5
1977–78	1,400	2,411	58.1
1978–79	1,600	2,587	61.8
1979–80	1,800	2,809	64.1
1980–81	1,750	3,101	56.4
1981–82	1,670	3,489	47.9
1982–83	1,800	3,877	46.4
1983–84	1,800	4,167	43.2
1984–85	1,900	4,563	41.6
1985–86[a]	2,100	4,885	43.0
1986–87[a]	2,100	5,206	40.3
1987–88[a]	2,100	5,510	38.1

Sources: Pell grant data are from College Board (1989b, table 8, p. 12). Cost data for all institutions are from National Center for Education Statistics (1989, table 258, p. 281).

a. Figures for 1985–86, 1986–87, and 1987–88 are estimates. Because of revisions in data collection procedures, figures for 1986–87 and 1987–88 are not entirely comparable with those for previous years (board rates are somewhat higher than in earlier years because they reflect a greater number of meals per week).

impression that the future of federal financial aid was uncertain. Indeed, many parents and students probably believed that the actual cuts were more substantial than they really were.

Regarding the goal of simplicity in the financing system, two trends have inhibited it. First, the federal effort has been divided among a number of programs. Besides the Pell grant program and the Stafford guaranteed loan program, undergraduate students may be eligible for any of several campus-based programs, providing grants, direct loans, or work-study support. In addition, a student may be eligible for a combination of different kinds of student aid support from state governments, institutions, and private charitable organizations. The principal mechanism for integrating these different sources of support is the needs-analysis system. For any student receiving federal assistance, the combination of other awards must not exceed the student's "demonstrated need" for financial assistance. Yet, to turn to the second point, needs analysis has itself become more complicated over time. Indeed, the system used in determining Pell eligibility is different from the congressionally mandated system used in awarding other federal as well as nonfederal dollars. As noted in chapter 8, the attempt to ensure horizontal equity in the face of increasingly complicated financial arrangements for parents, and in the face of the "need" for assistance's reaching higher into the income distribution, has compelled the needs-analysis system to inquire more and more deeply into the details of a family's financial status and history.

Goals for Reform in the Finance of Undergraduate Education

This analysis of the strengths and weaknesses of the existing financing system suggests that current arrangements accomplish a lot. Access to at least some form of higher education is widespread, certain components of the financing system respond well to differences in family circumstances, and diverse financing arrangements support a wide variety of types of postsecondary alternatives. Still, there is substantial room for improvement. We suggest that reform be directed toward the following four goals.

— Target the overall pattern of subsidies in the system (not only federal subsidies) more effectively on lower-income students.

— Ensure high quality educational alternatives for lower-income students and expand their range of choice.

— Reduce inequities that may result from state-to-state differences in educational opportunities for less advantaged students.

— Simplify the federal aid system, and make its contribution to overall educational policy goals more comprehensible.

In the following section, we lay out an ambitious proposal for long-run structural reform in the existing federal and state financing systems. The value of the proposal, in our opinion, is that it provides a clear-cut view of the existing system, and that it provides a useful standard for long-run reform. After laying out this proposal for structural change, we describe some incremental steps that are consistent with this longer-run approach.

Federalizing Student Aid for Lower-Income Students

Our proposal is, in a word, to *federalize* the financing of higher education for lower-income students. In doing this, the proposal would also *simplify* the federal effort by concentrating all federal student aid subsidies in a single grant program. Unsubsidized credit would be made available to all students through a federally guaranteed loan program. It may appear that support for lower-income students is already "federalized," since for many students a combination of Pell grants and Stafford loans comes close to covering the direct costs of attendance at a public in-state institution. Notice, however, that "costs" here are costs to students. Much of the operating cost of public institutions is borne by states, so that, in effect, the financing of lower-income students relies on a combination of state and federal support. Since state support is mostly reflected in artificially low tuitions (they are set substantially below cost), the effect of this system, as noted in chapter 7, is that subsidizing lower-income students produces substantial subsidies for all students.

We propose, in effect, a new division of labor between the states and the federal government in providing and paying for higher education. Maximum federal grants to undergraduate students should be set at a level that approximates the costs of *providing* a year's education at a typical public two-year institution, less a student contribution. In the 1985–86 academic year, average educational and general expenditures at public two-year colleges were $4,223; average room and board costs at those schools were $2,479.[3] Given inflation of about 17 percent between the 1985–86 and 1989–90 academic years, this implies a total cost in 1989–90 dollars of about $7,800. For students from the lowest-income families, we would propose that the student contribution should be set quite modestly, at $2,000.[4] Awards to individual students would be limited in two ways: first, no award could exceed the net costs of attendance facing the student at that institution (after taking account of other student aid and the $2,000 student contribution); and second, the award offered to a student would decline with increases in the student's family income. A reasonable schedule might have awards falling with increasing income at a rate that would have a typical family with one child in college become ineligible for a grant when annual income

3. National Center for Education Statistics (1989, pp. 307 and 281). The 1985–86 academic year is the most recent year for which expenditure data are available.

4. Students could meet this contribution through a combination of summer work, term-time work, and loans. It is important to note that under current procedures, a substantial part of the student contribution is expected to be met through student borrowing at subsidized rates. Such subsidized loans would not exist under our plan. Thus, although our student contribution is lower than that typically included in the existing approach, any borrowing included in it would be at market rates.

reachs $45,000—which is roughly the median U.S. income for families headed by parents aged 45–64 (the group most likely to have children in college).[5]

Such a change in federal policy would provide states with a powerful incentive to raise their tuitions to cover a much more substantial percentage of their costs. States that did not do so would be forgoing substantial federal revenue, owing to the rule that awards cannot exceed student cost of attendance. To the extent that states did respond by raising tuition, our proposal would involve a shift in the fiscal responsibility for paying for the education of lower-income students from the states to the federal government.

Our proposed policy change would also federalize the costs of education for lower-income students attending private colleges and universities. Since most such students in nonprofit institutions are already receiving substantial institution-based aid, increased federal aid would substitute for these institutional contributions. Is such a transfer to private institutions justified? Two considerations argue in favor of it. First, a disproportionately large share of lower-income students are enrolled in public institutions.[6] Thus, most of the revenue that private institutions would receive from this program would be from increases in the numbers of lower-income students they enrolled—and these payments should not be seen as transfers. Second, and more fundamentally, there is no reason to think the education that lower-income students receive at private institutions is less valuable than that provided at public institutions; therefore, for those who need subsidies, it is just as productive for society to support their education in private as well as public institutions.

5. This is roughly the income level at which the parental contribution for a family of four with two children, one of whom is in college, would reach $5,800 under the congressional methodology. See College Scholarship Service (1990a, table F-1). This parental contribution, plus a $2,000 student contribution, would equal the $7,800 average cost for a public two-year college that was cited earlier. Obviously, this parameter could be set differently depending on social judgments about subsidy targeting and expectations about appropriate levels of student contributions. We would propose that award levels be sensitive to many of the factors tracked in both the Pell methodology and the congressional methodology for determining ability to pay for college—factors such as assets, number of children in college, and so on. Notice, however, that we do *not* want the award level to be sensitive to the actual tuition level of the institution (excepting the requirement that awards not exceed an institution's costs).

6. According to the American Freshman Survey, in the fall of 1988, 74 percent of all full-time freshmen were enrolled at public institutions, but 80 percent of those with annual family

Generally speaking, then, this new program is in effect a dramatic expansion of the Pell program. We would suggest, in the interests of simplifying the federal effort, that this new program simply replace the existing campus-based programs for direct lending, supplementary educational opportunity grants, and work-study.

Why Enhance the Federal Government's Role?

Why transfer fiscal responsibility for the education of lower-income students from the states to the federal government? At base, we would argue that fairness, equal opportunity, and human capital development—those fundamental concerns underpinning federal student aid— are national concerns whose costs should be borne by the federal government. More specifically, we believe that our proposals would set up desirable incentives regarding the performance of all segments of the higher education system.

Many economists over the years have complained that the low-tuition policies pursued by most states have significant disadvantages.[7] Subsidies tend to be poorly targeted on needy individuals, institutions are insulated from competitive pressures in the provision of educational services to undergraduates, and private institutions are disadvantaged in competing with their public counterparts. The argument about competitive pressures is probably most telling at institutions that serve a predominantly lower-income clientele. Lower-income students typically have had little choice about where to enroll, particularly because they may be financially compelled to live at home. Because of this, it has been argued that states should reduce operating subsidies to public institutions, thus causing tuitions to rise, and should use the resulting savings to provide more need-based aid to their citizens regardless of where they choose to enroll.

Our proposal accepts this reasoning and suggests that the best route to getting a more attractive nationwide system of subsidies is to have

incomes below $20,000 were enrolled at these schools. See Astin, Korn, and Berz (1989, pp. 48 and 104).

7. For a classic statement, see Hansen and Weisbrod (1971). See also Karelis and Sabot (1987). Fischer (1990) has recently argued that federal student aid programs should be redesigned to give states incentives to raise tuition and to return the increase to students in the form of increased student aid.

the federal government step forward and assume the burden of student aid for lower-income students. What about the alternative of inducing the states to reform their own funding programs, reducing operating subsidies and expanding income-tested student aid? This might be accomplished by instituting federal grant programs that made the receipt of funds contingent on states' reforming their higher-education financing programs in the prescribed way.[8] That would certainly be worth doing and might well be a plausible alternative to our proposal. However, two considerations lead us to prefer the approach we do. First, we believe that financing the education of lower-income students *is* fundamentally a national responsibility, and that the clearest and most straightforward way for the federal government to discharge that responsibility is to fund these students directly. Second, the indirect route of providing incentives to states would probably lead to uneven responses across states, with the possible result of exacerbating the already considerable inequalities in opportunity facing students who happen to reside in different states.

If our proposal to expand federal need-based aid were enacted, how would states be likely to respond? It seems probable to us that most states would raise their tuitions substantially in order to capture this federal revenue. There is evidence that at least some states deliberately raised tuition rates when the Pell program was initiated, for precisely this reason.[9] Moreover, the analysis and evidence concerning institutional behavior in chapter 4 suggest that states would be disposed to respond positively to these incentives: according to our estimates, a one dollar increase in federal financial aid leads to a tuition increase at public four-year institutions of 50 cents. If states raised tuition by enough to capture the increased federal spending fully, increased reve-

8. Fischer (1990).

9. The argument that federal student aid would tend to induce states to move away from their low-tuition policies was deployed by both supporters and critics of federal student aid at the time the BEOG program was being debated in Congress in the early 1970s. In fact, ceiling levels in the BEOG program have been low enough to make these incentive effects relatively unimportant. There is some evidence that the decision of public institutions in New York State to abandon their zero-tuition policy was influenced by these incentives. In 1972, the Keppel Task Force recommended the introduction of tuition at City University of New York, arguing that "New York State students and institutions will fail to some degree to qualify for Federal funds under the new statutes unless the public institutions charge higher tuitions than they do at present. . . . [We] consider it extremely important that the State take maximum advantage of Federal funding in order to reduce the burden on State taxpayers." See Task Force on Financing Higher Education (1972, pp. 5 and 15).

nue to the states would in fact substantially exceed the additional federal spending on student aid for students at public institutions—since higher tuitions would be paid by a great many students at public institutions who would not receive federal aid. This rearrangement of federal and state fiscal responsibilities might work best as part of some larger package of changes in federal and state fiscal relationships—as federal responsibility for paying for higher education expanded, states might assume increased responsibilities in other areas. Some possibilities are discussed in the later section on budgetary implications. In the absence of a larger package, states might respond to reduced funding responsibilities for higher education by reducing taxes or by increasing spending on nonhigher education programs. Correspondingly, unless the federal government transferred other responsibilities to the states, it would either have to raise taxes, reduce other spending, or increase the deficit to finance its increased student aid obligations. If the overall rearrangement of federal and state finances left the states with more revenue, it is likely that some part of the "windfall" to states would be returned to higher-education spending.

Two particular possibilities for the "new" state revenue are worth noting. First, the states might well devote some resources to helping more affluent students, who are not eligible for federal student aid, cope with the higher tuitions. If, for example, states developed or expanded need-based aid programs for state residents, the new, higher tuitions at state institutions would imply that even middle- or upper-middle-income students might qualify for aid, as is now true at many private institutions. (Note that, even if states raised tuition by the full amount of the recommended increase in federal aid, this would by no means eliminate the operating subsidies at public institutions; some subsidy would persist, keeping attendance costs for nonaided students below their true cost.) Providing need-based aid to middle- and upper-middle-income students would, it is true, partially undo the favorable redistributive consequences of expanding federal income-tested aid and raising tuition. However, this arrangement would have some important advantages over the present one. First, states would need to be explicit about whom they were electing to subsidize, and why, thus encouraging more enlightening public discussion of this issue. Second, it seems unlikely that any explicit program of subsidized tuition would reach as far up the income distribution as the present program does. Finally, if states were to provide these subsidies through *portable* student aid instead, they would make the competition for students between public and private institutions more even-handed.

A second possibility is that states might use the additional revenue from higher tuition to permit more rapid spending increases at these institutions. This outcome seems less likely to us than the one above, partly because states will be under pressure both to reduce taxes and to reduce payment burdens for parents in the face of higher tuition, and partly because prevailing levels of spending at public institutions presumably reflect some political accommodation about the appropriate level of such spending. It is not obvious that changing the financing mechanism as we describe would affect that political "equilibrium" substantially. Our empirical work in chapter 4 shows that, at current levels of federal spending, there is no tendency for public (or private) institutions that receive more federal student aid to spend more on instruction.

A major impact of our program, then, will be to target more governmental assistance on lower-income students and (to the extent that states allow public tuitions to rise) to reduce the assistance now going to relatively affluent students. This redistribution of higher-education subsidies advances the goal of improving access to postsecondary education generally and of broadening the range of higher-education alternatives for lower-income students. Evidence in chapter 3 shows that this group is sensitive to net price when deciding both whether to and where to attend college. The evidence also suggests that middle- and upper-income students are not discouraged from enrolling in college by increases in net price.

The Effect on Private Institutions

How would private institutions be affected by the reform we propose? To answer that, it is important to clarify one feature of the proposed federal aid program. Awards in our program would be proportioned to family *income* (or some broader measure of financial capacity), not to "need" as conventionally defined in higher education.[10] The usual needs analysis has a family's need for assistance rising dollar for dollar with the tuition of the institution attended. To adopt this principle for a program with very high maximum award levels, like the ones that we

10. For further discussion of need versus income testing, see chapter 7.

propose, would have two significant drawbacks. First, for students at relatively costly private institutions, such an arrangement could make even affluent students eligible for federal grant aid. Depending on exactly how award rates were set, it would not be implausible for families with incomes in excess of $75,000 and with multiple siblings in college to receive significant amounts of government grant aid. This does not seem a justifiable use of scarce federal grant resources. Moreover, private institutions will often commit considerable resources to the financial assistance of middle-income students. These funds are usually distributed according to measures of "ability to pay," and do take college costs into account. Thus, while chapter 5 does note that there has been some movement of middle-income students away from the "elite" private institutions, we argued there that a significant part of this movement probably results from a misperception among families about the availability of aid at these schools. Therefore, despite concerns about college affordability for the middle class, it is lower-income families who are asked to pay the largest fraction of their incomes to cover college costs at high-cost private institutions.

"Needs" testing, which as we noted takes price into account, would be an unattractive addition to our proposed federal program not only because it would mistarget funds, but also because it could provide a substantial incentive for private institutions to raise prices. We have shown that there is no evidence that existing student aid programs have a measurable tuition-raising effect at private institutions. We have further argued that the program we are describing here *would* have a tuition-raising effect at public institutions, and we consider that a good thing. Note, however, that higher tuition at private institutions has different implications from higher tuition at public institutions. Higher public tuition is likely to reflect lower state expenditures and no net increase in resources devoted to higher education. In private higher education, however, higher tuition is likely to translate into higher institutional spending and thus greater resource use in higher education. Our results in chapter 4 indicate that a one-dollar increase in gross tuition and fees at a four-year private institution increases instructional expenditure by about 31 cents. Without evidence that instructional spending at private institutions is too low, we believe there is a broad consensus that such increases would be undesirable. As we argued in chapter 7, an income-tested program would avoid these incentives to raise price for all but a handful of private institutions. Most private institutions currently charge more than the maximum grant aid we are proposing, and so these institutions would not be able to capture additional federal aid by raising prices. There are, however, a small number of institutions currently charging less than $7,800 (including residence costs) that would have an incentive to raise prices under our proposed policy, but this is not obviously a bad thing, since spending levels at these institutions are currently quite low, and higher tuition and spending might well bring commensurate quality improvements.

Private institutions, then, would not have incentives to raise tuitions to capture the increases in student aid. The policy might have the effect of increasing the demand for private higher education, both by adding to the purchasing power of lower-income students and by raising the price at public institutions. This higher demand might have the indirect effect of tending to raise prices at private institutions. Ironically, perhaps, the most important effect on private institutions may be the increased price charged by their public competition—closing the price differential between the two sectors would presumably increase demand for private higher education among fee-paying students and would thus be a benefit to private colleges and universities.

A second consequence of our proposed policy would be a change in the way private institutions allocate their own aid funds. Institutions whose costs were roughly comparable to those of public institutions would find most of the financial need of lower-income students met by federal aid. Under current arrangements, institutions usually have to supplement available federal aid significantly to make attendance possible for lower-income students. "Federalizing" college finance for lower-income students would relieve the moderately priced private institutions of this burden. At the same time, since few private institutions can completely meet the needs of lower-income students under present arrangements, this change would expand the range of choice for these students.

High-cost private institutions would face a somewhat different set of incentives. Because the proposed grant program would not be tuition-sensitive (above the ceiling set by the maximum award amount), high-cost institutions would not receive more federal student aid to finance the education of a given student than would less costly institutions. More expensive institutions would find, under this regime as under the present policy, that (holding income constant) their students have greater "unmet need" than students at cheaper institutions. It would make sense, then, for these institutions to continue to operate need-based student aid programs "on top of" the foundation support provided by the proposed federal grant program.

DEALING WITH NONTRADITIONAL STUDENTS AND INSTITU-TIONS. Under existing eligibility criteria, it is likely that a significant fraction of awards under the expanded federal program we describe would go to nontraditional students—independent adult students, part-time students, and students in nondegree vocational programs at community colleges and proprietary trade schools. From the standpoints of equity and efficiency, it is not clear that this is a desirable result.

Considering equity first, there is reason to doubt the effectiveness of the existing needs-analysis system in identifying needy adults compared with needy families of dependent students. On the social efficiency side, there is reason to question the level of social returns to at least some postsecondary vocational programs as well as to some of the many activities pursued by adults as continuing education. At a minimum, it is not clear that all these activities are equally worthy of federal subsidy.

A final concern is that proprietary vocational schools are the set of institutions most likely to increase their total claim on national resources if federal aid became more generous. As we have shown, in the face of increased federal aid, public institutions would raise tuition to capture that aid, while most private nonprofit institutions, whose tuitions already exceed the proposed increases in federal aid, would have little direct impetus to raise tuition. For proprietary institutions—many of whose student charges and expenditures roughly equal the sum of the current Pell and GSL maxima, about $5,000 per student—the outcome is different.[11] These institutions would have strong incentives to raise their charges to capture added federal support, but whether this additional revenue would translate into expenditures on higher-quality programs is doubtful. To the extent that competitive pressures from well-

11. Students in the 1986–87 academic year reported that total charges at proprietary institutions, including tuition, room, and board, averaged $5,188 a student. (Institution-reported cost estimates were much higher, since the institutions estimated costs for room and board at a figure $3,177 higher than the students estimated.) The figures reported here are for full-time, full-year students living off campus, but not with their parents—the housing situation of the majority of proprietary school students. See Korb and others (1988, p. 17). Since proprietary institutions generally get almost all their revenues from student dollars (typically subsidized by federal student aid), their institutional costs and student charges will be close to equal.

informed consumers are effective, there would be pressure in this direction. However, to the extent that proprietary institutions could capture the added revenue as profit, they would plainly try to do so.

All these concerns, about equity, efficiency, and levels of resource use, exist in the present system, but are rendered less visible by the fact that the mechanisms for providing educational subsidies to needy students are more indirect and complex than they would be under our proposal. Indeed, from some points of view, making social choices about what kinds of educational activities to subsidize, and for whom, might be seen as a virtue of our proposal.

The point is this: if the proposal is a good one with regard to the education of "traditional" college-age students at academic institutions, the "needs" of other groups of students and other kinds of institutions should not be treated as insurmountable obstacles to the reform. If the goals of adult and vocational education are well served by grants to individual students, and if the social judgment is that these activities and populations should be as well supported as traditional students and institutions, then so be it. But it should be clear to all that this is a costly proposition. If, on the other hand, other delivery mechanisms seem preferable, or if, on balance, society is inclined to support these activities less generously than traditional student aid, then the necessary programmatic distinctions have to be made.

It is worth emphasizing that our proposed reform might make more traditional academic programs attractive to some of the students who now enroll in vocational programs. More substantial grant-based funding would widen the range of academic alternatives that disadvantaged students now consider. Raising the purchasing power available to these students might also make institutions more responsive to these students' capacities. Undoubtedly, however, a substantial number of potential students will continue to believe that their best course is to pursue vocational training, and for many students this may indeed be best.

Our tentative recommendation is that, under our structural reform, federal support for nondegree-oriented programs and short-term vocational training should be administered and funded separately from academic postsecondary education. The voucher mechanism implicit in current student aid funding, coupled with minimal regulatory oversight, does not appear to have worked well in this area. As an alternative, the funding of vocational efforts through contracts with providers, as discussed in chapter 7, may well have merit. Institutions offering vocational training would contract with the federal government, or perhaps with federally funded state agencies, to supply such an education to persons whose eligibility would be decided jointly by the funding agency and the provider. Students would not pay tuition; rather, educational costs would be covered by the contract. Living costs might be subsidized directly by the government. These arrangements have potential advantages over the existing system: in permitting the government to impose performance standards, in allowing the supply of training in various fields to be tailored to regional labor market conditions, and in regulating the costs of the training.[12]

Placing these programs under a separate authority would, in itself, introduce a significant change in the treatment of adult and independent students, since a large fraction of them are enrolled in vocational and other nondegree programs. Indeed, an advantage of such a reorganization is that it might encourage more effective techniques for determining an adult's eligibility for such programs. If people were admitted to federally supported programs on the basis of such criteria as technology-related job loss or long-term economic disadvantage, or the like, this might provide a better measure of economic need than the current needs-analysis standards, which are less reliable when used for independent students.

At the same time, a number of adult and independent students will remain interested in pursuing academic postsecondary alternatives, and their numbers may increase if federal grant support for such programs becomes more generous. We believe that educational opportunity is quite important for disadvantaged adults, and that access to federal support through the expanded grant program should be provided. A needs-analysis system for adult and independent students should, however, aim to meet three criteria that the existing system meets only imperfectly.

— The subsidy system should avoid creating substantial incentives for students to move voluntarily from dependent to independent status.

12. Why wouldn't this be a suitable mechanism for all federal educational support? If it is good enough for vocational training, why should it not be applied to academic postsecondary education as well? We make several points in reply. First, traditional concerns with academic freedom are much more salient in academic than vocational contexts, and these argue for a funding mechanism that is more neutral with regard to program content and method than a contract approach would be. Second, because academic education is typically more nearly "general" human capital than the "job-specific" human capital provided in short-term vocational programs, there is less need to worry about the suitability of training students to meet short-term labor market

— The system should expect a larger contribution from independent students than from the parents of dependent students, since the student is the principal beneficiary of the education.

— Because a person's short-term economic status is reduced by returning to school, the system should attempt to base its assessment of the student's ability to pay on information extending over several years prior to the resumption of schooling.

The nuances of designing a system that meets these criteria, especially since it must deal with married as well as single people and parents as well as childless adults, are complicated, and we will not pause for a detailed discussion here.[13]

REFORMING FEDERAL LOAN FINANCE. Accompanying the substantial increase in federal grant support of higher education would be a reform in the federal loan programs. We advocate that federal loans should continue to carry a guarantee, but should not be subsidized in any other way, and that anticipated default costs should be built into a fee to be charged at the time loans are initiated.[14] The basic reasoning here is that current loans, which carry interest rate subsidies, can combine a grant and a smaller unsubsidized loan. Packaging the two together makes it hard to target both subsidies and credit access at the right groups, and confuses both policymakers and borrowers about just where the aid is going. Our proposal is to give grants to those who need subsidies, loans to those who need credit, and some of each to those who need both.

As noted in chapter 8, unsubsidized loans could be provided either through a guarantee mechanism for privately generated loans, as in the present GSL system, or through a direct lending system, presumably operated through schools, which would rely on federally provided capital. In terms of the fundamental economics of the matter, there is

---

conditions. Finally, both state-run and nonprofit suppliers have built in regulatory mechanisms in the form of governing boards, which help to supervise the use of voucher funds. These mechanisms are absent in profit-seeking institutions, which provide a large share of short-term vocational training.

13. Useful discussion of policy issues and alternatives in independent student needs analysis can be found in College Scholarship Service (1990b) and Hansen and Stampen (1986).

14. Since the exact definition of "unsubsidized" in this context is ambiguous, we recognize some room for variation here. Some people would argue that the very fact of guaranteeing the loans amounts to subsidizing them, relative to the rate an unregulated market would provide. Others would say that the loans are unsubsidized so long as a fair estimate of future default costs is built into the charges to students. Another view would have it that even if the government absorbs default costs, the loans can be viewed as unsubsidized for those who pay them back.

little to distinguish between these two arrangements. Our discussion in chapter 8 reviews some of the pros and cons of the two alternatives, as well as some reforms that would be useful if the guarantee mechanism is maintained. Specifically, we would urge that the payments to banks to compensate their costs in offering these loans—if any are needed in an unsubsidized system—should be set through an auction mechanism. We would further urge that a healthy direct lending mechanism be developed in parallel with the guarantee system, partly as a potential source of institutional innovation and partly as an alternative source of credit should banks for one reason or another withdraw from the program or fail to provide credit to certain groups of students.

A possible reason for concern about offering unsubsidized loans is that they would generate unreasonably large repayment burdens for students. This worry, however, neglects the point that the resources currently used to subsidize loans would become direct grant subsidies instead. Suppose, for example, that a particular student would qualify for a grant equal in value to the loan subsidy she would otherwise have received and that her costs of attending college are not otherwise affected. Then, her borrowing requirement is reduced by the grant just enough to make the repayment burden for her loan exactly what it would have been before. Obviously, if this equality held for everyone, there would be little point in changing the loan subsidies into grants. The advantage of making the separation, however, is precisely that it is possible to make a direct policy judgment about the best way to target all the grant funds, and then meet the credit needs that remain.

ESTIMATED BUDGETARY AND ENROLLMENT IMPLICATIONS. Both the budgetary and enrollment consequences of implementing our proposed plan would depend critically on the responses of students and of institutions to changed student financing incentives. For the purpose of getting a sense of the likely implications for the federal budget, it is useful to consider two extreme cases: first, that public institutions do not raise prices at all in response to increases in federal grant ceilings, and second, that prices rise enough so that all institutions would qualify their students for the largest available federal grants. This latter assumption would imply that no institution would charge less than $7,800 (including room and board). The real outcome would presumably lie between these extremes, although we both expect and hope that it would lie closer to the latter than the former.

Suppose, first, that there is no increase in public tuitions. In this case, the increased federal grant awards, if the maximum rose to $5,800, would mostly affect students in private higher education. If students currently receiving awards in private institutions had award increases that preserved the current ratio of average to maximum awards, we estimate that additional spending on these students would come to $1.0 billion.[15] In addition, some students at private institutions who are not currently eligible for awards would qualify when the maximum rises. These students would have higher incomes than current Pell recipients, and therefore the average award for them would be a smaller fraction of the maximum than is true for current recipients. For purposes of this calculation, we will assume that the average for these added students would be one-half the maximum ($2,900) and that all students from families with incomes below $40,000 would qualify for awards. This would add another $1.1 billion to federal costs.[16] Thus the total cost of Pell grants to the private, nonprofit sector would rise by $2.1 billion. Note that these costs are independent of how public tuition responds: students in private institutions would qualify for the aid regardless.[17]

If public institutions do not raise prices, students at these institutions would not be able to qualify for much additional federal aid. As a rough approximation, we assume that average awards in public higher education would rise from $1,435 (in the fall of 1986) to $2,000.[18] We estimate that this would add about $0.8 billion to Pell costs.[19]

Alternatively, suppose that public institutions raise their prices enough to fully qualify their students for increased federal aid. In that event, assuming the current ratio of average to maximum awards is preserved, the increase in Pell awards to current award recipients in

15. This calculation relies on data from the NPSAS survey, as reported in Korb and others (1988, tables 5.1 and 5.2, pp. 48 and 49). In the fall of 1986, the Pell maximum was $2,100, and the average award to a full-time student in private, nonprofit higher education was $1,551. There were 353,000 students in private, nonprofit institutions receiving Pell grants at that time, according to the survey report.

16. According to American Freshman Survey data for 1989, about 36 percent of freshmen at private institutions had annual family incomes below $40,000. If all students with incomes below $40,000 qualified for grants, we estimate that this would add about 383,000 students to the total.

17. This reasoning neglects any effects resulting from increases in private relative to public enrollment. Such effects are more likely if public institutions raise prices than if they do not.

18. Korb and others (1988, table 5.2, p. 49).

19. This estimate is based on enrollments and award levels from Korb and others (1988). Notice that with no increase in public tuitions, the number of students qualifying for awards in public higher education would not increase substantially.

public higher education would be about $3.4 billion.[20] In addition, a number of new students would qualify for grants, which we again assume would average half the maximum.[21] We estimate that this would add $8.8 billion to program costs, for a total increment at public institutions of $12.2 billion.[22]

Thus the increase in the cost of the Pell program, assuming that public institutions raise tuition to fully capture additional federal funding, would total $14.3 billion. If public institutions did not raise tuition, Pell costs would rise by about $2.9 billion. In turn, the cost of other federal programs would be reduced under our proposal. The three "campus-based" programs would be eliminated, resulting in savings of about $1.2 billion. Elimination of interest subsidies in the Stafford program would also bring substantial savings: although present federal accounting practices do not properly reflect the costs, between 30 and 50 percent of the cost of a new loan is now borne by the federal government, with more than half of that being subsidized interest cost.[23] Thus, with no change in loan volume, eliminating the interest subsidy would save the federal government between $1.4 billion and $2.3 billion. Therefore, if the states did not raise tuition, most or all of the increased cost of the Pell program would be offset by reductions in other federal student aid spending. If the states did raise tuition, costs to the federal government would rise by about $11.0 billion to $11.5 billion.

However, additional revenue from tuition increases would offset some of these costs. In the 1987–88 academic year, the average cost of attendance (tuition plus room and board) at public institutions was $3,960.[24] If this rose to an average $7,800, the resulting revenue increase would be about $23.2 billion.[25] Thus, unless states rebate

20. According to Korb and others (1988), average Pell awards in public higher education were $1,435 in 1986, and about 1.3 million students received awards.

21. American Freshman Survey data indicate that 51 percent of freshmen at public institutions (including public two-year colleges) had annual family incomes below $40,000 in the 1989–90 academic year.

22. If students in short-term vocational programs were supported separately, rather than through this grant mechanism, program costs would rise by less than this estimate indicates.

23. The remainder of the federal cost is default cost, which the government would continue to bear under our proposed reform.

24. National Center for Education Statistics (1989, table 258, pp. 281–82). At private institutions, the average cost of attendance was $10,390.

25. In the fall of 1986 (the most recent available year) full-time-equivalent enrollments in public higher education were 6.0 million students. See National Center for Education Statistics (1989, table 154, p. 173).

part of the increased tuition through expanding their own student aid programs or through increasing spending, the net effect of our proposed policy would be to reduce combined government spending on undergraduate education by around $12.0 billion. Most likely, the actual outcome would lie somewhere between the two extreme cases, with some but not all public institutions raising prices to qualify their students for additional federal aid.

Changes of this magnitude in the net prices facing different groups of students would probably have substantial effects on enrollment. The projections examined in chapter 6, which discusses the consequences of a "swap" of funding between federal and state governments, provide a useful basis for examining the likely enrollment consequences of our proposal. Those projections assume that as federal need-based aid expands, state operating subsidies are reduced dollar-for-dollar, with the result that the national cost of student finance is held constant. This scenario can serve as an intermediate case in terms of projecting enrollment effects.

These projections show that such a swap, averaging over sectors, would reduce the net price facing aided students, reducing the net price to income ratio for these students from 22 percent in 1990 to 21 percent in 2010, whereas it rises to 26 percent in the baseline scenario. The net price facing nonaided students would rise, moving the net price to income ratio from 12 percent to 22 percent, rather than rising to 17 percent as it does in the baseline scenario. The enrollment effect of the price reduction for aided students, based on the demand elasticity estimates from chapter 3, would be substantial. We estimate that the "swap" would raise the enrollment rate of aided students by about 12 percent. The evidence from chapter 3 also suggests that the price rise for nonaided students would not reduce their enrollment.

Our proposal, then, would involve a large increase in federal budgetary commitments, compensated by reductions in state spending. In recent years, much of the fiscal movement has been in the opposite direction, with federal budgetary constraints leading to increasing fiscal burdens on state governments. Over much of the 1980s, state budgets appeared to be in much better shape than the federal budget, and this was one important impetus for the shift in fiscal responsibilities. However, although the federal budget continues to be in substantial deficit, there are growing signs that the ability of state governments to increase their budgets is reaching its limits. Thus, a proposal like ours, which would move some responsibilities away from state budgets toward the federal budget, may be more plausible in the 1990s than it would have seemed in the recent past. Moreover, some of the most pressing needs facing the nation fall into areas that are more clearly state and local responsibilities than is the financing of higher education. Among those under local purview are the improvement of elementary and secondary education and investments in various forms of "infrastructure." As proposals to address these and other areas of need continue to come forward, the idea of directing some fiscal movements in the other direction may have appeal. Further pressure in this direction might arise from state-level "tax resistance" and from national-level proposals, such as restricting the federal deductibility of state tax payments, which make it more difficult for states to raise taxes.

The kind of structural reform we have outlined could be accomplished only over a substantial period of time. Although the proposal would not raise the national public costs of higher education—and could conceivably lower them—it would call for a major redistribution of financing responsibilities among levels of government, and would probably need to be worked out as part of a larger package of fiscal reorganization.

Moreover, the proposal would conflict with the real or perceived interests of some major political elements in the national college finance effort: banks will not want to lose student loan subsidies; public colleges will not uniformly welcome incentives to raise prices (even if they are compensated through higher aid received by some students); private colleges will be concerned about the lack of tuition sensitivity in our proposed grant program; and proprietary vocational schools and community colleges will be unsettled by the thought of having their support diverted to other funding channels.

We believe our proposal would actually have considerable benefits for some of the groups that might focus on these costs. Private colleges, for example, might benefit significantly from higher public tuition; those public colleges and universities that succeed in serving students well will benefit from funding mechanisms that are more sensitive to student choice; some proprietary institutions and community colleges might find a contract funding mechanism quite effective for their purposes. More important than its appeal to various interest groups, we believe the proposed revision in funding would advance the interests of students and of the nation in creating a more competitive and equitable higher-education system.

Incremental Reforms

The long-run proposal we have sketched can also help in the short run by guiding the reform along the incremental steps necessary to advance the four major goals outlined above. We believe the following recommendations will help move reform efforts in the right direction.

1. *Sustain efforts for federal credit reform.* The best way to get Congress to make better informed and more balanced decisions about the relative role of grant and loan programs is to account for those programs in a way that reflects their true relative cost. As noted in chapter 8, the Budget Enforcement Act of 1990 has gone a long way in that direction. Under the new law, when Congress authorizes new loans, it must appropriate an amount equal to the expected present value of the stream of "special allowance" payments to banks and of future default costs. Under these rules, legislators will not be inclined to view lending as quite so cheap or grants as quite so expensive. It is important to keep these valuable provisions in place.

2. *Reduce subsidies in the loan programs and translate those subsidy dollars into larger grants.* A subsidized loan is equivalent to a grant plus a smaller loan. Unbundling these components is the best way of getting both subsidies and credit to the right people.

3. *Develop alternatives to the support of postsecondary vocational training through the student aid programs.* If, as we urge, the nation decides to fund short-term vocational training for postsecondary students through channels other than grants and loans to individual students, the transition to these other funding mechanisms should occur gradually. Although projects funded by the Job Training Partnership Act provide a useful model for an alternative funding mechanism, it would be useful for the Office of Postsecondary Education in the Department of Education, which funds the student aid programs, to initiate some experiments in funding short-term vocational training for postsecondary students. If such pilot efforts are successful, both in meeting student needs and in providing a viable means of supporting

effective institutions, they could lay the groundwork for a more ambitious recasting of the funding mechanisms.

4. *Eliminate the 60 percent of the cost provision in the Pell grant program.* The main effect of this provision is to reduce the size of Pell grants going to the neediest students at the lowest-priced community colleges. At the same time, because the Pell grant can increase by only 60 cents for each dollar that the school's tuition increases, this provision reduces the incentives for these schools to raise tuitions. If, as we argue, it is desirable in the long run for public tuitions to rise closer to cost-covering levels, this ceiling on aid is counterproductive.

5. *Focus discussion explicitly on the level and distribution of federal grants.* Early in the development of the federal Pell grant program, a good deal of attention was focused on the appropriate schedule for determining award eligibility under the program—how large the maximum grant should be; how grant size should decline with rising income; and what income level should be the maximum for grant recipients. In recent years, these debates have faded into the background, with the result that the distribution of Pell funds across income classes is largely a by-product of the overall appropriation level. More explicit discussion of these key policy variables would help contribute to more intelligent decisions about how to target federal subsidies.

In line with the longer-term reform we have outlined, we would argue that the maximum Pell grant should be raised significantly, but that the rate at which awards are reduced for higher-income families should be great enough to prevent the maximum income level for a family qualifying for a grant from increasing substantially. While any student's total aid package, including a Pell grant, should continue to be limited by the total cost of attending the institution, the formula for awarding Pell grants should be revised to eliminate other elements of tuition sensitivity. In other words, Pell grants should be made an "income-tested" (or more generally a "family-resources-tested") rather than a "needs-tested" program.

6. *Maintain a broad-based notion of family resources in assessing family ability to pay and eligibility for federal grants.* Both the "Pell eligibility index" and the congressional methodology for performing needs analysis incorporate a fairly comprehensive view of family income and assets into their formulae. Keeping track both of assets and of tax-preferred sources of income, such as the income from tax-exempt bonds, is very important in assessing family ability to pay, since a

family's taxable income in a particular year is sometimes a poor measure of its underlying financial strength. Congress has repeatedly entertained attempts to revise the underlying conception of family resources in order to respond to the perceived needs of some constituent groups. In the summer of 1990, for example, there was pressure to remove the value of owner-occupied housing from the list of assets counted in family wealth. Such a step would plainly introduce horizontal inequity by discriminating among families who hold similar amounts of wealth but in different forms and vertical inequity by disregarding an asset that is held in disproportionately higher amounts by more affluent groups.

Conclusion

In this final chapter, we have outlined the strengths and weaknesses of the existing system of undergraduate student finance in the United States, and put forward a proposal for structural reform. This proposal is built around a basic conclusion: student aid works. Need-based student aid, particularly aid in the form of income-tested federal grants, encourages the enrollment of lower-income students, makes the profile of net prices facing students from different income backgrounds fairer, and does not generate the perverse incentives regarding institutional behavior that some have worried about. Our proposal, in effect, seeks to bolster the role of income-tested aid in the overall student financing picture, focusing it better and making it more effective.

As our projections of college affordability documented, a prolonged period of slow growth in output and productivity would put substantial stress on our existing system for paying for college. Although no one can be sure what the future holds, the ability of state governments, in particular, to finance high-quality education while keeping tuitions low for all students may be severely tested. Without significant changes in the financing system, lower-income students would be most severely threatened by such a development. Our proposed reforms would help considerably to reduce the threats to these students' educational opportunities.

Although it is our judgment that the evidence developed in this volume provides strong support for our recommended policy, we stress the need for additional research on certain fundamental aspects of the existing postsecondary education system. It is hard not to be impressed by the gaps in knowledge about some central matters involved in the design of intelligent policy for postsecondary education, and this is one place where further research might make a real difference. We single out two areas especially deserving of further attention.

The first is the proprietary sector—a sector that has grown up almost overnight. It receives a remarkably large amount of federal support and educates a significant portion of our most disadvantaged youth. Yet the information needed to address even the most elementary questions about this sector—the rate at which enrollments have grown, the income distribution of its students, the way in which institutional resources are deployed—is only beginning to become available. We are even less able to evaluate the effectiveness of these programs—questions like program completion and job placement rates, future incomes of graduates of these programs, suitability of training to labor market conditions, and the like. Although observers often rightly decry the poor state of knowledge concerning these same questions in traditional higher education, our ignorance concerning this newly emerging sector is much deeper.

The second area deserving attention is the comparative returns to different forms of postsecondary education. Broadening the point about the proprietary sector, it is indeed of policywise interest to know something about the relative "payoff" of different types of postsecondary experience. "Payoffs" here include not only monetary outcomes in terms of better wages, lower unemployment rates, and the like, but also less tangible items including job satisfaction, levels of community service, and so on. What are the comparative returns to technical and liberal arts training? To two years at a community college compared with two years at a traditional four-year institution? To public compared with private higher education? Do students with particular backgrounds do better at particular kinds of schools? In principle, the answers to these questions would go a long way toward shaping desirable national policies toward postsecondary finance. Currently we know almost nothing about these issues, yet meaningful research on them is certainly possible.

In fact, the work we have done on the economics of student finance increases our confidence that meaningful results can be obtained through well-designed empirical investigations. Our empirical work shows that increased student aid does induce greater enrollments among students from lower-income backgrounds, and suggests that a consistent picture of the impact of aid on enrollment can be derived from both time-series and cross-section evidence. While our analysis of the supply-side effects of student aid is more preliminary, it nevertheless indicates that we can also measure institutional responses to changes in external educational funding. Moreover, we have been able to subject some familiar conjectures about perverse institutional impacts of such funding to empirical tests, and have found these conjectures unsupported in the data.

Of course, not all useful research on higher-education finance need involve econometrics. In fact, we believe that our findings about the distribution of college choice, which rely on a careful description of available data about patterns of student enrollment, shed considerable light on the alternatives facing exceptionally qualified students and on the enrollment behavior of students of differing economic backgrounds. Similarly, our efforts to project future patterns of affordability attempt to draw out systematically the implications of emerging trends and of alternative possible future developments in the economy that impinge on higher education. We hope that the impact of our empirical studies on our policy recommendations is evident: it has been our aim when assessing current policies and suggesting alternatives to ground our judgments in an empirical understanding both of the particulars of existing policies and of the likely behavioral responses of both students and institutions to policy change.

Appendix A

An Empirical Analysis of Financial Aid, College Costs, and Enrollment: Technical Report

BECAUSE we use a relatively unusual data set, it may be worthwhile first to spell out how the regressions should be interpreted. The individual data points in our regressions are an average enrollment rate and an average net cost for a particular population subgroup—classified by demographic characteristic and income; an example might be white women with annual incomes below $10,000—in a particular year. We then organize the data into three institutional categories: one for public schools, one for private schools, and one that averages over the two. Sample sizes in the underlying Current Population Survey (CPS) data base, from which the enrollment rate series is constructed, are not large enough to permit meaningful analyses of annual variations in the enrollment experience of blacks and other nonwhites. Therefore, the results we report here are limited to whites only. In the regressions that report on enrollments at public and private institutions separately, we are forced to exclude data for 1980 because mistakes made by the Bureau of the Census in coding the 1980 survey make it impossible to distinguish public from private enrollment. Thus, regressions using the combined data set are based on sixty-six observations (three income groups, two genders, and eleven years). Regressions for public and for private institutions have sixty observations (three income groups, two genders, and ten years). Dummy variables and interaction terms are used to control for differences among income groups in the strength of the relationship between net cost and enrollment and in the average

217

propensity to enroll. Differences between men and women in the average propensity to enroll are controlled for through the use of a gender dummy. Finally, the regressions contain a time trend which tests for secular changes in enrollment propensities that are not captured by our other independent variables.

As noted earlier, the data on student aid and family income in the American Freshman Survey are self-reported by students. No doubt this self-reporting introduces measurement error in these variables. Nevertheless, we use these data for several reasons. First, they are the only consistently reported annual data on net costs and income. After the National Postsecondary Student Aid Survey (NPSAS) has been replicated several times, this data file will provide a useful, and probably statistically superior, source for time-series analysis. Since at this point that survey has only been conducted once, it cannot be used in time-series analysis. Second, there is no reason to expect the biases in student reporting of income and costs to vary systematically over time. While it is likely that student-reported data on family income and ways of paying for college are inaccurate in any particular year, their variation over time should be more reliable. Finally, we know of no reason why any systematic biases in these variables should be correlated with time-series variations in the dependent variable (the enrollment rate). Note that the dependent variable is obtained from a data set (the Current Population Survey) that is collected separately from these independent variables.

Table A-1 presents regression results in which enrollment rates averaged across public and private institutions are explained by time-series changes in net cost and other variables.[1] Given the nature of the data set, heteroskedasticity is a natural worry. Therefore, for all of the regression results that follow, estimated asymptotic covariance matrices were computed under the assumption of heteroskedasticity in order to calculate the standard errors.[2] These adjusted standard errors were used in all tests of significance. The regression equation includes a time trend along with a dummy variable for gender (1 for females and 0 for males) and dummy variables for the middle-income group (income between $10,000 and $30,000 in 1978–79 dollars) and for the upper-

1. A more technical presentation of this analysis is in McPherson and Schapiro (1991).
2. For the derivation of this technique, see White (1980).

Table A-1. *Regression Explaining Enrollment Rates at Private and Public Institutions*

| | Test statistics | | | | |
Independent variable	Parameter estimate	Standard error	t-statistic	Chi-square value	Summary statistic
Constant (α)	0.461157	0.049629	9.292[a]	. . .	. . .
Net cost (C)	-0.000068	0.000023	-2.952[a]	. . .	. . .
Time (t)	-0.003645	0.001755	-2.077[b]	. . .	. . .
Female (F)	0.048680	0.008753	5.561[a]	. . .	. . .
Middle income (M)	-0.142580	0.063266	-2.254[b]	. . .	. . .
Upper income (U)	-0.209977	0.073307	-2.864[a]	. . .	. . .
Net cost, upper income (C_U)	0.000155	0.000028	5.526[a]	. . .	. . .
Net cost, middle income (C_M)	0.000091	0.000027	3.357[a]	. . .	. . .
Time, upper income (t_U)	-0.003005	0.002773	-1.084	. . .	. . .
Time, middle income (t_M)	0.002917	0.002096	1.392	. . .	. . .
Female, upper income (F_U)	-0.001193	0.013238	-0.090	. . .	. . .
Female, middle income (F_M)	-0.000261	0.010992	-0.024	. . .	. . .
Chi-square tests					
$C + C_U = 0$	. . .	. . .	. . .	32.57[a]	. . .
$C + C_M = 0$	. . .	. . .	. . .	2.85[c]	. . .
$t + t_U = 0$	. . .	. . .	. . .	9.59[a]	. . .
$t + t_M = 0$	. . .	. . .	. . .	0.40	. . .
$F + F_U = 0$	. . .	. . .	. . .	22.86[a]	. . .
$F + F_M = 0$	. . .	. . .	. . .	53.02[a]	. . .
Number of observations	. . .	. . .	. . .	. . .	66
R^2	. . .	. . .	. . .	. . .	0.968
$\bar{R}^2$	. . .	. . .	. . .	. . .	0.962
Root MSE	. . .	. . .	. . .	. . .	0.022826
Dep Mean	. . .	. . .	. . .	. . .	0.427174
C.V.	. . .	. . .	. . .	. . .	5.344

Source: Author's calculations as described in text. The *t*-values resulted from a test of the null hypothesis that the indicated parameter is equal to zero.
a. Significant at 0.01 level.
b. Significant at 0.05 level.
c. Significant at 0.10 level.

income group (income over \$30,000).[3] The two sets of dummies allow the constant term in the regression to vary for different income groups and genders. In addition, the equation includes terms that interact income with the net cost variable, the gender dummy, and the time trend. These interaction terms permit the enrollment impact of net cost to vary across income groups, and also allow us to test for differences across income groups in the time trend and in the impact of gender

3. The omitted categories for the dummy variables are annual incomes below \$10,000 and males. The coefficients on the dummy variables in the regression predict differences relative to these omitted categories. Note that in the text, incomes are reported in 1990 dollars.

differences on enrollment. The variable C_U interacts C, the net cost variable, with the dummy variable U representing upper income. The variable C_M interacts C with the middle-income dummy variable M. The variables t_U and t_M interact t with the income dummies, while F^U and F_M interact F, the gender dummy, with the income dummies.

An example may clarify the interpretation of these interaction effects. The coefficient on C measures the effect of changes in net cost on enrollment among lower-income students. The coefficient on C_U measures the *difference* between the effect of net cost on upper-income and on lower-income students, while the standard error on C_U indicates the precision with which this difference is measured. The net effect of changes in net cost on enrollment for upper-income students is the algebraic sum of C and C_U. The statistical significance of this net effect cannot be read directly from the t-tests on the individual variables; instead, it is determined by testing the hypothesis that the sum of C and C_U is equal to zero. As seen in table A-1, the chi-square value equals 32.57, which is large enough to reject the hypothesis that the sum of C and C_U equals zero. Hence, there is a statistically significant effect of net cost on enrollment for upper-income students.

We have the following expectations about the signs of the coefficients. The C coefficient, which measures the responsiveness of enrollment to net cost for the lower-income group, should be negative (higher net cost discourages enrollment). The coefficient on C_M measures the difference between the responsiveness of lower- and middle-income students' enrollment to changes in net cost. Cross-section studies generally indicate that upper-income students are less responsive to price than lower-income students. We therefore expect the coefficient on C_M to be positive, muting the negative effect of net cost on enrollment relative to that of lower-income students. For the same reason we expect the coefficient on C_U to be positive (and larger than that on C_M).

As table A-1 shows, all the estimated coefficients on these net cost variables are significant with the expected sign. Increases in net cost lead to lower enrollment for the lower-income group, and the interaction effects are positive and significant, showing that this effect is smaller for middle- and upper-income students. In fact, the coefficients on the net cost–income interaction terms are larger in absolute value than the coefficient on net cost, implying that the predicted effect of net cost on enrollment in this equation is positive for middle- and upper-income students.[4] For both groups, the net-cost coefficient is statistically significant as well as positive. It is possible that this unexpected result for more affluent students is explained by a supply rather than a demand effect: a positive relationship between enrollment and net cost may come about because (particularly in the 1980s) a strong demand among middle- and upper-income students for higher education has caused colleges and universities to raise their prices.[5]

The negative coefficient on net cost implies that for lower-income students a $100 increase in net cost results in an enrollment decline of about 0.7 percentage point, which is about a 2.2 percent decline in enrollment for that income group. We noted earlier that Leslie and Brinkman find a consensus in the literature that a $100 increase in net cost reduces enrollment rates by 1.8 percent. Converting our estimates in 1978–79 dollars to the 1982–83 equivalent relied on by Leslie and Brinkman, we find that a $100 cost increase results in a 1.6 percent enrollment decline for lower-income students. The Leslie-Brinkman figure is, in effect, averaged over all income groups. As also noted, most studies find greater responsiveness to price among lower-income students. Manski and Wise's results, for example, suggest that a $100 net cost increase for lower-income students (in 1979 dollars) leads to a 4.9 percent decline in enrollment.[6] Our result, while lower than the Manski-Wise estimate, seems broadly consistent with typical cross-section findings. The important point is that our econometrically controlled time-series analysis supports the view that changes in costs lead to changes in enrollment for lower-income students.

We turn next to the coefficients relating to gender and to the time

4. The values of the constant, middle-income, and upper-income dummies imply that for all three income groups the constant terms are positive but are a declining function of income. This may seem surprising, since we expect enrollment rates to vary positively with income. However, the presence of a negative net-cost effect for the lower-income group, coupled with positive effects for the other income groups, means that predicted levels of enrollment evaluated at means in fact increase with income.

5. Because enrollment rates are substantially higher for middle- and upper-income students than for lower-income students, and because these more affluent students generally pay higher net costs than lower-income students, it is more plausible to expect a supply response to the behavior of middle- and upper-income students than to that of the lower-income group. Ideally, we could test this conjecture about supply-side effects by including demand-shift variables in a multi-equation analysis; this, however, is beyond the scope of the present study.

6. This coefficient is computed from information in Manski and Wise (1983, tables 7.2 and 7.4).

trend. The coefficient on the female variable F indicates that over the 1974–84 period the enrollment rate for lower-income women tended to be about 5 percentage points higher than that for men. The fact that the variables interacting F with income are close to zero and statistically insignificant indicates that this gender effect is constant across income groups. (Chi-square values show that the net effect of the female variable on enrollment is positive and significant for all three income groups.) The time trend is negative and significant for the lower-income group, suggesting a tendency for the enrollment propensity for that group to fall over time, but it is important to note that the coefficient is small, with the estimated rate of decline being just 0.4 percentage point a year. The interaction effects imply that there is no significant time trend for middle-income students, but that there is a significant negative time trend of 0.7 percentage point a year for upper-income students.

Tables A-2 and A-3 examine private enrollment and public enrollment separately. This breakdown is potentially important because the earlier analysis, in averaging over enrollments and costs in the two sectors, may distort the picture of behavior in each of the sectors separately. The structure of the equations is similar to that in table A-1, which combines public and private enrollment, except that the net cost variables (C_{pub} and C_{priv}) and the net cost-income interaction terms ($C_{pub, M}$ and $C_{pub, U}$) for public middle and upper incomes and $C_{priv, M}$ and $C_{priv, U}$ for private middle and upper incomes) are specific to the sector whose enrollment is being explained. It would be natural to test for the significance of variables measuring cross-price effects (for example, the effect of public sector prices on private enrollment). Unfortunately, a high correlation between the time series for public and private net costs (on the order of 90 percent) makes it impossible to include both variables in the same equation.

As in the combined equation, all the coefficients in the private and public equations that are significant have the expected sign. For private enrollment, we estimate that a $100 increase in net cost lowers enrollment by about 6 percent for lower-income students. In the private equation the net cost–middle income interaction is significant, implying that the price responsiveness of students from middle-income families differs significantly from that of students from lower-income families. The overall net effect of cost on private enrollment for middle-income

Table A-2. *Regression Explaining Enrollment Rates at Private Institutions*

Independent variable	Parameter estimate	Standard error	t-statistic	Chi-square value	Summary statistic
			Test statistic		
Constant (α)	0.164585	0.019427	8.472[a]	. . .	. . .
Net cost, private (C_{priv})	−0.000036	0.000006	−6.272[a]	. . .	. . .
Time (t)	0.000487	0.000551	0.884	. . .	. . .
Female (F)	0.015657	0.004125	3.796[a]	. . .	. . .
Middle income (M)	−0.027524	0.027085	−1.016	. . .	. . .
Upper income (U)	−0.069076	0.053513	−1.291	. . .	. . .
Net cost, private, upper income ($C_{priv, U}$)	0.000052	0.000012	4.234[a]	. . .	. . .
Net cost, private, middle income ($C_{priv, M}$)	0.000023	0.000008	2.947[a]	. . .	. . .
Time, upper income (t_U)	−0.003880	0.002022	−1.918[c]	. . .	. . .
Time, middle income (t_M)	0.000156	0.000802	0.195	. . .	. . .
Female, upper income (F_U)	0.011529	0.009027	1.277	. . .	. . .
Female, middle income (F_M)	0.005081	0.005152	0.986	. . .	. . .
Chi-square tests					
$C_{priv} + C_{priv, U} = 0$	. . .	. . .	. . .	2.22	. . .
$C_{priv} + C_{priv, M} = 0$	. . .	. . .	. . .	6.65[a]	. . .
$t + t_U = 0$	. . .	. . .	. . .	3.04[c]	. . .
$t + t_M = 0$	. . .	. . .	. . .	1.22	. . .
$F + F_U = 0$	. . .	. . .	. . .	11.46[a]	. . .
$F + F_M = 0$	. . .	. . .	. . .	45.11[a]	. . .
Number of observations	. . .	. . .	. . .	. . .	60
R^2	. . .	. . .	. . .	. . .	0.940
$\bar{R}^2$	. . .	. . .	. . .	. . .	0.927
Root MSE	. . .	. . .	. . .	. . .	0.013794
Dep Mean	. . .	. . .	. . .	. . .	0.110864
C.V.	. . .	. . .	. . .	. . .	12.442

Source: See table A-1.
a. Significant at 0.01 level.
b. Significant at 0.05 level.
c. Significant at 0.10 level.

families is negative and significant, indicating that, as for lower-income students, rises in net cost reduce enrollment for middle-income students as well. The net cost–income interaction variable for students from upper-income families is also positive and significant, indicating that they are less responsive to price. However, the overall net effect of cost increases on upper-income private enrollment is not significantly different from zero.

Continuing with the results for private enrollment in table A-2, we find that lower-income women have a significantly higher enrollment propensity than lower-income men—that is, the coefficient on F is

Table A-3. *Regression Explaining Enrollment Rates at Public Institutions*

Independent variable	Parameter estimate	Standard error	t- statistic	Chi-square value	Summary statistic
			Test statistic		
Constant (α)	0.327110	0.059491	5.498[a]	. . .	. . .
Net cost, public (C_{pub})	−0.000038	0.000034	−1.121	. . .	. . .
Time (t)	−0.003646	0.001960	−1.860[c]	. . .	. . .
Female (F)	0.028666	0.008981	3.192[a]	. . .	. . .
Middle income (M)	−0.178774	0.072434	−2.468[b]	. . .	. . .
Upper income (U)	−0.256200	0.076028	−3.370[a]	. . .	. . .
Net cost, public, upper income ($C_{pub, U}$)	0.000149	0.000038	3.905[a]	. . .	. . .
Net cost, public, middle income ($C_{pub, M}$)	0.000098	0.000038	2.588[b]	. . .	. . .
Time, upper income (t_U)	0.003209	0.002350	1.365	. . .	. . .
Time, middle income (t_M)	0.002631	0.002246	1.171	. . .	. . .
Female, upper income (F_U)	−0.007328	0.012655	−0.579	. . .	. . .
Female, middle income (F_M)	0.001272	0.011050	0.115	. . .	. . .
Chi-square tests					
$C_{pub} + C_{pub, U} = 0$	. . .	. . .	. . .	43.17[a]	. . .
$C_{pub} + C_{pub, M} = 0$	. . .	. . .	. . .	13.84[a]	. . .
$t + t_U = 0$	. . .	. . .	. . .	0.11	. . .
$t + t_M = 0$	. . .	. . .	. . .	0.86	. . .
$F + F_U = 0$	. . .	. . .	. . .	5.73[b]	. . .
$F + F_M = 0$	. . .	. . .	. . .	21.63[a]	. . .
Number of observations	. . .	. . .	. . .	. . .	60
R^2	. . .	. . .	. . .	. . .	0.928
$\bar{R}^2$	. . .	. . .	. . .	. . .	0.912
Root MSE	. . .	. . .	. . .	. . .	0.020841
Dep Mean	. . .	. . .	. . .	. . .	0.317772
C.V.	. . .	. . .	. . .	. . .	6.559

Source: See table A-1.
a. Significant at 0.01 level.
b. Significant at 0.05 level.
c. Significant at 0.10 level.

significantly different from zero. Moreover, chi-square values indicate that enrollment propensities in private colleges are also significantly higher for middle-income and upper-income women than for men of the same income class. We find a 0.3 percentage point negative and significant time trend for upper-income students. The time trends for the lower-income and middle-income groups are not significant.

Turning to the results for public enrollment in table A-3, we find that the coefficient on net cost for lower-income students has the expected negative sign but is not significant. As expected, the coefficients on the net cost-income interactions are both positive and significant. For both middle- and upper-income groups, chi-square values indicate that the net effect of cost on enrollment is positive and statistically significant. The F variable is significant for all income groups. The only significant time trend is a small negative one (-0.4 percentage point a year) for lower-income students at public institutions.

In a further refinement of the analysis, we break down net cost into its two components—the gross tuition (the sticker price, called P in the table) and the subsidy value of aid (A). This step serves the purposes, first, of shedding light on the relative magnitudes of the aid and sticker price effects and, second, of pushing the data to see if anomalies or inconsistencies surface. Table A-4 reports these results for equations that average over public and private institutions. The coefficients on P and A, which indicate effects for lower-income students, have the expected sign—a higher "sticker price" lowers enrollment, and more aid raises enrollment. The sticker price coefficient is significant, but the aid coefficient fails to be significant at the 10 percent level. It is interesting to note that the parameter estimates are virtually identical (and the same as the net-cost coefficient reported above), suggesting that aid and sticker price variations have similar effects.[7] The interaction coefficients all have the expected signs, indicating that both the negative effect of price and the positive effect of aid are muted as income rises. The interactions of P with income are statistically significant, while the interactions of A with income are not. Considering the overall effects of the A and P variables on the enrollment of middle- and upper-income students, we find no significant effect of aid for either group, while sticker price has a perverse positive effect for middle-and high-income students.

Tables A-5 and A-6 report the effect of distinguishing sticker price and aid in the equations that examine private and public enrollment separately. These variables are called P_{pub} and P_{priv} and A_{pub} and A_{priv}. Table A-5 reports results for private institutions. We find that for low-income students, aid has the expected positive sign and is significant; sticker price has the expected negative sign and is also significant. Again, the aid effect and the price effect are almost identical. The aid-income interaction terms are not significant; the overall effect of aid on enrollment is not significant for middle-income or upper-income students. As expected, the interaction terms for sticker price and upper-income and sticker price and middle-income are positive and signifi-

---

7. The last test statement on table A-4 verifies that the difference in absolute value between the P and the A coefficients is not statistically significant.

Table A-4. *Regression Explaining Enrollment Rates at Private and Public Institutions, Price and Aid Variables Considered*

Independent variable	Parameter estimate	Standard error	t-statistic	Chi-square value	Summary statistic
		Test statistic			
Constant (α)	0.459218	0.114308	4.017[a]	. . .	. . .
Sticker price (P)	−0.000068	0.000024	−2.818[a]	. . .	. . .
Aid (A)	0.000069	0.000051	1.344	. . .	. . .
Time (t)	−0.003635	0.001989	−1.828[c]	. . .	. . .
Female (F)	0.048684	0.008704	5.593[a]	. . .	. . .
Middle income (M)	−0.278997	0.142833	−1.953[c]	. . .	. . .
Upper income (U)	−0.189528	0.176219	−1.076	. . .	. . .
Aid, upper income (A_U)	−0.000172	0.000106	−1.624	. . .	. . .
Aid, middle income (A_M)	−0.000014	0.000064	−0.225	. . .	. . .
Sticker price, upper income (P_U)	0.000150	0.000039	3.855[a]	. . .	. . .
Sticker price, middle income (P_M)	0.000114	0.000031	3.683[a]	. . .	. . .
Time, upper income (t_U)	−0.002410	0.004400	−0.548	. . .	. . .
Time, middle income (t_M)	0.001500	0.002349	0.639	. . .	. . .
Female, upper income (F_U)	−0.001494	0.013533	−0.110	. . .	. . .
Female, middle income (F_M)	0.000664	0.010839	0.061	. . .	. . .
Chi-square tests					
$P + P_U = 0$	. . .	. . .	. . .	6.93[a]	. . .
$P + P_M = 0$	. . .	. . .	. . .	5.75[b]	. . .
$A + A_U = 0$	. . .	. . .	. . .	1.23	. . .
$A + A_M = 0$	. . .	. . .	. . .	2.02	. . .
$t + t_U = 0$	. . .	. . .	. . .	2.37	. . .
$t + t_M = 0$	. . .	. . .	. . .	2.92[c]	. . .
$F + F_U = 0$	. . .	. . .	. . .	20.74[a]	. . .
$F + F_M = 0$	. . .	. . .	. . .	58.36[a]	. . .
$P + A = 0$	. . .	. . .	. . .	0.0003	. . .
Number of observations	. . .	. . .	. . .	. . .	66
R^2	. . .	. . .	. . .	. . .	0.969
$\bar{R}^2$	. . .	. . .	. . .	. . .	0.960
Root MSE	. . .	. . .	. . .	. . .	0.023296
Dep Mean	. . .	. . .	. . .	. . .	0.427174
C.V.	. . .	. . .	. . .	. . .	5.454

Source: See table A-1.
a. Significant at 0.01 level.
b. Significant at 0.05 level.
c. Significant at 0.10 level.

cant, while the overall effect of price for middle- and upper-income students is insignificant.

Table A-6 reports results for public institutions. For lower-income students, the signs on P_{pub} and A_{pub} are as expected but are not statistically significant. The interaction term with A for the upper-income group is negative and significant, as we expect. The overall effect of

Table A-5. *Regression Explaining Enrollment Rates at Private Institutions, Price and Aid Variables Considered*

Independent variable	Parameter estimate	Standard error	Test statistic t- statistic	Chi-square value	Summary statistic
Constant (α)	0.151874	0.049227	3.085[a]	. . .	. . .
Sticker price, private (P_{priv})	−0.000034	0.000008	−4.449[a]	. . .	. . .
Aid, private (A_{priv})	0.000038	0.000011	3.337[a]	. . .	. . .
Time (t)	0.000468	0.000536	0.872	. . .	. . .
Female (F)	0.015830	0.004210	3.760[a]	. . .	. . .
Middle income (M)	−0.039105	0.082808	−0.472	. . .	. . .
Upper income (U)	−0.134988	0.121489	−1.111	. . .	. . .
Aid, upper income ($A_{priv, U}$)	0.000015	0.000108	0.140	. . .	. . .
Aid, middle income ($A_{priv, M}$)	−0.000017	0.000024	−0.727	. . .	. . .
Sticker price, upper income ($P_{priv, U}$)	0.000063	0.000020	3.209[a]	. . .	. . .
Sticker price, middle income ($P_{priv, M}$)	0.000024	0.000012	1.957[c]	. . .	. . .
Time, upper income (t_U)	−0.007402	0.004866	−1.521	. . .	. . .
Time, middle income (t_M)	−0.000183	0.001097	−0.167	. . .	. . .
Female, upper income (F_U)	0.013390	0.010638	1.259	. . .	. . .
Female, middle income (F_M)	0.005357	0.005301	1.011	. . .	. . .
Chi-square tests					
$P_{priv} + P_{priv, U} = 0$	. . .	. . .	. . .	2.55	. . .
$P_{priv} + P_{priv, M} = 0$	. . .	. . .	. . .	1.10	. . .
$A_{priv} + A_{priv, U} = 0$	. . .	. . .	. . .	0.25	. . .
$A_{priv} + A_{priv, M} = 0$	. . .	. . .	. . .	1.02	. . .
$t + t_U = 0$	. . .	. . .	. . .	2.06	. . .
$t + t_M = 0$	. . .	. . .	. . .	0.09	. . .
$F + F_U = 0$	. . .	. . .	. . .	8.95[a]	. . .
$F + F_M = 0$	. . .	. . .	. . .	43.29[a]	. . .
$P_{priv} + A_{priv} = 0$	. . .	. . .	. . .	0.06	. . .
Number of observations	. . .	. . .	. . .	. . .	60
R^2	. . .	. . .	. . .	. . .	0.942
$\bar{R}^2$	. . .	. . .	. . .	. . .	0.924
Root MSE	. . .	. . .	. . .	. . .	0.014054
Dep Mean	. . .	. . .	. . .	. . .	0.110864
C.V.	. . .	. . .	. . .	. . .	12.677

Source: See table A-1.
a. Significant at 0.01 level.
b. Significant at 0.05 level.
c. Significant at 0.10 level.

aid for the middle-income group is positive and significant, while for the upper-income group, the overall effect is (perversely) negative and significant. The interaction effects for sticker price and income are both significant with the expected positive signs; the overall effects of sticker price are significant and (perversely) positive for both income groups.

Table A-6. *Regression Explaining Enrollment Rates at Public Institutions, Price and Aid Variables Considered*

Independent variable	Parameter estimate	Standard error	t-statistic	Chi-square value	Summary statistic
			Test statistic		
Constant (α)	0.380366	0.125456	3.032[a]	...	...
Sticker price, public (P_{pub})	−0.000049	0.000037	−1.352	...	...
Aid, public (A_{pub})	0.000020	0.000066	0.310	...	...
Time (t)	−0.003868	0.002240	−1.727[c]	...	...
Female (F)	0.028309	0.008917	3.175[a]	...	...
Middle income (M)	−0.438030	0.157962	−2.773[a]	...	...
Upper income (U)	−0.092041	0.149601	−0.615	...	...
Aid, upper income ($A_{pub, U}$)	−0.000343	0.000106	−3.230[a]	...	...
Aid, middle income ($A_{pub, M}$)	0.000080	0.000086	0.926	...	...
Sticker price, upper income ($P_{pub, U}$)	0.000098	0.000043	2.275[b]	...	...
Sticker price, middle income ($P_{pub, M}$)	0.000152	0.000044	3.442[a]	...	...
Time, upper income (t_U)	0.006152	0.002430	2.532[b]	...	...
Time, middle income (t_M)	0.001606	0.002439	0.658	...	...
Female, upper income (F_U)	−0.012045	0.011502	−1.047	...	...
Female, middle income (F_M)	0.003761	0.010841	0.347	...	...
Chi-square tests					
$P_{pub} + P_{pub, U} = 0$	...	...	...	4.49[b]	...
$P_{pub} + P_{pub, M} = 0$	...	...	...	17.03[a]	...
$A_{pub} + A_{pub, U} = 0$	...	...	...	14.95[a]	...
$A_{pub} + A_{pub, M} = 0$	...	...	...	3.24[c]	...
$t + t_U = 0$	...	...	...	5.90[b]	...
$t + t_M = 0$	...	...	...	5.52[b]	...
$F + F_U = 0$	...	...	...	5.01[b]	...
$F + F_M = 0$	...	...	...	27.05[a]	...
$P_{pub} + A_{pub} = 0$	...	...	...	0.17	...
Number of observations	...	...	...	...	60
R^2	...	...	...	...	0.935
$\bar{R}^2$	...	...	...	...	0.914
Root MSE	...	...	...	...	0.020537
Dep Mean	...	...	...	...	0.317772
C.V.	...	...	...	...	6.463

Source: See table A-1.
a. Significant at 0.01 level.
b. Significant at 0.05 level.
c. Significant at 0.10 level.

Description of Variables Used in Analysis of Institutional Behavior

IN THIS appendix we describe the methods used to calculate our variables as well as the relationships among several of the financial variables.

Description of General Variables[1]

Gross tuition and fees (P): This variable measures gross tuition and fee revenue per full-time-equivalent (FTE) student; it has also been referred to as the sticker price in previous sections. By convention, academic institutions calculate this amount by assuming that every student pays the sticker, or list, price—hence this variable does not deduct for any financial aid received. Charges for room, board, and other services rendered by auxiliary enterprises are excluded.

Institutional financial aid (A_i): This variable measures total scholarship aid from institutional funds per FTE student. We add scholarships and fellowships awarded from unrestricted and restricted funds (these include moneys given in the form of outright grants and trainee stipends to individuals enrolled in formal coursework, whether for credit or not). Aid to students in the form of tuition or fee remissions is included (except those remissions granted because of faculty or staff status). College work-study program expenses are not included here. Pell and supplemental educational opportunity grants (SEOG) are removed from the amount of restricted scholarships.

---

1. Variables used in the regression analysis are calculated as the difference in value between the beginning and the end of the period; the values are adjusted for inflation over the period. As an example, ΔP is used in the estimated model. It is the real change in gross tuition and fee revenue (P) per full-time equivalent student between the 1978–79 and 1985–86 academic years.

Federal financial aid (A_f): This variable equals the sum of Pell and SEOG grants disbursed per FTE student. Administrative expenses are included for the SEOG grants.

Income from gift and endowment earnings (*EARN*): This variable measures the addition to institutional resources per FTE student resulting from gifts and endowment earnings. It equals the sum of gifts to the endowment, gifts to the operating budget, realized and unrealized capital gains, interest, and dividends.

Federal government grants and contracts (*FED*): This variable measures federal financial support for higher education excluding student aid and direct federal appropriations: *FED* equals federal grants and contracts per FTE student less Pell and SEOG grants. Projects that might be supported by these funds include research projects, training programs, and similar activities for which amounts are received or expenditures are reimbursable under the terms of a government grant or contract.

State and local government grants and contracts $(S\&L_g)$: This variable measures state and local grants and contracts per FTE student.

State and local government appropriations $(S\&L_{app})$: This variable measures state and local appropriations per FTE student. It includes all amounts received or made available to an institution through acts of a legislative body, except grants or contracts. These funds go to meet current operating expenses and not specific projects or programs.

Instructional expenditures (EXP_{instr}): This variable measures institutions' instructional and self-supported research expenditures per FTE student. Included in this variable are expenditures of the colleges, schools, departments, and other instructional divisions of the institution, as well as expenditures for departmental research and public service that are not separately budgeted. Expenditures for academic administration where the primary function is administration (for example, the salaries and expenditures of academic deans) are excluded.

Variables Used in the Trend Analysis Only

Net tuition and fees: This variable measures net tuition and fee payments per FTE student. We subtract A_i and A_f from P to calculate the net price figure.

Academic support expenditures: This variable measures academic support expenditures per FTE student. Items included in this variable concern those expenditures for support services integral to the institution's primary missions of instruction, research, or public service; examples of such services are libraries, museums, galleries, audiovisual services, academic computing support, ancillary support, academic administration, personnel development, and course and curriculum development.

Student service expenditures: This variable measures student service expenditures per FTE student. This category includes funds expended for admissions, registrar activities, and activities whose primary purpose is to contribute to students' emotional and physical well-being and to their intellectual, cultural, and social development outside the context of the formal instruction program. Examples are career guidance, counseling, financial aid administration, student health services (except when operated as a self-supporting auxiliary enterprise), and the administrative allowance for Pell grants.

Institutional support expenditures: This variable measures institutional support expenditures per FTE student. Included are expenditures for the day-to-day operational support of the institution, excluding expenditures for physical plant operations. Examples are general administrative services, executive direction and planning, legal and fiscal operations, and community relations.

Operation and maintenance expenditures: This variable measures operation and maintenance expenditures per FTE student. Included are all expenditures for operations established to provide service and maintenance related to campus grounds and facilities used for educational and general purposes. Expenditures made from institutional plant funds accounts are excluded.

Additions to physical plant: This variable measures expenditures per FTE student on additional physical plant. We compute this number by summing over the three categories of physical plant additions during the year—land, buildings, and equipment. Additions during the year are additions to plant made through purchase, by gift-in-kind from donors, and from other sources. Construction-in-progress and plant expenditures that represent capital fund investments in real estate are excluded.

Variables Used in the Regression Analysis Only

Market value of the endowment (*ENDOW*): This variable measures the market value of the endowment per FTE student at the start of the fiscal year.

State income per capita (*INC*): This variable measures per capita income for the state in which each institution is located.

Enrollment in the 1978–79 academic year (*ENR79*): This variable measures FTE student enrollment in the 1978–79 academic year.

Percentage change in enrollment (Δ*ENR*): This variable measures the percentage change in FTE student enrollment over the period.

Relationships among Financial Variables

The accounting conventions of colleges and universities include some peculiarities that require mention. We assume in the following discussion that "auxiliary enterprises" run by universities, such as dormitories and hospitals, just break even. They can, therefore, be ignored.

Revenue

The principal sources of revenue for colleges and universities are tuition payments, funds supplied to institutions to support financial aid provided to students, government appropriations, grants and contracts, gifts to the schools, and earnings on endowments.

Accounting for tuition receipts properly is a tricky business. Colleges set a "sticker price" and report their tuition revenue as that sticker price multiplied by the number of students. However, many students receive discounts from that nominal price, discounts which the institution labels as "student aid expenditures." Part of this "expenditure" is simply revenue that the institution has forgone by accepting a lower tuition payment. Another part of the student aid expenditure, however, reflects grant money provided by the federal government. One part of this grant money takes the form of Pell grants, which are awarded directly to students but administered through the institution. A second part of the money is the SEOG program. These funds are awarded to the institution to be spent only for grants to needy students.[2]

2. Grant and scholarship funds may also be provided to students by state and local governments and by private organizations. Some of these funds, which pass through the institution, may appear

Thus, there are three different concepts of tuition revenue that might be distinguished. First is "gross tuition and fee revenue": the sticker price times the enrollment. Second is what we might call "net tuition receipts" (by institutions): gross tuition less amounts paid from the institution's own resources. Finally, we might define "net tuition payments" (from families): the amounts families actually pay for tuition. The difference between the last two is that net tuition receipts include federal student aid spending and net tuition payments exclude them.[3] The variable "net tuition and fees" in our data set corresponds to "net tuition payments."

Other revenue categories are more straightforward, although they raise some noteworthy problems. In standard higher-education accounting, federal student-aid grant moneys will be counted as student aid expenditures and as federal grant and contract revenue. For our purposes, we have removed federal student aid from both figures.

Regarding gifts and endowment earnings, it is important to note that universities and colleges divide their total revenue from these sources in fairly arbitrary ways, between "current operating income" and "additions to endowment." Conceptually, we view the earnings of the endowment as the sum of the capital gains on the assets owned at the beginning of the accounting period and the total dividends and interest generated by those assets. We regard gifts as the total of giving—physical and financial—to the institution for all purposes. The sum of these two minus any increase in indebtedness—what we call "increase in resources"—is the total income provided to the university in a particular year from past and present philanthropy. Data reported on the federal accounting forms do not allow us to get these figures directly, but we are able to estimate them from data that are provided.[4]

Spending

Expenditures can be broadly divided between those for current purposes and those for capital purposes. We define an institution's *saving*

---

in the accounts as institutional expenditure on student aid; others will simply be incorporated in tuition revenue. Our data set does not allow us to trace these amounts.

3. We treat federally guaranteed student loans as payments by families. They should really be viewed as partly that and partly federal student aid, but our data set does not include any information about the amounts of these loans.

4. The federal form asks institutions to report both endowment earnings and gift income. The former, however, are limited to dividends and interest, and the latter is only that portion of all giving that is allocated to the operating budget. Our computation of increased resources relies on

as the difference between its total revenue and its total expenditure for current purposes. This saving will then equal the sum of the increase of the value of the endowment (subtracting for any increased indebtedness) and the amount of "physical saving" the institution has done through the purchase or construction of land, buildings, or durable plant and equipment.[5]

The Budget Identity

The following budget identity summarizes the financial relationships on which we focus.

Net tuition payments by parents + government student aid + other government and private grants and contracts + government appropriations + gifts + endowment earnings = current expenditures + saving, where current expenditures are defined to exclude spending from institutional resources on student aid.

Equivalently, gross tuition revenue + government and private grants and contracts (other than student aid) + government appropriations + gifts + endowment earnings = current expenditures (including student aid expenditure) + saving.

---

figures for changes in the value of the endowment, total current revenue and spending of the institution, changes in physical asset holdings, and changes in net indebtedness.

5. At private institutions, the financing of such construction usually involves either an increase in debt or a reduction in endowment. In some public higher education systems, however, much addition of new capital assets takes the form, from an accounting point of view, of a "gift" from the state. The accounting practices we use will capture such a gift as a building as both an increase in resources and an equal amount of new saving.

Appendix C

Notes on the Modeling Strategy: The Question of Fungibility

TO BEGIN, assume that the university simply maximizes a set of objectives subject to an income constraint. Call the set of objectives $\{X_i\}$. Assume that the costs associated with these objectives are additively separable, so that the cost of X_i is $C_i(X_i)$ and the university's budget constraint is

$$\sum_i C_i(X_i) \leq I,$$

where I is the university's income.

If the X_i objectives enter a utility function for the university in which each counts positively with diminishing marginal rates of substitution, and if costs rise with higher levels of X_i at a diminishing rate, the university will select optimum levels of activities, X_i^*, with associated cost levels $C_i X_i^*)$.

Suppose the university has an increase of unrestricted income in the amount g. Assuming all activities, also called objectives in their more theoretical form, are "normal," each will increase to a new equilibrium level $X_i^{**} > X_i^*$.

What if, instead, the institution receives revenue in amount g that is targeted to be spent on a particular activity, say X_1? If this increase in "earmarked" funds does not change the cost or utility functions, the university's response will depend on whether $C_i(X_i^{**})$ is greater or less than g. If the earmarked revenue is less than or equal to the amount that would be spent on X_1 from a total income of $I + g$, then the "earmarking" constraint is not binding, and the university will spend the added revenue exactly as if it had come as unrestricted income. If, instead, the earmarked revenue exceeds $C_i(X_1^{**})$, then the constraint

235

implied by the earmarking becomes binding. The university will then spend g on X_1, and will maximize its utility subject to that constraint and a constraint that its total spending on other activities cannot exceed I. Obviously, this added constraint will result in both more spending on X_1 and a lower "utility" level for the institution than it would attain from an increase in unrestricted income equal to g.

This is a familiar but still striking result: earmarked gifts or transfers are equivalent to unrestricted gifts provided that their implied spending constraints are slack. To the extent that higher-education finance meets the conditions of this model, analyses of higher-education policy that neglect the point may be misleading. Consider federal student aid as an example. Many institutions award aid from their own resources according to principles that are similar to those constraining the distribution of federal aid. If federal aid substituted perfectly for institutional aid spending (which can be seen as a form of price discounting), then the effects of an increase in federal aid should be exactly the same as those of any increase in unrestricted income to universities, only a small portion of which would presumably be used to reduce the price facing disadvantaged students. Most analyses of the enrollment impact of federal student aid assume that an increase in aid results in a dollar-for-dollar reduction in the price facing lower-income students, which, based on this analysis, would be a substantial overestimate.

The same kind of point may apply to research spending in areas where universities devote some of their own resources to research. Increases in federal funding up to the amount the university would have spent without that funding will release university resources, and hence result in a reallocation of resources throughout the institution without any reason to expect larger increases in the funded area than elsewhere. Thus, a simple optimizing model of the university would imply perfect "fungibility" of earmarked dollars up to the point where earmarked funds match the amount the university would spend in the absence of such support, and zero fungibility thereafter.

However, as we have already noted, we do not believe that this model adequately captures the reality of university decisionmaking. Introducing some reasonable complications to the model modifies these simple and strong conclusions: there are reasons to expect less-than-perfect fungibility below the level of an activity that would be chosen in the absence of external finance, and more-than-zero fungibility above that level.

The first complication arises even within the simple maximizing model. Within relatively broadly defined activities, sources of external support are likely to impose constraints that blur the picture of a sharp dividing line after which external support ceases to replace internal spending. Formally, one could say that each broadly defined activity is composed of a number of more narrowly defined activities (for example, aiding this student versus aiding that student). At any given level of earmarked external support for the broadly defined activity, some of the narrow activities will have been fully funded externally, while others will not. As the overall level of external funding increases, the number of narrow activities that can still "absorb" funding will decrease, so that the degree of fungibility will decline more smoothly than the discontinuous result of the simple model.

Second, recognition of political elements in the allocation of resources within a university suggests less-than-perfect fungibility. The simple model assumes a unified objective function which "the university" is maximizing. In fact, while there may be broad consensus within a university on what objectives are worth pursuing, it is implausible to suppose that such an institution puts stable and agreed weights on these objectives. The availability of external funding is likely to increase the political influence of a constituency that favors a particular objective. This makes it likely that such a group could "capture" more of the benefits of increased external funding than the simple model implies.

A distinct but related point pertains to the incentives the university provides to those who seek and obtain external funding. Unless gains in external funding are shared with those who obtain them, the incentive to seek such funding will be small. Although, in principle, such rewards could take the form of direct side payments, it seems more plausible that a successful constituency will be rewarded by letting a larger share of the increased funding remain with that area than strict short-run optimizing would imply.

Finally, we should note that the simple model assumes that the cost functions facing the university are insensitive to changes in external funding. But this obviously depends on the form that the external funding takes. Suppose, for example, that research funding took the form of "matching grants," with, say, half the marginal cost of a research project being provided externally on condition that the rest is provided internally. Such regulation would reduce the marginal cost of research activities and increase the level of research activity the institution would undertake. Such linkages will clearly increase the responsiveness of activity levels to changes in external funding for them, relative to the simple model sketched above.

The clearest case of this kind of funding arrangement in higher education is probably state appropriations to public colleges and universities, which are often tied closely to enrollment levels. Research funding and federal student aid funding may similarly provide marginal incentives to expand the activities they support. Thus, with regard to research, a tendency to award research grants to institutions that display a strong commitment to research may provide a marginal incentive to expand research efforts. Similarly, federal grants to institutions to finance their student aid efforts under the SEOG program are, in principle, responsive to the "neediness" of the institution's student body, thereby aiming to provide more resources at the margin to institutions that enroll more needy students. In practice, "grandfathering" rules and funding limitations have largely blocked these marginal responses for most of the program's existence.

An Empirical Analysis of Government Support and Institutional Behavior

THE MODEL presented below examines the behavior of a panel of institutions over a seven-year period, the 1978–79 to the 1985–86 academic years. All our variables are calculated as the difference in value between the beginning and end of the period, and are adjusted for inflation over the period. For example, ΔP measures the real change in gross tuition and fee revenue per full-time-equivalent (FTE) student between the two years.

There are three equations in our model. The dependent variables are the change in total scholarship aid per FTE student from institutional resources (ΔA_i); the change in gross tuition and fees per FTE student received by the institution (ΔP); and the change in instructional expenditures per FTE student (ΔEXP_{instr}). These variables along with the rest of the variables included in the empirical analysis below are defined in appendix B, which also contains a detailed examination of the accounting relationships among all the variables.

The dependent variables in the three equations in our model are related to the objectives identified in the text. The three equations, including our theoretical expectations about signs, are displayed in table D-1.

A number of our expected signs follow directly from wealth effects in the theoretical model described in appendix C. Institutions experiencing more rapid increases over the period in state and local appropriations ($\Delta S\&L_{app}$), federal grants and contracts (ΔFED), or state and local grants and contracts ($\Delta S\&L_g$) will gain more in institutional wealth, and, given the objectives described above, are expected to increase institution-based scholarship aid more rapidly, to raise tuition and fees

Table D-1. *Expected Signs for Regression Analysis*

Independent variable[a]	Dependent variables[a]		
	ΔA_i	ΔP	ΔEXP_{instr}
ΔA_f	?	?	+
$\Delta ENDOW$	+	. . .	. . .
$\Delta EARN$	. . .	−	+
$\Delta S\&L_{app}$	+	−	+
ΔFED	+	−	+
$\Delta S\&L_g$	+	−	+
ΔINC	−	+	. . .
$ENR\ 79$	. . .	. . .	−
ΔENR	. . .	. . .	?
ΔP	+	. . .	+
ΔA_i	. . .	+	. . .

Source: Authors' calculations as described in text.

a. See appendix B for definition of variables. Greek delta signifies the level change of a variable, except for ΔENR where it signifies the percent change.

more slowly, and to raise instructional expenditures more rapidly than other institutions. Similarly, more rapid growth in endowment ($\Delta ENDOW$) or more rapid increases in income from gifts and endowment ($\Delta EARN$) should add to the growth in wealth and have the same effects on institutional behavior.[1]

More rapid increases in federal financial aid (ΔA_f) also have a positive wealth effect, which explains the expected positive sign for this variable in the equation for changes in instructional expenditures.[2] However, in explaining changes in tuition and in institution-based aid expenditures, changes in federal financial aid have effects additional to the wealth

1. We postulate that changes in tuition and fees and instructional expenditures are based on changes in the flow of earnings—that is, when the sum of gifts, interest, and dividends declines from one year to the next, institutions respond by increasing the sticker price and lowering instructional expenditures. On the other hand, we assume that changes in the amount of institutional financial aid depend more on changes in the long-run financial situation of an institution as reflected in changes in the stock of wealth rather than changes in year-to-year gifts and earnings. Thus, $\Delta ENDOW$ is included as an independent variable in the ΔA_i equation while $\Delta EARN$ is included as an independent variable in the ΔP and ΔEXP_{instr} equations. It should be noted that the high correlation between $\Delta ENDOW$ and $\Delta EARN$ implies that they cannot both be included as exogenous variables in a particular equation and that these assumptions are basically consistent with ordinary least squares regression results.

2. A large positive effect would imply that increases in federal student aid induce institutions to increase their instructional expenditures substantially. This might be viewed as a good thing if one believes that at the margin society would benefit from more resources' being devoted to student instruction. Yet it might be seen as a negative outcome, to the degree that it implies that university expenditures, and hence the cost to the nation of higher education, tend to be pushed up by higher student aid.

effect. In the case of institution-based aid, this wealth effect may be augmented by the effect of federal aid in making it easier for institutions to attract more lower-income students, who may then receive additional institution-based aid.[3] However, these complementary effects may be offset by a tendency for federal aid to substitute for institutional aid spending, tending to counteract the positive effects and leaving the expected sign ambiguous.

The effects of increased federal aid on rates of growth in tuition are similarly ambiguous. Although the wealth effect of more rapid federal aid growth, given the assumed objectives of the institutions, will tend to reduce tuition, some observers have suggested that increased federal aid availability may tend to raise tuitions, as institutions attempt to "capture" more aid through setting a higher sticker price.

State income per capita (ΔINC) is included in these equations as an indicator of the make-up of the student population of institutions. Institutions from states where income is growing more rapidly are expected to be able to raise tuition more rapidly while sustaining any given level of demand for enrollment, and we can expect institutions to attempt to gain added revenue in this way. Thus we expect a positive effect of ΔINC on ΔP. Similarly, institutions should be able to attain any given level of diversity in the student population at lower cost in terms of institution-based aid if they are located in a state where incomes are rising. Thus we expect the sign on ΔINC to be negative in the ΔA_i equation.

Measures of the level and the rate of growth of enrollment ($ENR79$ and ΔENR) are included in the equation explaining instructional expenditures in order to capture possible scale or capacity effects. For any given percentage growth in enrollment, the presence of economies of scale would imply that institutions with smaller enrollments at the beginning of the period would experience larger increases in instructional spending than those with larger enrollments; thus the sign on the 1978–79 enrollment level in the ΔEXP_{instr} equation is expected to be negative.[4] The impact of the percentage growth in enrollment

3. There are actually two forces at work here. First, as was seen in chapter 3, enrollment demand among lower-income students is increased by larger federal student aid awards. Second, the cost to an institution of recruiting a lower-income student (thereby pursuing its objective of promoting diversity) is reduced by the presence of larger amounts of federal student aid.

4. For a review of the literature on the economies of scale in higher education, see Brinkman and Leslie (1986).

depends on whether institutions have excess capacity; if so, we expect a negative impact of more rapid growth in enrollment on expenditure growth; if not, rising short-run marginal costs should lead to a positive effect.

Finally, two endogenous variables, ΔP and ΔA_i, enter as explanatory variables in our equations. In explaining changes in instructional expenditures, we assume that more rapid increases in tuition and fees cause instructional expenditures to rise more rapidly through an income effect; a further effect is that institutions with more rapidly growing tuitions may need to increase their instructional expenditures more rapidly to ensure adequate demand. More rapid increases in tuition and fees are also expected to have a positive effect on the growth of institution-based student aid spending, both through an income effect and because more rapid tuition growth will require more rapid increases in spending on student aid to maintain diversity. There is also a reverse causal effect: given the long-run solvency objective of the university, we expect that more rapid growth in institution-based student aid leads to more rapid growth in tuition.

Table D-2 presents descriptive statistics for each of these variables for the three categories of institutions considered in the empirical analysis—private four-year colleges and universities, public four-year colleges and universities, and public two-year colleges.[5] The simultaneous structure of the model implies that ordinary least squares (OLS) estimates are biased and inconsistent. A popular alternative, which we adopt, is a two-stage least squares (2SLS) procedure, which takes into account the presence of endogenous right-hand-side variables.[6] Estimation results are presented in table D-3.

As should be obvious from this discussion, a central concern of ours is the degree to which government funds affect the finances of institutions of higher learning. These funds can be divided into the

5. We also explored the use of a variable representing the proportion of an institution's students who are graduate students, with the expectation that an increase in the percentage of graduate students will, over time, all else equal, increase ΔA_i, ΔP, and ΔEXP_{instr}. However, it turned out that there was virtually no change in the proportion of graduate students during the period. This finding, along with a substantial number of missing values for this variable in any case, led us to exclude this variable from our regressions.

6. This procedure involves a first-stage regression of each of the endogenous variables on a set of instruments that includes all of the exogenous variables. The subsequent second-stage regressions use the predicted values from the first stage for the endogenous regressors. For each equation, the order condition for identification is met.

Table D-2. *Descriptive Statistics for Regression Analysis*

Variable[a]	Descriptive statistic			
	Mean	Standard deviation	Minimum	Maximum
Private four-year institutions[b]				
ΔA_i	266.1	374.0	−4099.0	1907.7
ΔP	768.3	665.2	−3617.4	4249.9
ΔEXP_{instr}	250.6	634.3	−6499.9	5701.0
ΔA_f	9.3	147.8	−1139.8	1616.7
$\Delta ENDOW$	1983.1	5013.4	−10119.7	58201.1
$\Delta EARN$	1298.0	4877.2	−13895.4	84721.5
$\Delta S\&L_{app}$	−7.1	113.1	−1237.5	1377.9
ΔFED	−73.3	482.2	−4031.9	7106.8
$\Delta S\&L_g$	45.8	504.2	−3026.9	13857.1
ΔINC	1009.1	659.2	−798.8	2548.1
$ENR79$	1721.1	2307.3	201.0	25131.0
ΔENR	5.2	32.2	−75.9	374.8
Public four-year institutions[b]				
ΔA_i	28.9	130.4	−1036.8	1298.2
ΔP	219.8	224.2	−1297.8	1339.0
ΔEXP_{instr}	132.0	574.1	−1866.5	5896.1
ΔA_f	37.9	85.0	−305.3	455.8
$\Delta ENDOW$	78.4	401.1	−3657.9	3021.8
$\Delta EARN$	−188.6	2244.7	−10858.0	29768.2
$\Delta S\&L_{app}$	187.9	1549.0	−5346.2	25363.0
ΔFED	−103.4	477.6	−7287.1	1554.4
$\Delta S\&L_g$	8.9	178.7	−1767.6	1465.3
ΔINC	890.1	660.4	−953.4	2548.1
$ENR79$	7792.0	7343.7	203.0	46485.0
ΔENR	8.0	16.6	−44.5	70.0
Public two-year institutions[b]				
ΔA_i	9.5	118.4	−1234.3	487.6
ΔP	86.2	153.7	−936.4	1088.4
ΔEXP_{instr}	89.5	472.3	−4683.3	3151.2
ΔA_f	52.0	99.4	−571.4	457.3
$\Delta ENDOW$	20.9	155.0	−248.8	2800.9
$\Delta EARN$	−231.5	1201.6	−8993.8	13434.8
$\Delta S\&L_{app}$	120.7	572.8	−2966.8	3217.2
ΔFED	−20.8	287.0	−2287.8	2467.7
$\Delta S\&L_g$	28.3	243.5	−1569.7	2655.7
ΔINC	968.3	641.5	−717.4	2548.1
$ENR79$	2423.5	2292.1	215.0	14091.0
ΔENR	11.8	32.2	−57.0	268.7

Source: Authors' calculations as described in text.

a. See appendix B for definition of variables. Greek delta signifies the level change of a variable, except for ΔENR where it signifies the percent change.

b. Sample sizes are as follows: 896 observations for four-year private institutions; 371 observations for four-year public institutions; and 667 observations for two-year public institutions.

Table D-3. Regression Results: Parameter Estimates for Explanatory Variables and Summary Statistics

Equation		Explanatory variable											Summary statistic	
	Constant	ΔA_f	$\Delta ENDOW$	$\Delta EARN$	$\Delta S\&L_{app}$	ΔFED	$\Delta S\&L_g$	ΔINC	ΔP	ΔA_i	$ENR79$	ΔENR	F-value	$\bar{R}^2$
Dependent variable—ΔA_i														
Private four-year	137.0	0.203	0.009	...	0.215	0.108	0.057	−0.061	0.232	...	...	...	20.60[a]	0.133
	(35.8)[a]	(0.091)[b]	(0.003)[a]		(0.111)[c]	(0.027)[a]	(0.024)[b]	(0.023)[a]	(0.064)[a]					
Public four-year	45.2	−0.154	0.050	...	0.008	0.040	0.063	0.001	−0.061	...	...	...	2.67[b]	0.031
	(33.5)	(0.097)	(0.029)[c]		(0.006)	(0.014)[a]	(0.040)	(0.011)	(0.156)					
Public two-year	−15.8	−0.006	−0.012	...	−0.008	0.076	−0.106	−0.011	0.489	...	...	...	9.54[a]	0.082
	(10.3)	(0.092)	(0.032)		(0.013)	(0.018)[a]	(0.025)[a]	(0.013)	(0.195)[b]					
Dependent variable—ΔP														
Private four-year	−173.9	−0.197	...	−0.016	−0.861	−0.220	−0.132	0.264	...	2.565	...	...	14.64[a]	0.096
	(138.4)	(0.274)		(0.011)	(0.297)[a]	(0.104)[b]	(0.078)[c]	(0.047)[a]		(0.488)[a]				
Public four-year	156.5	0.502	...	−0.007	0.010	−0.047	−0.021	−0.004	...	1.388	...	...	1.01	0.000
	(39.5)[a]	(0.221)[b]		(0.009)	(0.012)	(0.039)	(0.084)	(0.023)		(0.681)[b]				
Public two-year	25.7	0.135	...	0.002	0.027	−0.099	0.170	0.032	...	1.388	...	...	7.87[a]	0.067
	(17.2)	(0.130)		(0.007)	(0.017)[c]	(0.055)[c]	(0.051)[c]	(0.015)[b]		(0.539)[b]				
Dependent variable—ΔEXP_{instr}														
Private four-year	−43.8	−0.047	...	0.025	1.389	0.220	−0.017	...	0.314	...	0.035	−2.216	46.30[a]	0.288
	(68.5)	(0.128)		(0.004)[a]	(0.163)[a]	(0.041)[a]	(0.037)		(0.098)[a]		(0.009)[a]	(0.689)[a]		
Public four-year	−317.2	−0.240	...	−0.038	0.299	0.132	−0.310	...	2.237	...	−0.013	2.364	37.94[a]	0.444
	(108.9)[a]	(0.343)		(0.014)[a]	(0.021)[a]	(0.055)[b]	(0.146)[b]		(0.617)[a]		(0.006)[b]	(1.691)		
Public two-year	49.9	−0.031	...	0.054	0.377	0.311	0.377	...	0.299	...	−0.003	−1.142	47.74[a]	0.360
	(40.7)	(0.215)		(0.012)[a]	(0.034)[a]	(0.051)[a]	(0.069)[a]		(0.488)		(0.007)	(0.656)[c]		

Source: Authors' calculations as described in text. Standard errors are in parentheses. Sample sizes are as follows: 896 observations for four-year private institutions; 371 observations for four-year publics; and 667 observations for two-year publics. $\bar{R}^2$ adjusted for degrees of freedom. Greek delta signifies level change of a variable, except for ΔENR where it signifies the percent change.

a. Significant at 0.01 level.
b. Significant at 0.05 level.
c. Significant at 0.10 level.

following categories: federal financial aid (ΔA_f); direct state and local government support ($\Delta S \& L_{app}$); and government grants and contracts ($\Delta FED + \Delta S \& L_g$).

In terms of federal financial aid, we find an effect on the change in institution-based student aid for the private sample as well as an effect on the change in tuition and fees for public four-year institutions. Specifically, an increase in federal financial aid of $1 leads to a 20-cent increase in scholarship expenditures from institutional funds for four-year private colleges and universities (hence, federal financial aid and institutional aid are complements rather than substitutes) and an increase in tuition and fees of 50 cents for their public counterparts.[7] We find no effects of changes in federal financial aid on changes in instruction for any of the samples, on changes in scholarships for either four-year or two-year publics, or on changes in tuition and fees for either four-year privates or two-year publics. The finding that there is no statistically significant relationship between changes in federal financial aid and changes in the "sticker" price at private four-year institutions is consistent with our description of the historical data and our discussion of program incentives. This finding argues against the "Bennett hypothesis." This result, along with evidence of a positive link between changes in federal financial aid and changes in gross tuition at public four-year institutions, is helpful in formulating our plan for reform of federal student aid.

Unlike federal financial aid, changes in direct state and local educational appropriations lead to changes in instructional expenditures in all three samples. An increase in direct state and local expenditures of $1 leads to increases in instructional expenditures of $1.39, 30 cents, and 38 cents at four-year privates, four-year publics, and two-year publics, respectively. While the first coefficient is unexpectedly high, the general finding that state and local appropriations support instructional expenditures is not surprising. At private four-year institutions, changes in state and local appropriations also translate into increased scholarship aid: a $1 increase in these appropriations leads to a 22-cent increase in scholarships. A $1 increase in state and local appropriations also reduces the increase in tuition and fees at

---

7. The F-value for the tuition and fees equation for four-year publics is insignificant. However, when the equation is run again with all the right-hand-side variables except ΔA_f and ΔA_i, the F-value equals 3.38, which is statistically significant at the 5 percent level. The coefficient on ΔA_f is 0.377, also significant at the 5 percent level.

four-year privates by 86 cents. The effect on tuition and fees at two-year publics is unexpectedly positive but quite close to zero: a $1 increase in state and local appropriations leads to an increase in tuition and fees of less than 3 cents.[8]

Turning to the third category of government expenditure variables, government grants and contracts, we find significant effects of changes in federal grants and contracts on changes in scholarships, tuition and fees, and instructional expenditures. A $1 increase in federal grants and contracts leads to increases in scholarships of 11 cents, 4 cents, and 8 cents, and to increases in instructional expenditures of 22 cents, 13 cents, and 31 cents at four-year privates, four-year publics, and two-year publics. It leads to a decline in tuition and fees of 22 cents at four-year privates and 10 cents at two-year publics. This suggests that federal grant and contract awards have substantial fungibility, with a sizable portion of each dollar in grants going to reduce revenue or increase other spending. A $1 increase in state and local grants and contracts at four-year private institutions increases total scholarships by 6 cents and lowers tuition and fees by 13 cents. The only significant effect of state and local grants and contracts at four-year publics is an unexpected negative effect on instruction: a $1 increase leads to a 31-cent decline in instructional expenditures.[9] On the other hand, a $1 increase in state and local grants and contracts at two-year publics increases instructional expenditures by 38 cents, although it unexpectedly lowers scholarships by 11 cents and raises tuition and fees by 17 cents.

Besides the results relating to external funding reported above, there are a number of other interesting findings. As expected, changes in state income affect scholarships and tuition and fees—a $1 increase in per capita income lowers scholarships at four-year private institutions by 6 cents and raises tuition and fees by 26 cents, while increasing

8. Putting aside scale effects, all five of the unexpected signs in our regressions were in the public sector regressions—two in the tuition and fee equation for two-year publics, one in the institutional scholarship equation for two-year publics, and two in the instruction equation for four-year publics—where behavior is not always based on institutional discretion (particularly in the case of setting tuition and fees). For the privates, where institutional sovereignty is the governing mechanism, all fifteen of the significant variables for which we had predicted the signs based on our theoretical model had the expected sign.

9. However, the causality may run from low instructional expenditures to high levels of state and local grants and contracts. That is, state and local governments may allocate these funds to institutions in which instructional spending is quite low, in an effort to increase these expenditures.

tuition and fees at two-year publics by 3 cents. An increase in institutional wealth also leads to an increase in scholarships, with a $1 rise in the market value of the endowment raising scholarships by 1 cent at four-year privates and 5 cents at four-year publics. A $1 increase in annual income (*EARN*) raises instructional expenditures by 3 cents at four-year privates and 5 cents at two-year publics, but unexpectedly leads to a decline in instructional expenditures at four-year publics of 4 cents. The results relating to the scale effects on instructional expenditures are somewhat surprising: at four-year publics, the larger the enrollment at the beginning of the period (a higher value of *ENR79*), the smaller the increase in instructional expenditures, indicating that there are significant economies of scale in instruction, as we expected. However, for four-year privates, we find that the larger the enrollment, the larger the increase in these expenditures.[10] Moreover, at both four-year privates and two-year publics, the larger the percentage increase in enrollment over the period, the smaller the increase in instructional expenditures, which would be consistent with the presence of substantial excess capacity in these sectors at the beginning of the period. Our finding that excess capacity existed in the private sector supports the result of Cohn, Rhine, and Santos that economies of scale persist for the private sector even at 600 percent of the output means.[11]

Finally, the relationship among the endogenous variables deserves some attention. A $1 increase in tuition and fees raises scholarships by 23 cents at four-year privates and 49 cents at two-year publics. On the other hand, a $1 increase in scholarships raises tuition and fees by $2.57 at four-year privates and by $1.39 at both four-year and two-year publics. A $1 increase in tuition and fees increases instructional expenditures by 31 cents at four-year privates and $2.24 at four-year publics.

10. We suspect that in private higher education, enrollment levels may be functioning as a proxy for "quality" or expenditure levels per student. There are a great many very small private institutions with low expenditures per student. Thus, our finding may suggest that higher "quality" institutions had more rapid increases in instructional spending over this period.

11. Cohn, Rhine, and Santos (1989) examined data for the academic year 1981–82. While they did not distinguish between four-year and two-year public institutions, they found that economies of scale in the public sector were exhausted around the output means. Note that their analysis, because it relies on data for a single year, is unable to distinguish between shorter-run capacity effects and longer-run scale economies.

References

Arfin, David M. 1986. "The Use of Financial Aid to Attract Talented Students to Teaching: Lessons from Other Fields." *Elementary School Journal* 86: 405–23.

Arrow, Kenneth J. 1974. *The Limits of Organization.* Norton.

Astin, Alexander W., Williams S. Korn, and Ellyne R. Berz. 1989. *The American Freshman: National Norms for Fall 1989.* Los Angeles, Calif.: Higher Education Research Institute.

Barnett, Lance C., and Ira S. Lowry. 1979. "How Housing Allowances Affect Housing Prices: Housing Assistance Supply Experiment." Santa Monica, Calif.: Rand Corporation.

Becker, Gary Stanley. 1975. *Human Capital: A Theoretical and Empirical Analysis with Special Reference to Education.* Columbia University Press.

Berne, Robert. 1980. "Net Price Effects on Two-Year College Attendance Decisions." *Journal of Education Finance* 5: 391–414.

Blakemore, Arthur E., and Stuart A. Low. 1985. "Public Expenditures on Higher Education and Their Impact on Enrollment Patterns." *Applied Economics* 17: 331–40.

Bosworth, Barry P., Andrew S. Carron, and Elisabeth B. Rhyne. 1987. *The Economics of Federal Credit Programs.* Brookings.

Bowen, Howard R. 1974. "Financing Higher Education: The Current State of the Debate." In *Exploring the Case for Low Tuition in Public Higher Education,* edited by Kenneth E. Young, pp. 11–32. Washington: American Association of State Colleges and Universities.

———. 1977. *Investment in Learning: The Individual and Social Value of American Higher Education.* San Francisco: Jossey-Bass.

Breneman, David W. 1976. "The Ph.D. Production Process." In *Education as an Industry,* edited by Joseph T. Froomkin, Dean T. Jamison, and Roy Radner, pp. 3–52. Ballinger.

Breneman, David W., and Chester E. Finn, Jr., eds. 1978. *Public Policy and Private Higher Education.* Brookings.

Brinkman, Paul T., and Larry L. Leslie. 1986. "Economies of Scale in Higher Education: Sixty Years of Research." *Review of Higher Education* 10:1–28.

Byron, William J. 1989. "Neither Grant nor Loan: New Ground for Federal Student Aid Policy." In *Radical Reform or Incremental Change? Student Loan Policy Alternatives for the Federal Government,* edited by Lawrence E. Gladieux, pp. 25–32. New York: College Board.

249

Carlson, Daryl E. 1975. *A Flow of Funds Model for Assessing the Impact of Alternative Student Aid Programs*. Stanford, Calif.: Stanford Research Institute.

Carnegie Council. 1980. *Three Thousand Futures: The Next Twenty Years for Higher Education*. San Francisco: Jossey-Bass.

Carroll, Stephen J., and others. 1977. *The Enrollment Effects of Federal Student Aid Policies*. Santa Monica, Calif.: Rand Corporation.

Case, Karl E., and Michael S. McPherson. 1986. "Does Need-Based Student Aid Discourage Saving for College?" Washington Office of the College Board.

Cohn, Elchanan, Sherrie L. W. Rhine, and Maria C. Santos. 1989. "Institutions of Higher Education as Multi-Product Firms: Economies of Scale and Scope." *Review of Economics and Statistics* 71:284–90.

College Board. 1986. *Who Receives Federal Student Aid?* Washington Office of the College Board.

———. 1988. *Annual Survey of Colleges 1988–1989: Summary Statistics*. New York.

———. 1989a. *College Cost Book, 1989–90*. New York.

———. 1989b. *Trends in Student Aid, 1980 to 1989*. New York.

College Scholarship Service. 1990a. *Manual for Student Aid Administrators, 1991–92: Policies and Procedures*. New York: College Board.

———. 1990b. "Preparing for the Next Reauthorization: Need Analysis Issues." *CCS Reports*, no. 3. New York: College Board.

Craig, Steven G., and Robert P. Inman. 1982. "Federal Aid and Public Education: An Empirical Look at the New Fiscal Federalism." *Review of Economics and Statistics* 64: 541–52.

Crawford, Norman C., Jr. 1966. *Effects of Offers of Financial Assistance on the College-Going Decisions of Talented Students with Limited Financial Means*. National Merit Scholarship Corporation.

Davis, Jerry S., and Kingston Johns, Jr. 1982. "Low Family Income: A Continuing Barrier to College Enrollment?" *Journal of Student Financial Aid* 12:5–10.

Ehrenberg, Ronald G., and Daniel R. Sherman. 1984. "Optimal Financial Aid Policies for a Selective University." *Journal of Human Resources* 19: 202–30.

Eureka Project. 1988. "The Critical Difference: Student Financial Aid and Educational Opportunities in California." Sacramento, Calif.

Feldstein, Martin. 1978. "The Effect of a Differential Add-On Grant: Title I and Local Education Spending." *Journal of Human Resources*. 13:443–58.

Finn, Chester E., Jr. 1978. *Scholars, Dollars, and Bureaucrats*. Brookings.

Fischer, Frederick J. 1990. "State Financing of Higher Education: A New Look at an Old Problem." *Change* (January–February): 42–56.

Freeman, Richard B. 1971. *The Market for College-Trained Manpower: A Study in the Economics of Career Choice*. Harvard University Press.

———. 1976. *The Over-educated American*. New York: Academic Press.

Freeman, Richard B., and David W. Breneman. 1974. "Forecasting the Ph.D.

Labor Market: Pitfalls for Policy." Washington: National Board on Graduate Education.

Friedman, Milton, and Rose D. Friedman. 1962. *Capitalism and Freedom*. University of Chicago Press.

Garvin, David A. 1980. *The Economics of University Behavior*. New York: Academic Press.

Gillespie, Donald A., and Nancy Carlson. 1983. *Trends in Student Aid, 1963 to 1983*. Washington Office of the College Board.

Gladieux, Lawrence E., and Thomas R. Wolanin. 1976. *Congress and the Colleges: The National Politics of Higher Education*. Lexington, Mass.: Heath.

Gurwitz, Aaron S. 1980. "The Capitalization of School Finance Reform." *Journal of Education Finance* 5: 297–319.

Gutmann, Amy. 1987. *Democratic Education*. Princeton University Press.

Hansen, Janet S. 1987. *Student Loans: Are They Overburdening a Generation?* New York: College Board.

Hansen, W. Lee. 1983. "Impact of Student Financial Aid on Access." In *The Crisis in Higher Education*, edited by Joseph Froomkin, pp. 84–96. New York: Academy of Political Science.

Hansen, W. Lee, and Jacob O. Stampen. 1986. "Independent Students at Two-Year Institutions and the Future of Financial Aid." In *The Community College and Its Critics*, edited by L. Steven Zwerling, pp. 81–90. San Francisco: Jossey-Bass.

Hansen, W. Lee, and Burton A. Weisbrod. 1971. "A New Approach to Higher Education Finance." In *Financing Higher Education: Alternatives for the Federal Government*, edited by M. D. Orvig, pp. 117–42. Iowa City: American College Testing Program, 1971.

Hartman, Robert. 1973. "The Rationale for Federal Support for Higher Education." In *Does College Matter? Some Evidence of the Impacts of Higher Education*, edited by Lewis C. Solomon and Paul J. Taubman. New York: Academic Press.

Hauptman, Arthur M. 1985. "Federal Costs for Student Loans: Is There a Role for Institution-based Lending?" Washington: American Council on Education.

———. 1989. "The National Student Loan Bank: Adapting an Old Idea for Future Needs." In *Radical Reform or Incremental Change? Student Loan Policy Alternatives for the Federal Government*, edited by Lawrence E. Gladieux, pp. 75–92. New York: College Board.

———. 1990a. *The College Tuition Spiral: An Examination of Why Charges Are Increasing*. Macmillan.

———. 1990b. *The Tuition Dilemma: Assessing New Ways to Pay for College*. Brookings.

Hauptman, Arthur M., and Maureen McLaughlin. 1988. "Is the Goal of Access to Postsecondary Education Being Met?" Background paper prepared for the Education Policy seminar, Aspen Institute. Washington: American Council on Education.

Hayek, Friedrich A. 1945. "The Use of Knowledge in Society." *American Economic Review* 35: 519–30.

Hearn, James C., and Sharon L. Wilford. 1985. "A Commitment to Opportunity: The Impacts of Federal Student Financial Aid Programs." Report prepared for the 20th Anniversary Observance of the Signing of the Higher Education Act of 1965, Southwest Texas State University, San Marcos, Texas, November 7–8.

Hodgkinson, Harold L. 1985. "The Changing Face of Tomorrow's Student," *Change* 17:38–41.

Hoenack, Stephen A., and Daniel J. Pierro. 1986. "An Econometric Model of a Public University's Income and Enrollments." University of Minnesota.

Hopkins, David S. P., and William F. Massy. 1981. *Planning Models for Universities and Colleges*. Stanford University Press.

Jackson, Gregory A. 1978. "Financial Aid and Student Enrollment." *Journal of Higher Education* 49: 548–74.

James, Estelle. 1978. "Product Mix and Cost Disaggregation: A Reinterpretation of the Economics of Higher Education." *Journal of Human Resources* 13: 157–86.

James, Estelle, and others. 1989. "College Quality and Future Earnings: Where Should You Send Your Child to College?" *American Economic Review* 79: 247–52 (*Papers and Proceedings, 1988*).

Jensen, Eric L. 1983. "Financial Aid and Educational Outcomes: A Review." *College and University* (Spring): 287–302.

Johnstone, D. Bruce. 1986. *Sharing the Costs of Higher Education: Student Financial Assistance in the United Kingdom, the Federal Republic of Germany, France, Sweden, and the United States*. New York: College Board.

Kane, Thomas. [Forthcoming]. "College Entry by Blacks since 1970: The Role of Tuition, Financial Aid, Local Economic Conditions and Family Background." Ph.D dissertation, Harvard University.

Karelis, Charles H., and Richard O. Sabot. 1987. "Financing Higher Education: A Proposal for Reform." *Liberal Education* 73: 40–42.

Katz, Lawrence F., and Kevin M. Murphy. 1990. "Changes in Relative Wages, 1963–1987: Supply and Demand Factors." National Bureau of Economic Research, Cambridge, Mass.

Korb, Roslyn, and others. 1988. *Undergraduate Financing of Postsecondary Education: A Report of the 1987 National Postsecondary Student Aid Study*. U.S. Department of Education.

Lee, John B. 1987. "The Distribution of Higher Education Subsidies." Working paper, Center for Higher Education, Management, Finance, and Governance, University of Maryland.

Leslie, Larry L., and Paul T. Brinkman. 1987. "Student Price Response in Higher Education: The Student Demand Studies." *Journal of Higher Education* 58: 181–204.

———. 1988. *The Economic Value of Higher Education*. Macmillan.

Levin, Henry. 1983. "Individual Entitlements." In *Financing Recurrent Educa-*

tion: Strategies for Increasing Employment, Job Opportunities, and Productivity, edited by Henry M. Levin and Hans G. Schütze, pp. 39–66. Beverly Hills: Sage Publications.

Lewis, Gwendolyn L. 1988. *Trends in Student Aid, 1980 to 1988*. Washington Office of the College Board.

Lewis, Lionel S., and Paul W. Kingston. 1989. "The Best, the Brightest, and the Most Affluent: Undergraduates at Elite Institutions." *Academe* (November–December): 28–33.

McGuinness, Aims, and Christine Paulson. 1990. "A Survey of College Prepayment and Savings Plans in the States." In *College Savings Plans: Public Policy Choices,* edited by Janet S. Hansen, pp. 44–77. New York: College Board.

Manski, Charles F., and David A. Wise. 1983. *College Choice in America.* Harvard University Press.

McPherson, Michael S. 1978. "The Demand for Higher Education." In *Public Policy and Private Higher Education,* edited by David W. Breneman and Chester E. Finn, pp. 143–96. Brookings.

———. 1987. "Family Ability to Pay: A Lifetime Perspective." Williams College, Department of Economics.

———. 1988. "On Assessing the Impact of Federal Student Aid." *Economics of Education Review* 7: 77–84.

———. 1989. "Appearance and Reality in the Guaranteed Student Loan Program." In *Radical Reform or Incremental Change? Student Loan Policy Alternatives for the Federal Government,* edited by Lawrence E. Gladieux, pp. 11–24. New York: College Board.

McPherson, Michael S., and Morton Owen Schapiro. 1990. *Selective Admission and the Public Interest.* New York: College Board.

———. 1991. "Does Student Aid Affect College Enrollment? New Evidence on a Persistent Controversy." *American Economic Review* 81: 309–18.

McPherson, Michael S., and Mary S. Skinner. 1986. "Paying for College: A Lifetime Proposition." *Brookings Review* 4: 29–36 (Fall).

Miller, Scott E., and Holly Hexter. 1985a. "How Low-Income Families Pay for College." Washington: American Council on Education.

———. 1985b. "How Middle-Income Families Pay for College." Washington: American Council on Education.

Moll, Richard. 1985. *The Public Ivys: A Guide to America's Best Public Undergraduate Colleges and Universities.* Viking.

Mortenson, Thomas G. 1990. "The Impact of Increased Loan Utilization Among Low Family Income Students." Iowa City: American College Testing Program.

Murnane, Richard J., and Randall J. Olsen. 1989. "Will There Be Enough Teachers?" *American Economic Review* 79: 242–46 (*Papers and Proceedings, 1988*).

National Center for Education Statistics. 1989. *Digest of Educational Statistics.* U.S. Department of Education.

National Institute of Independent Colleges and Universities. 1990. *A Commit-*

ment to Access: Undergraduate Student Financial Assistance Provided Directly by Independent Colleges and Universities. Washington.

Nerlove, Marc. 1972. "On Tuition and the Costs of Higher Education: Prolegomena to a Conceptual Framework." Journal of Political Economy 80 (supplement): S: 178–218.

O'Keefe, Michael. 1985. "What Ever Happened to the Crash of '80 '81 '82 '83 '84 '85?" Change 17: 37–38.

O'Neill, June A. 1971. "Resource Use in Higher Education: Trends in Output and Inputs, 1930 to 1967." Report prepared for the Carnegie Commission on Higher Education, Berkeley, Calif.

———. 1973. "Sources of Funds to Colleges and Universities." A technical report sponsored by the Carnegie Commission on Higher Education, Berkeley, Calif.

Porter, Oscar F. 1989. Undergraduate Completion and Persistence at Four-Year Colleges and Universities: Completers, Persisters, Stopouts, and Dropouts. Washington: National Institute of Independent Colleges and Universities.

Psacharopoulos, George. 1981. "Returns to Education: An Updated International Comparison." Comparative Education 17: 321–41.

Reischauer, Robert D. 1989. "HELP: A Student Loan Program for the Twenty-first Century." In Radical Reform or Incremental Change? Student Loan Policy Alternatives for the Federal Government, edited by Lawrence E. Gladieux, pp. 33–56. New York: College Board.

Rose-Ackerman, Susan, ed. 1986. The Economics of Nonprofit Institutions: Studies in Structure and Policy. Oxford University Press.

Samuelson, Paul A. 1958. "An Exact Consumption-Loan Model of Interest with or without the Social Contrivance of Money." Journal of Political Economy 66: 467–82.

Schapiro, Morton O., Michael P. O'Malley, and Larry H. Litten. 1991. "Progression to Graduate School from the 'Elite' Colleges and Universities." Economics of Education Review (forthcoming).

Schwartz, J. Brad. 1985. "Student Financial Aid and the College Enrollment Decision: The Effects of Public and Private Grants and Interest Subsidies." Economics of Education Review 4: 129–44.

———. 1986. "Wealth Neutrality in Higher Education: The Effects of Student Grants." Economics of Education Review 5: 107–17.

Sloan, Frank A., Jerry Cromwell, and Janet B. Mitchell. 1978. Private Physicians and Public Programs. Lexington, Mass.: Heath.

Spies, Richard R. 1978. "The Effect of Rising Costs on College Choice: A Study of the Application Decisions of High-Ability Students." New York: College Board.

———. 1990. "The Effect of Rising Costs on College Choice: The Third in a Series of Studies on This Subject." Princeton University.

St. John, Edward P., Rita J. Kirshstein, and Jay Noell. 1988. "The Effects of Student Financial Aid on Persistence: A Sequential Analysis." Paper presented at the American Educational Research Association, Annual Meeting, New Orleans.

St. John, Edward P., and Jay Noell. 1988. "The Effects of Student Aid on Access to Higher Education: An Analysis of Progress with Special Considerations to Minority Enrollment." Paper presented at the American Educational Research Association, Annual Meeting, New Orleans.

Sullivan, A. Charlene. 1990. "Saving for College: The Investment Challenge," In *College Savings Plans: Public Policy Choices,* edited by Janet S. Hansen, pp. 18–39. New York: College Board.

Task Force on Financing Higher Education. 1972. *Higher Education in New York State.* A Report to Governor Nelson A. Rockefeller.

Thurow, Lester. 1975. *Generating Inequality: Mechanisms of Distribution in the U.S. Economy.* Basic Books.

Tierney, Michael L. 1980. "Student Matriculation Decisions and Financial Aid." *Review of Higher Education* 3: 14–25.

Tsang, Mun, and Henry M. Levin. 1983. "The Impact of Intergovernmental Grants on Educational Expenditure." *Review of Educational Research* 53: 329–67.

U.S. Bureau of the Census. 1975. *Money Income of Households, Families, and Persons in the United States.* Series P-60. Department of Commerce.

White, Halbert. 1980. "A Heteroskedasticity-Consistent Covariance Matrix Estimator and a Direct Test for Heteroskedasticity." *Econometrica* 48: 817–38.

Williamson, Oliver E. 1975. *Markets and Hierarchies: Analysis and Antitrust Implications: A Study in the Economics of Internal Organization.* Free Press.

Index

Affordability: federal financing and projections of, 131; government financing of colleges and, 122; impact of aid on, 34; living at home and, 38; worrisome trends, 132. *See also* Future affordability of college

American Freshman Survey, 30, 79, 87, 88, 108–09

Basic education opportunity grant (BEOG) program, 192. *See also* Pell grant program

Bennett, William, 13

Bennett hypothesis, 72; institutional incentives and, 69

Borrowing. *See* Loans

Brinkman, Paul, 37, 47, 50, 52

Budget Enforcement Act, 171–72

College education. *See* Higher education; Postsecondary education

College financing: as an intergenerational compact, 174–80; long-run perspective, 20–25; overview, 3–8; trends since *1965*, 25, 27–30; trends since *1974*, 30–37; trends inhibiting simplicity in, 193

Colleges and universities: analysis of trends in finance, 60–65; econometric model of finance, 65–73; elite, 75, 76 (*see also* Consortium for Financing Higher Education); growth of revenues (*1939–80*), 24; prestigious public, 97; rates of change in revenue and expenditure categories (*1970s–80s*), 63–64; tuition-sensitive student aid as incentive for price raising, 135

Community colleges, 38, 46, 188

Consortium for Financing Higher Education (COFHE), 76–78, 81–83, 86–91, 93–99, 100–05

Cost of attending college: effect on enrollment, 38–39, 52–54; forecasts, 113, 114; model for determining, 107–09; net, 34, 36, 39

Craig, Stephen, 59

Current Population Survey (CPS), 40, 217, 218

Debt burden, occupational choice and, 182–85

Disadvantaged students, subsidization of vocational training, 141–42. *See also* Low-income students

Educational investment: economic returns, 2, 154–56, 185

Educational opportunity: access for lower-income students and, 188–89; options and, 75, 104, 188

Educational sector, national economy and, 111–12, 115, 117, 121

Educational subsidies. *See* Pell grants; Student aid

Elite four-year institutions: alternatives (for high-achieving students), 94–97; enrollment, 76–78, 79, 81–83, 86–89, 89–91, 93–99, 101–05; financial aid, 99, 102; tuition increases, 76. *See also* Consortium for Financing Higher Education

Enrollment: financial aid and, 45–50; fluctuations in black and white compared, 41; fluctuations in upper- and lower-income groups compared, 41–42; full-time vs. total, 4; of high-achieving students, 89–91, 93–99, 101–02; influences of price cuts and

257